TOWARD A TRINITARIAN THEOLOGY
OF LITURGICAL PARTICIPATION

R. Gabriel Pivarnik, OP

Foreword by Rev. Msgr. Kevin W. Irwin

Toward a Trinitarian Theology of Liturgical Participation

A PUEBLO BOOK

Liturgical Press   Collegeville, Minnesota

www.litpress.org

A Pueblo Book published by Liturgical Press

Cover design by David Manahan, OSB. Cover photo: Thinkstock Photos. Cover Illustration: Frank Kacmarcik, OblSB, used with permission.

Excerpts from documents of the Second Vatican Council are from *Vatican Council II. Volume 1, The Conciliar and Post Conciliar Documents*, ed. Austin Flannery, OP, © 1996 (Costello Publishing Company, Inc.). Used with permission.

1	2	3	4	5	6	7	8

Library of Congress Control Number: 2012950684

ISBN 978-0-8146-6285-4

For my parents,
William and Barbara

Contents

Foreword   ix
  Kevin W. Irwin

List of Abbreviations   xiii

Acknowledgments   xv

Introduction: The Search for Meaning within Liturgical
                Participation   xvii

Chapter 1:   The Unfolding of a Trinitarian Narrative in the
             Concept of Liturgical Participation   1

Chapter 2:   Attempts at Creating a Trinitarian Approach to
             Participation I: Cipriano Vagaggini   53

Chapter 3:   Attempts at Creating a Trinitarian Approach to
             Participation II: Edward Kilmartin   101

Chapter 4:   Later Attempts to Articulate a Trinitarian Theology
             of Participation   143

Chapter 5:   Toward a Trinitarian Theology of Liturgical
             Participation   165

Epilogue: The Emergence of a Trinitarian Language of
             Liturgical Participation   235

Bibliography   241

Index   255

Foreword

From a pastoral as well as a theological point of view probably no one word typifies what the liturgical reforms of Vatican II were primarily concerned with than the word "participation." While adding up the number of times a word is used in any document and on that basis suggesting its importance can be very deceptive, nonetheless the fact that the term "participation" is used sixteen times in the liturgy constitution from Vatican II (*Sacrosanctum Concilium*) and that its modifier is "active" on twelve of those occasions and that "liturgical instruction and active participation" is cited as one of the three principles on which the restoration and promotion of the sacred liturgy is based is very significant.[1] After the reformed rites were published and subsequently translated into vernacular languages, enormous efforts were undertaken to invite those who participated in the former liturgy to engage themselves now more fully in the sacred liturgy by using their voices and bodies to experience the action of nothing less than the Trinity at work among us through the rites and prayers of the sacred liturgy, well understood.[2]

That the term "participation" has been used and fostered since the first part of the twentieth century in the papal magisterium is clear.[3] That the vernacular was cited by the pioneers of the liturgical movement as a means to this end is also clear. But what is less clear is what the term "participation" actually means in its breadth and depth. Some have recently argued (not without value) that there was so much emphasis placed on the externals of the reformed liturgy that physical activity seemed to be what active participation meant as envisioned by the council. Some have taken this more than a precipitous step further and written that what really matters is "to take part in" Christ's paschal mystery interiorly and internally and that the *means* to do this through the liturgy did not matter. In fact, the *means* to participate *do*

---

[1] See http://www.vatican.va/archive/hist_councils/ii_vatican_council/documents/vat-ii_const_19631204_sacrosanctum-concilium_en.html, 14, 19, 27, 30, 41, 50, 113, 114, 121, 124, and the title preceding 14.

[2] *Sacrosanctum Concilium* refers to *per ritus et preces* (48).

[3] See this often repeated phrase from *Tra le sollecitudini* of Pope Pius X (1903).

matter a great deal, because the sacred liturgy matters a great deal. The means we use are based on two important and classic Catholic principles—of sacramentality and of the incarnation. This is to say that the way we participate in the liturgy, through rites and prayers, matters a great deal. The principle of sacramentality means, among other things, that we use the things of this good earth and the work of human hands to worship God and be sanctified by him through his Son. The incarnational principle means, among other things, that God sent his Son to be incarnate among us, to take on our flesh and to live, obey, suffer, die, rise, and ascend to the Father's right hand so that we, in and through our bodies, through the liturgy's rites and prayers, could participate in the very divinity of God.

Despite the frequency with which the phrase "active participation" was used in *Sacrosanctum Concilium*, what was needed then and what is needed still are theological explorations of its meaning both then and now. Father Pivarnik offers us rich fare in this solidly grounded, thoroughly researched, densely argued, but eminently readable monograph. It is a work of true theological scholarship that will serve the ongoing renewal of the church for years to come, derived from the church's participation in the sacred liturgy.

In placing Cipriano Vagaggini, OSB, and Edward Kilmartin, SJ, in dialogue with the church's magisterium, Father Pivarnik accomplishes what Catholic theologians often strive to do, that is, to offer arguments and perspectives on a topic simply not available through the magisterium alone because of the nature of magisterial statements. At times reactive (as at the Council of Trent) and at times deliberately pithy and open-ended (as in *Sacrosanctum Concilium*), magisterial statements deserve fuller theological exploration and explanation from within the Catholic theological tradition. In Cipriano Vagaggini, Father Pivarnik has chosen a classically trained theologian, an expert in liturgical texts (both East and West), and an esteemed *peritus* at Vatican II. In Edward Kilmartin, Father Pivarnik has chosen a premier sacramental theologian of the twentieth century whose knowledge and use of insights from several German trinitarian theologians to help explain what the liturgy is remains unsurpassed. In summarizing and using both Vagaggini's and Kilmartin's *oeuvre*, he provides the great service of condensing the rather diffuse and numerous articles and books from each author and in the process offers the next generation of liturgical scholars important bibliographical material for future research. (While both Vagaggini and Kilmartin have left us key books, i.e., Vagaggini's

Theological Dimensions of the Liturgy in its various editions from 1957 on and Kilmartin's *Christian Liturgy*, Father Pivarnik has brought them into dialogue with the rest of their articles and books, in some cases updating and nuancing the originals.)

And yet, Father Pivarnik is not uncritical of even these giants in the constellation of important twentieth-century liturgical theologians. His assessments and evaluations are precise and invitational in the sense that when he offers what are still underdeveloped ideas from each author, he invites the reader to think about and, yes, to contemplate what trinitarian participation in the sacred liturgy really means. The words of the sixth preface in Ordinary Time (from Acts 17:28) have obvious perennial value and always ring true:

> . . . in you we live and move and have our being,
> and while in this body
> we not only experience the daily effects of your care,
> but even now possess the pledge of life eternal.

It is especially in chapter 5 of this book that we benefit from Father Pivarnik's linguistic abilities, as well as his philosophical and theological training as a son of St. Thomas and as a teacher who himself has already drawn many into appreciating more fully what it means to *participate* in the sacred liturgy. I anticipate that this study will make him an invaluable dialogue partner in future debates about the ongoing renewal of the church as based on liturgical participation—a major point of what liturgical participation means, which is unfortunately often lost in some contemporary debates. His theological expertise abounds on every page of this book.

The liturgy is a many splendored thing. It can be viewed and grasped from a variety of viewpoints and perspectives. In choosing the lens of *"trinitarian liturgical participation"* Father Pivarnik has chosen one of the foundations on which the entire enterprise of liturgy is based. We are in his debt for inviting us to go beyond the externals and the ephemeral and to drink deeply of the liturgy at its source—in and through the triune God. This book should become a model for others trying to help us all appreciate what it means to *participate* in the sacred liturgy.

Rev. Msgr. Kevin W. Irwin
Walter J. Schmitz Chair in Liturgical Studies
School of Theology and Religious Studies
The Catholic University of America
Washington, DC

Abbreviations

Documents of the Second Vatican Council:

AA   *Apostolicam Actuositatem*
AG   *Ad Gentes*
CD   *Christus Dominus*
DV   *Dei Verbum*
GE   *Gravissimum Educationis*
GS   *Gaudium et Spes*
LG   *Lumen Gentium*
OT   *Optatum Totius*
PO   *Presbyterorum Ordinis*
SC   *Sacrosanctum Concilium*

Other abbreviations:

AAS   *Acta Apostolicae Sedis*
AS   *Acta Synodalia (Sacrosancti Concilii Oecumenici Vaticani II)*
ASS   *Acta Sanctae Sedis*
CCC   *Catechism of the Catholic Church*
CCCB   Canadian Conference of Catholic Bishops
CCL   *Corpus Christianorum (Series) Latina*
MR   *Missale Romanum*
PG   *Patrologia Greaca*
ST   *Summa theologiae*

Acknowledgments

The process of rewriting and revising a doctoral dissertation is something akin to telling parents that their beautiful infant child looks like Lyndon Johnson and needs to have plastic surgery—it doesn't sit well with anyone and may, in fact, cause the parents a certain amount of grief, frustration, and angst. While my characterization of the revision process might be somewhat hyperbolic, there are those I need to thank who helped me through this "rebirth."

First and foremost, I would like to thank my mentor and friend, Kevin W. Irwin, who has continued to provide me with needed insight and advice over the years. Without his guidance, I would never have moved forward with bringing this manuscript to light. He has been a part of my writing career since its earliest stages and has always encouraged me to "sharpen the pencil" as I sought to put words on paper. Any student will agree that there is something remarkable and amazing that happens when a former teacher tells you that you have something worthwhile to say to the academy.

My special thanks to Robert Daly, professor emeritus at Boston College, and the other members of the Eucharistic Prayer and Theology Seminar of the North American Academy of Liturgy who encouraged me to seek the publication of this revision. It was their guidance and motivation after a paper presentation at an annual meeting that moved me to begin talking to Liturgical Press.

It is important for me to recognize as well the great witness and encouragement that have been shown to me by my colleagues and friends at Providence College. The chair of my department, Aurelie Hagstrom, was a constant source of strength and an even more constant reminder that patience is necessary in all things. Richard Grace, Laurie Grupp, Mark Caprio, and Siobhan Ross-Humphries have each provided the gifts of friendship and wisdom. As the revisions to this manuscript began, I also became the director for the Center for Catholic and Dominican Studies. In that arena, I have to thank Margaret Wakelee and Kevin Smith, who were diligent enough in their job as my graduate assistants to keep things off of my desk that did not need to be there.

I would also like to acknowledge the ongoing support and friendship of my Dominican community in Providence, Rhode Island. Through their forbearance, their patience, their laughter, and their witness, I have been sustained and nourished. To Brian, Ken, James, and Joe, I can only express the greatest of thanks. They have provided me with the fruits of their contemplation, and that has become the source of my own relief, refreshment, and rebirth.

* * *

Excerpts from Pope Pius XII, *Mediator Dei*, in *The Papal Encyclicals, 1939–1958*, ed. Claudia Carlen, IHM (Ann Arbor, MI: Pierian Press, reprint, 1990), 119–54. Used by permission of the Sisters, Servants of the Immaculate Heart of Mary (print rights) and Pierian Press (electronic rights).

Excerpts from Edward J. Kilmartin, "*Sacrificium Laudis*: Content and Function of Early Eucharistic Prayers," *Theological Studies* 35 (1974): 268–87; and "Sacraments as Liturgy of the Church," *Theological Studies* 50 (1980): 527–47. Used by permission.

Excerpts from Edward J. Kilmartin, "A Modern Approach to the World of God and Sacraments of Christ: Perspectives and Principles," in *The Sacraments: God's Love and Mercy Actualized; Proceedings of the Theological Institute 11*, ed. F. A. Eigo (Villanova, PA: Villanova University Press, 1979), 59–109. Used by permission.

Excerpts from Edward J. Kilmartin, *Christian Liturgy 1: Theology and Practice* (Kansas City, MO: Sheed and Ward, 1988). Used by permission of Rowman and Littlefield Publishing Group.

Excerpts from William J. Hill, *The Three-Personed God* (Washington, DC: The Catholic University of America Press, 1982). Used by permission.

Introduction

The Search for Meaning within Liturgical Participation

THE CONTEMPORARY SHIFT IN SACRAMENTAL AND LITURGICAL METHODOLOGY

Change never comes easily—nor does it come in neat linear developments that are packaged nicely for assimilation and approbation. By the time the Second Vatican Council (1961–1965) had completed its sessions, any observer could recognize that what the council attempted was nothing less than the fostering of a renewal in every avenue of the church's life. At the close of the council Pope Paul VI commented:

> May it (the greeting of Christ) rise as a new spark of divine charity in our hearts, a spark which may enkindle the principles, doctrine and proposals which the council has organized and which, thus inflamed by charity, may really produce in the church and in the world that renewal of thoughts, activities, conduct, moral force and hope and joy which was the very scope of the council.[1]

This renewal would prove to have definite ramifications for sacramental theology and methodology, but it would also recognize a change that had begun decades before. In the first constitution promulgated by the council, *Sacrosanctum Concilium* (December 4, 1963), an intentional shift from the Tridentine liturgy was made regarding the participation of the faithful in the liturgical action in three basic areas.

---

[1] Pope Paul VI, "Closing Homily to the Second Vatican Council," December 8, 1965, http:www.vatican.va/holy_father/paul_vi/homilies/1965/documents/hf_p-vi_hom_19651208_epilogo-concilio-immacolata_en.html (accessed February 8, 2009).

First, the council maintained that "all the faithful should be led to that full, conscious, and active participation in liturgical celebrations which is demanded by the very nature of the liturgy."[2] The council's insistence on the necessity of "active participation" became the guiding norm for postconciliar liturgical renewal and sacramental theology.

Second, the council emphasized the particular relationship between the Word and the sacramental ritual. *Sacrosanctum Concilium* asserts that "Sacred Scripture is of the greatest importance in the celebration of the liturgy" (SC 24). The emphasis on the Word underscores the dialogical nature of the sacramental celebration, for the proclamation of the Word necessitates an engagement of the faithful in the act of hearing. In the reform of the rites that followed the council each of the sacraments is given a distinct collection of scriptural texts (for a liturgy of the Word) that are meant to act as an essential part of the sacramental rite. In this way Word and sacrament become inextricably linked—the hearing of the Word is viewed as an essential part of the celebration of the sacrament. Such a position already moves the council's theology past the minimalistic canonical approach to sacraments that had dominated the manual teaching of the previous century. In fact, the Sacred Congregation for Divine Worship asserts in *Liturgicae Instaurationes* (The Third Instruction on the Correct Implementation of the Constitution of the Sacred Liturgy—September 5, 1970) that the effectiveness of the liturgy lies "solely in entering more deeply into the Word of God and the mystery being celebrated."[3]

The third major factor emanating from the council surrounding the concept of liturgical participation involves the relationship between the unity of the church and the fruitfulness of the sacrament. In the same instruction the Sacred Congregation for Divine Worship says that the unity of the body protects the authenticity of the liturgy. It asserts: "The present renewal offers liturgical prayer as it should be, flowing out of a living and time-honored spiritual tradition. And with it brought forward, this prayer must be made manifest as the work of the entire people of God in all their different orders and ministries. The power and authenticity of this prayer has as its sole guarantee the

[2] SC 14. For all references to the documents of the Second Vatican Council, see Austin Flannery, OP, ed., *Vatican Council II: Volume I, The Conciliar and Post Conciliar Documents* (Northport, NY: Costello Publishing Co., 2004).

[3] Sacred Congregation for Divine Worship, "*Liturgicae Instaurationes*," AAS 62 (1970): 695.

unity of the entire ecclesial body."[4] Such a statement goes well beyond the original declaration of the council that "liturgical services are not private functions but are celebrations of the Church which is the 'sacrament of unity'" (SC 26). But the statement by the congregation also demands some explanation, since the church does not present itself as the "sacrament of unity" strictly through the work or operation of its human constituents whenever they gather. Rather, the unity of the church is guaranteed by the Holy Spirit. The *General Instruction on the Liturgy of the Hours* (1970) makes this clear: "The unity of the Church at prayer is brought about by the Holy Spirit, who is the same in Christ, in the whole Church, and in every baptized person. . . . There can be therefore no Christian prayer without the action of the Holy Spirit, who unites the whole Church and leads it through the Son to the Father."[5] This emphasis on the unity of the faithful with regard to the efficacy of the liturgy adds a heretofore neglected dimension to sacramental theology in the West—a dimension intimately connected to the action of the Holy Spirit.

While these three areas provided new material for theological reflection on the sacraments after the council, the actual pathway to a new sacramental methodology (or methodologies!) was not an easy task then, and it continues to be a challenge. In some ways the council and its reform perhaps raise more questions than they answer. New attempts to explain and explicate the sacraments have necessarily moved theological discussion into new arenas of thought and conjecture. The very language of sacraments has been revolutionized.

THE SEARCH FOR MEANING IN THE CONCEPT OF "*ACTUOSA PARTICIPATIO*"

During his plenary address to the 2009 Meeting of the North American Academy of Liturgy, noted French sacramental theologian Louis-Marie Chauvet observed that the very concept of participation in the liturgy defies any easy kind of comprehensible expression. He argued: "The 'active participation' desired by the Second Vatican Council appears difficult to many, if not impossible, because of the

---

[4] Ibid., 703–4.

[5] Sacred Congregation for Divine Worship, *General Instruction on the Liturgy of the Hours*, in *Documents on the Liturgy, 1963–1979*, ed. Denis E. Hurley (Collegeville, MN: Liturgical Press, 1971), 1094. See paragraph 8 in particular.

very difficulty of liturgical language."[6] His "diagnosis" of the problem stems from the crucial difference between the liturgical action and the everyday or ordinary actions that form the frame of reference for the majority of Christians. Liturgical language does, in fact, have its own tenor and hue, at times poetic and expressive, at times lyrical and melodious. At other times it appears brusque and nondescript, functional without excess. The current debates over the implementation of the new English translation of the Roman Missal provide more than ample evidence of the difficulties in appropriating and absorbing liturgical language. Such a language, even when it is placed in the vernacular, defies the straightforwardness of newspaper journalism, the sometimes baffling abridged text-speak of electronic instant messaging, and the sound-byte mentality of modern commercial media. Liturgical language is characteristically atypical in the human experience. In this sense participation in the liturgy can imply an engagement with a milieu that is not familiar or, even worse, seemingly alien.

Chauvet's observation on the twenty-first-century dilemma is neither new nor unique. In his book *Toward a Renewal of Sacramental Theology*, Raymond Vaillancourt maintains that any change in Christology, ecclesiology, or anthropology will demand a comprehensively new way of looking at sacramental theology because each of those elements is constitutive of a sacramental order.[7] Since the liturgical renewal of the Second Vatican Council there has been a growing need for new sacramental methodologies that meet the needs of the modern critical mind and experience. Vaillancourt notes that the ambiguity of rituals, an individualistic conception of sacraments, and a sense of separation from the sacramental liturgy by the faithful shed light on the inadequacies of a sacramental theology that has not renewed itself. Vaillancourt surmises that the mission of the modern-day theologian lies in bridging that gap between sacramental theology and the expression of sacramental faith in the lives of believers:

> It is true that in and through Christ, God had addressed a definitive message to the human race. But even in its primary expression, the New Testament, the message bears the mark of a particular culture and

[6] Louis-Marie Chauvet, "Are the Words of the Liturgy Worn Out?" *Worship* 84 (January 2010): 25–37, at 25.

[7] Raymond Vaillancourt, *Toward a Renewal of Sacramental Theology*, trans. Matthew J. O'Connell (Collegeville, MN: Liturgical Press, 1979), iv–v.

a particular way of experiencing life in the world. Successive Christian traditions have endeavored to give the unique and decisive event of Christ's coming and presence in the world an expression that satisfied their contemporaries, using categories of thought familiar to them. Our age in its turn must do what previous generations did: give the sacramental reality a concrete form which is capable of stimulating the faith of our contemporaries and enabling them to express it in a truly concrete way.[8]

Thus the question of the meaning of liturgical participation in the contemporary cultural shift in theological method implies not only a redefinition of terms but also a reframing of the scope of the discussion.

CREATING A NEW METHODOLOGY FOR THE SACRAMENTS

The modern theologian faces a noticeable dilemma. Is it possible to reinvent the parameters for a discussion of liturgical participation in a way that helps to elucidate the very mystery being celebrated? At least a first stage of development must include a thorough unpacking of the term *actuosa participatio* in both its historical significance and its more contemporary usage. The phrase "active participation" can, as Chauvet points out, have various different meanings and shades of understanding if the understanding of it is not rooted in something deeper—an overarching narrative that acts as its foundation and lens. In this case one can see that the grammar of salvation history, the self-communication of the triune God, forms the crucial thread linking together the various images and perceptions of liturgical participation. That thread provides a pathway into the mystery being celebrated. While it is certainly not an exact blueprint for intellectual understanding, the trinitarian narrative at least provides a central frame of reference that can be commonly apprehended.

The first part of this work outlines the connection between the trinitarian narrative and the major theological developments of *actuosa participatio*. This is a crucial step in understanding the multifaceted dimensions of liturgical participation and the rich symbolic meaning such participation implies. To participate in the liturgy is synonymous with participating in the ecclesial reality of the church, in the ministry and priesthood of Christ, and ultimately in the divine life itself. The

[8] Ibid., 34.

search for meaning in the concept of *actuosa participatio* must recognize this multivalence. The trinitarian narrative in one sense holds that meaning together and forces the juxtaposition of multiple symbolic interpretations of liturgical participation. What becomes apparent, then, is that a trinitarian theology of participation is needed in order to sustain the myriad meanings of participation in the liturgy.

The second part of this work investigates the attempts of both Cipriano Vagaggini and Edward Kilmartin to wed a trinitarian narrative to a fuller understanding of the sacraments and to the notion of participation in the liturgical action. Both theologians link the active work of the Trinity within the sacraments themselves with the possible participation of the faithful in the life of that Trinity; that is, the purpose or end of the sacramental celebration is not self-enclosed. The ecclesial community never celebrates sacraments simply for the sake of celebration. Rather, participation in the sacramental-liturgical experience is meant to lead the participant into ever-greater union with the divine. Liturgical participation always points to a participation in the life of the Trinity. The work of both Vagaggini and Kilmartin can be seen as foundational to later attempts to evolve a deeper trinitarian understanding of the sacraments in statements by the magisterium and new methodologies of the past two decades. However, neither theologian is completely successful in elucidating a trinitarian theology of liturgical participation that can both hold together the various symbolic meanings of *actuosa participatio* and maintain a cogent trinitarian description of the action of God in the sacraments.

The third part of this work analyzes the scholarship of both these theologians from a series of critical focal points: the use of liturgical sources, consistency with the trinitarian theology of the tradition, and the ability to maintain a theology of liturgical participation. Such a critique can help determine the essential elements of any endeavor hoping to move *toward a trinitarian theology of liturgical participation*.

In the end, this work attempts to provide an intellectual framework for coming closer to the mystery that is celebrated within the sacramental action. It is a framework that recognizes the multivalence of the term *participatio* and provides an experiential node (the liturgical action itself) for the interpretation of that mystery. Creating such a framework may help bridge the gap mentioned by Chauvet between the intent and purpose of liturgical action and the daily life of Christians. The final intent here is not necessarily to provide a new systematic approach to the liturgy but rather to point to the elements that must be included in any such development or methodology: a return to baptismal imagery, a demarcation of the role of the active presence of each of the persons of the Trinity, and a movement toward the inclusion of eschatological participation within the realm of meaning of *actuosa participatio*.

If Chauvet is correct and the church currently suffers from an inability to understand the language of liturgical participation, then this present effort provides a possible theological locus in which to create a new liturgical language—one based on the experience of the liturgy itself. The ongoing revision of rites, the struggle of theologians and laity to inculcate these changes, and the recognition that the renewal initiated by the Second Vatican Council fifty years ago is still taking shape all point to a need for a theological language and method that can adapt and move with the modern world. That such a language is decidedly trinitarian only confirms that the grammar of salvation history is presented in the liturgical action that moves believers from this life into the eternal life of the triune God.

Chapter 1

The Unfolding of a Trinitarian Narrative in the Concept of Liturgical Participation

PARTICIPATION AND ITS COMPLEX OF INTERCONNECTED MEANING

In the Constitution on the Sacred Liturgy the Fathers of the Second Vatican Council declared that "the faithful should be led to the full, conscious and active participation in liturgical celebrations which is demanded by the very nature of the liturgy."[1] What is left unsaid is *why* such a participation is not only advantageous but also "demanded by the very nature of the liturgy." The concept of the active participation of the faithful was not new to the council, but in fact had been developing since the beginning of the twentieth century within both magisterial documents and the theological discourse of the liturgical movement. What makes any study of the council's insistence on "active participation" somewhat difficult is the clear polyvalence of the term *participation* within the theological arena, not just in liturgical studies but in areas of ecclesiology, soteriology, and metaphysics. Moreover, in order to appreciate fully the complexity of liturgical participation for the laity one has to look at both the theological development of the concept itself and its relationship to the *lex agendi*, that is, the way in which the liturgy is acted out in a given time period.[2] That

---

[1] *Sacrosanctum Concilium* (SC) 14. For all references to the documents of the Second Vatican Council, see Austin Flannery, OP, ed., *Vatican Council II: Volume I, The Conciliar and Post Conciliar Documents* (Northport, NY: Costello Publishing Co., 2004).

[2] Other scholars have used the term *lex agendi* to refer to the impact of the liturgy on the lived life of its participants, but here I take my cue from the distinction made by Kevin Irwin between *lex agendi* and *lex vivendi*, where *lex vivendi* is the life relation to the liturgy and *lex agendi* the way in which the liturgy is enacted and performed. See Kevin Irwin, *Context and Text: Method in Liturgical Theology* (Collegeville, MN: Liturgical Press, 1994), 55–56.

is, participation in the liturgy means one thing at the beginning of the twentieth century and takes on different shades of meaning and nuance at its close since the object of that participation, the liturgy itself, has undergone tremendous reform. In this sense the polyvalent nature of the term *participation* can be seen through at least two qualifying lenses: its temporal condition and its theological metaphors.

We must realize that certain temporal realities affect the developing theology of liturgical participation in the twentieth century. One cannot overlook the *lex agendi* of a specific time period—namely, that the celebration of the liturgy prior to the liturgical movement of the 1920s and 1930s had different concerns than the celebration of what was technically the same liturgical rite on the eve of the Second Vatican Council. Moreover, the council's insistence on "full, active, and conscious participation" was formulated in light of the Tridentine rite, not the rites that were produced by the reform after the council. In fact, the opposite is true. The reformed rites were formed under this principle enunciated by the council.

Among others, four theological metaphors that help us understand the concept of participation revolve around four distinct spheres: metaphysical (in the order of nature/being), soteriological (in the order of grace), ecclesiological (in the order of communion), and ritual-liturgical (in the order of activity). A brief look at each of these concepts of participation will help situate the council's call for "full, active, and conscious participation."

Participation first came to the foreground within the metaphysical context of Platonic philosophy. In Plato's understanding of the concept, metaphysical participation implies both a difference and a similarity between the reality and the thing in which it participates. David Schindler argues: "To speak of metaphysical participation is to say that one thing has what it is *with* and indeed *after* and *in pursuit of*, another: it has its reality, in other words, by virtue of something other than itself."[3] Such an approximation, however, does not easily translate into a Christian worldview. How does created reality tend toward the complete otherness of God while at the same time recognizing God's hand in creation's very existence? Also, how can one recognize

---

[3] David C. Schindler, "What's the Difference? On the Metaphysics of Participation in a Christian Context," *Saint Anselm Journal* 3 (2005): 1–27, at 1. Italics are Schindler's.

the individual uniqueness of a particular created reality (this tree, this frog, this human being) with its own particular nature without letting it be trivialized by a seemingly higher universal form? Aquinas sought to Christianize the participation of metaphysics by reverting to Aristotelian terms of substance. In his commentary on Boethius, *De Hebdomadibus*, Aquinas argues that someone can participate in three distinct ways: as a species to a genus, as a substance in its accidents, and as an effect in its cause.[4] For the sake of theological discourse he rightly asserts that the only way in which these metaphysical senses of participation can be linked to the divine is through the last of the three analogies—as the effect shares in its cause, especially in the case of one's *being*. Thus in the order of being one participates in God as an effect participates in its cause.

In his later work, the *Summa theologiae*, however, Aquinas also links this understanding of participation to the order of grace. In a soteriological framework Aquinas defines grace as a participation in the divine nature.[5] Grace is viewed as the self-communication of God to the human person with the intent to transform that person: grace building on nature. In the soteriological arena participation goes beyond the level of being and centers now on the deification of the human person, who becomes more like God by participating or sharing in the divine nature. William Hill clearly delineates the distinction Aquinas makes here. Hill asserts that the self-communication of the trinitarian God *qua* grace is radically different from participation in God on the level of being:

> Here, man is enabled to enter into intersubjective union with God in the depths of his own uncreated Trinitarian life—with the Father, the Son, and Spirit who can only be communicated to the world as God. In creation, (apart from grace) by contrast, all that is possible is man's imitation, in a way proper to the structures of his natural being and person, of God in his nature known by reason as the first source and last end of creatures. This is only to note the necessity of maintaining the real distinction between what have been designated traditionally as the order of nature and the order of grace. Both are gratuitous—since no one can make a claim on his own coming into existence—but differently so. On the level of nature, man participates in the divine

4 *De hebdom.*, lec. 2, n. 24.
5 ST, Ia IIae, q. 110.

being, but as it is imitable in finite ways; on the level of grace, he participates even in the uncreated mode of that being proper to God.[6]

This second understanding of participation, then, is intimately allied with the act of revelation—with the disclosure and communication of God to creation.

A third understanding of participation can also be linked to the ecclesial reality of an individual or group of individuals connected in communion to Christ and to one another. Participation within the order of communion implies an ecclesiological belonging: it goes beyond the sense of simply partaking in a certain group or becoming a member within a distinct club. Ecclesiological participation points to the unity of believers in Christ that is eternal and divinely formed. Jean-Marie Tillard asserts that one of the hallmarks of the early Christian church was the simple realization that one could not be *in Christo* unless one was also *in pneumati*.[7] The communion that is established with Christ encompasses the whole of his life—one with his suffering, one with his ministry, one with his Spirit. Thus the participation established in Christ has an ecclesial reality; it binds the members of the church together through the power of the Spirit. The *syndesmos*, or bond of unity, that unites the whole is only broken by human sin.[8] The ecclesiological sense of participation not only brings the individual out of isolation to realize his or her place within the church and salvation history but also provides an intimate link to the inner-trinitarian dynamic expressed in the unity between Son and Spirit in the church.

Finally, we must look at participation in a ritual-liturgical sense. It is too easy to oversimplify liturgical participation and see it in a minimalistic sense as how one behaves or acts in the context of the liturgical celebration: the priest presides, the lector reads, the cantor sings, etc. But liturgical participation cannot be envisioned as simply role fulfillment. Rather, liturgical participation roots itself in the sacramental life of the church and specifically in what the sacraments are meant to achieve in the lives of the faithful. In this sense liturgical participation is centered on the transformation of the human person through grace

---

[6] William J. Hill, *The Three-Personed God: The Trinity as a Mystery of Salvation* (Washington, DC: Catholic University of America Press, 1982), 291.

[7] Jean-Marie Roger Tillard, "Spirit, Reconciliation, Church," *Ecumenical Review* 42 (1990): 237–49, at 238.

[8] Ibid., 242.

in the medium of the church in order to bring the individual back to his or her Creator, the source of being. Thus liturgical participation presupposes the first three senses of participation we have discussed already. Through the sacramental life (liturgical) of the gathered church (ecclesiological) one participates in the divine life of God who created us (metaphysical) and is thus transformed in grace for beatitude (soteriological).

THE TRINITARIAN NARRATIVE
AT THE HEART OF PARTICIPATION

Woven through this comprehensive notion of liturgical participation is a trinitarian narrative that undergirds not only the liturgy that is celebrated but also the Christian life as it unfolds within salvation history. The polyvalent nature of participation mirrors the self-communication of the Trinity in human history. That self-communication begins in the very act of creation. All creation participates in the Triune God in the order of being, that is, every creature shares in being with God who is being itself. In this sense the metaphysical understanding of participation roots itself in the disclosure of the creator God. The trinitarian narrative continues in the act of revelation: God the Father reveals himself to humanity in the witness of the Old Testament and binds himself to that humanity by means of the covenant. Such a covenantal relationship lifts the notion of participation beyond the order of being and into the order of grace: at the heart of the covenant is the understanding of the human person's redemption and final end as union with God. The fullness of that revelation comes in the person of Christ, in the act of the Incarnation and the manifestation of the Paschal Mystery. In his death and resurrection Christ invites his disciples to be one with him through participating in his own suffering, death, and resurrection. Such a participation links the believer with the Son at a level of communion. The establishment of a living church in the power of the Spirit implies an ongoing participation in its sacramental-liturgical life. The work of the Spirit in the economy of salvation continues the work of Christ and undergirds the participation of the faithful in divine realities. Thus in order to understand the development of a theology of *liturgical* participation one must consider the trinitarian narrative that is inextricably linked to the very notion of participation in all of its nuanced meanings, whether it be in the act of creation, the establishment of the covenant, the fullness of the revelation of the Triune God in Christ, or the work of the Trinity in the sacramental life of the church. Inherent in the notion of liturgical participation is the simple reality that all liturgy manifests the self-communication of the Triune God in the Paschal Mystery. One cannot talk about the liturgical action without also talking about the work of the Trinity in the economy of salvation. In this sense the Second Vatican Council's call for "full, conscious, and active participation" carries with it implications of the trinitarian narrative that are inextricably linked to the liturgical action.

In order to understand fully how this trinitarian narrative operates in determining a theology of liturgical participation one must investigate the origin of the phrase "full, active, and conscious participation," the major influence of the encyclical *Mediator Dei* on this developing theology, the full context of the Second Vatican Council's formulation of the phrase, and its later development after the council. What is attempted here is not meant to be an exhaustive explication of every mention of "active participation" in magisterial and theological documents from the formulation of the phrase to the present. Such an attempt would necessarily be compromised by the sheer volume of instances, varied interpretations, and distinctions made among various kinds of magisterial documents. Instead, what is offered is a synopsis of both the major influences leading up to the council's formulation and the reaction to those influences from the theological arena.

EARLY ATTEMPTS AT DEFINING LITURGICAL PARTICIPATION

At the beginning of his *motu proprio* on the function of sacred music, *Tra le sollecitudini*, Pope Pius X noted the crucial role that active participation of the faithful could and must have in the life of the church. The *motu proprio* itself was geared toward the reestablishment of the use of Gregorian chant throughout the church and the respective roles of the faithful and musicians within the liturgy. Referring to the restoration of a true Christian spirit, the pope argued for the necessity of "acquiring this spirit from its foremost and indispensable fount, which is the active participation in the holy mysteries and in the public and solemn prayer of the Church."[9] This marked the first time the phrase "active

---

[9] Pope Pius X, "*Tra le sollecitudini,*" *Ephemerides Liturgicae* 18 (1904): 129–49, at 132. ". . . dove appunto i fedeli si radunano per attingere tale spirito dalla sua prima ed indispensabile fonte, che è la participazione attiva ai sacrosanti

participation" was used in any magisterial document of known record. Giacomo Cardinal Lercaro asserts that Pius X's use of the phrase was directly connected to what the pontiff sought to achieve during his pontificate: "the restoration of all things in Christ."[10] Here, then, there is an indirect reference to the soteriological and ecclesiological aspects of the trinitarian narrative: active participation in the liturgy leads to union with Christ, which has redemptive qualities. Pius X, responding to the Jansenist crisis of the decades preceding his papacy, attempted to articulate a theology that used the participation of the faithful as a means to achieve the reformation he desired. Lercaro argues that Jansenism, by "chilling the relations of the sons of God to their heavenly Father and terrorizing them into staying away from His holy Table, had inhibited or at least lessened their most intimate and concrete participation in 'Liturgy' *par excellence*."[11] Combined with his proposal to reform the Roman breviary and his attempt to restore the reception of frequent communion as a regular practice among the Christian faithful, Pius X's *motu proprio* helped set the stage for a renewal of the liturgy.

The theological reaction to Pius X's *motu proprio* was muted at best. Six years later, in 1909, at the Catholic Conference at Malines, Dom Lambert Beauduin from the Abbey of Mont César articulated a program whereby the liturgy could once again become central to the lives of the faithful. He used as the basis for his argument Pius X's call for "active participation," referring again and again to the one line noted above.[12] In the event, while the immediate reaction to Pius X's *motu*

---

misteri e alla preghiera pubblica e solenne della Chiesa." Pius X originally published the *motu proprio* in Italian. In this edition the Italian and the official Latin translation that appeared in ASS are published side by side.

[10] Giacomo Cardinal Lercaro, "Active Participation: The Basic Principle of the Pastoral-Liturgical Reforms of Pius X," *Worship* 28 (1954): 120–28, at 121.

[11] Ibid. For contrasting opinions regarding the Jansenist influence on liturgical participation of the faithful in the decades before Pius X's papacy, see Ralph W. Franklin, "The Peoples' Work: Anti-Jansenist Prejudice in the Benedictine Movement for Popular Participation in the 19th Century," *Studia Liturgica* 19 (1989): 60–77; Ellen Weaver, "Liturgy for the Laity: The Jansenist Case for Popular Participation in Worship in the Seventeenth and Eighteenth Centuries," *Studia Liturgica* 19 (1989): 47–59.

[12] Louis Bouyer, *Liturgical Piety* (Notre Dame, IN: University of Notre Dame Press, 1955), 60. Bouyer describes Beauduin and the Malines Conference in

proprio on sacred music was limited, within twenty years the liturgical movement had taken root across the world.[13]

By 1928, when Pius XI issued his apostolic constitution *Divini cultus*, the reaction was far different. Following the lead of his predecessor, Pius XI described in detail the participation of the faithful in liturgical music: "In order that the faithful may actively participate in divine worship, may Gregorian chant be restored to the use of the peoples . . . they should not be merely extraneous or silent spectators, but, filled with a deep sense of the beauty of the liturgy, should sing alternately with the clergy or with the choir, as it is prescribed."[14] This obvious allusion to the earlier statement of Pius X is then followed immediately by a statement of the need for catechesis, the simple recognition that clergy, bishops, and ordinaries must "devote their energies, either directly or through other trained teachers, to providing for the instruction of the people in the liturgy and in music."[15] It was in this arena of catechesis for the active participation of the faithful that many theologians and liturgists began to comment anew on the issue.

For instance, at the National Eucharistic Congress of South Africa in May 1929, just six months after the promulgation of the apostolic constitution on sacred music, Kenneth McMurtrie lamented the lack of participation of the faithful in the eucharistic celebration: "At the present day it has become very common for the laity to take very little active part indeed in the official prayers and ceremonies of the Church. Thus at holy Mass you will commonly find the congregation engaged in all kinds of private devotions . . . which are very different from the Mass prayers themselves."[16] But what McMurtrie did next in his address built on the work of the previous pontiffs to encourage participation as a way of restoring the church in Christ. Citing the

---

some detail and lists the fourfold program that comes out of the conference under Beauduin's direction; it mirrors the direction and work of Pius X.

[13] Bernard Botte, *From Silence to Participation: An Insider's View of Liturgical Renewal*, trans. John Sullivan, OCD (Washington, DC: Pastoral Press, 1988), 29–40.

[14] Pope Pius XI, *Divini Cultus*, AAS 21, no. 2 (1929): 33–41, at 39–40. For an English translation of the document, see also Kevin Seasoltz, *The New Liturgy: A Documentation, 1903–1965*, 58–63.

[15] Pope Pius XI, *Divini Cultus*, 40.

[16] Kenneth F. McMurtrie, "The Liturgy and the Laity," *Orate Fratres* 3 (1929): 414–20, at 414.

work of other theologians, McMurtrie added that "active participation in the liturgy will necessarily produce effects of social character which will overflow from the sphere of religion into the spheres of political, social, and economic life."[17] Liturgical participation has the ability to create an ethic of behavior; it transforms the participant. McMurtrie calls for a two-tiered level of catechesis to help the laity understand and thereby participate more fully in the celebration. The first tier involves the encouragement of the fruitful study of Latin for the laity because "at the present day the average layman, because of his ignorance of Latin, is inclined to perhaps think that the contents of the Missal are of no importance or interest to him."[18] The second tier involves the use of primers and missals to help aid the laity in their understanding of what is happening in the liturgical act. McMurtrie argued that most of the primers and missals for use by the laity included prayers and devotions extraneous to the prayers of the liturgy itself. His intent here was to reinsert the importance of the church's liturgical prayer as formative and he had moved beyond the simpler statements of both Pius X and Pius XI to equate at least some aspect of active participation with cognitive understanding of the liturgical action.

In a similar vein, William Busch responded quite dramatically to the apostolic constitution at the third annual Liturgical Day in 1931.[19] Citing Pius XI's comment about "mute spectators" in *Divini cultus*, Busch saw a call to demonstrable activity within the liturgy. He argued that what the liturgical movement sought to achieve was "not only instruction, but action also. The Mass is not only something to be understood; it is also something to be done; it is action, it is drama, and it is something to be done by all."[20] He noted that participation must have at least two dimensions: an outward one, in its actions and words, and an inward one, in the union with Christ in the sacrifice. But here

[17] Ibid., 415.

[18] Ibid., 418.

[19] The Liturgical Days began in the United States at Saint John's Abbey in Collegeville, Minnesota, the home of the liturgical movement in this country. At the third Liturgical Day the conference moved to St. Cloud, Minnesota, where a larger number of people could participate. This marked the beginning of the spread of the liturgical movement in this country from the Benedictine center at Collegeville.

[20] William Busch, " 'Do This in Commemoration of Me.' Popular Participation in the Sacrifice of the Mass," *Orate Fratres* 5, no. 10 (1931): 441–52.

is where a determined liturgical theology[21] of participation begins to develop—a theology drawn from the liturgical rites and the sacramental actions themselves that looks toward the mystery being celebrated. Busch repeatedly cited the liturgical texts themselves as the locus for understanding how participation must be both outward and inward: outward by the dialogical nature of the texts and inward from the obvious supplication and offering of the words of the texts. He asserted:

> Active participation of all the faithful means therefore that each one of us must come to the Mass not merely as passive recipients but as active givers, offering in union with our Lord the homage and devotion and service of our daily life, all our purposes and efforts, our endurances and abnegations. These we bring to the altar, represented outwardly by our gifts of bread and wine, so that as bread and wine are changed into the body and blood of Christ we ourselves may be embraced as victims in His great sacrifice.
>
> Such is the teaching of the official Mass-prayers if we will read them attentively and study and meditate them. Such is the main thought that runs all through the prayers of the Offertory and Canon of the Mass.[22]

In this way, Busch pointed to a twofold offering and receiving within his concept of active participation. The examples of Busch and McMurtrie are only two of the various theological opinions that surfaced during the 1920s and 1930s regarding the meaning of "active participation," not only in the United States but throughout the church worldwide.

---

[21] "Liturgical theology" is not a univocal expression. It can variously mean a theology about the liturgy itself or a theology derived from liturgical rites, actions, and text. In most recent theological discussions it has also taken on a third meaning: a theology that is doxological, that is, geared toward the praise of God inherent in liturgical action: it becomes both a moment of reflection on the faith act and a vehicle toward systematic discourse. When the phrase "liturgical theology" is used in this work the latter definition is implied. See especially Kevin Irwin, *Liturgical Theology: A Primer*, ed. Edward Foley, American Essays in Liturgy (Collegeville, MN: Liturgical Press, 1990). For other related interpretations of liturgical theology, see also Aidan Kavanagh, *On Liturgical Theology* (New York: Pueblo, 1984); Gordon W. Lathrop, *Holy Things: A Liturgical Theology* (Minneapolis: Fortress Press, 1993).

[22] Busch, "'Do This in Commemoration of Me,'" 450.

The Belgian Liturgical Movement that had begun at Mont César had now spread to nearly every institution of Catholic thought. New publications addressing specifically liturgical issues were introduced for nearly every language group in the Western world.[23] With the dramatic increase of scholarly debate and opinion on the matter of "active participation" it was seemingly only a matter of time before the church's magisterium would help bring clarity to the matter.

MEDIATOR DEI AND THE PRE-CONCILIAR DEFINITIONS OF ACTIVE PARTICIPATION

The encyclical on the sacred liturgy, *Mediator Dei*, promulgated by Pope Pius XII in November 1947,[24] sought to achieve that very clarity on the matter of participation. While the document as a whole is devoted to the entire liturgy, significant portions of the encyclical are geared specifically to the discussion of what it means for the faithful to participate in the sacraments, with primary attention being given to the celebration of the Eucharist. The encyclical itself follows from Pius XII's earlier encyclical *Mystici Corporis*, in which he presented the idea

[23] The first of these was *La vie liturgique*, which published the Sunday Masses for the dioceses of Belgium. It was replaced approximately five years later by the *Missel dominical*. Beginning in 1919, *Questions liturgiques et paroissiales* became the second publication of the Abbey of Mont César. Its Flemish counterpart was *Liturgisch Tijdschrift*. In Italy, *Rivista Liturgica* began publication in Padova in 1914. In Germany the *Jahrbuch für Liturgiewissenschaft* began under the editorship of Dom Odo Casel in 1921 and continued under that name until World War II. After Casel's death in 1948 a new publication, the *Archiv für Liturgiewissenschaft*, began in 1951. *Orate Fratres* began publication in the United States in 1926 at St. John's Abbey in Collegeville, Minnesota, and later, in 1945, the Centre de Pastorale Liturgique began *La Maison-Dieu* in Paris. *Sacris Erudiri* began three years later in the Netherlands.

[24] Pope Pius XII, *Mediator Dei*, in *The Papal Encyclicals, 1939–1958*, ed. Claudia Carlen, IHM (Ann Arbor, MI: Pierian Press, reprint, 1990), 119–54. In this compilation Carlen uses the translation by Gerald Ellard in *On the Sacred Liturgy: Encyclical Letter Mediator Dei (November 20, 1947) of Pope Pius XII* (New York: America Press, 1954). All English references are to the Carlen edition, which will hereafter be cited simply as *Mediator Dei*, followed by the paragraph number. For the Latin text, see also Pope Pius XII, *Mediator Dei*, AAS 39, no. 2:14 (1947): 521–600. All further references to this edition will be cited hereafter as AAS, followed by the issue number and then page number.

of the church as the Mystical Body of Christ and the ramifications of the identification of the church with Christ.

Before proceeding to his discussion of the role of liturgical participation in the Eucharist, Pius XII asserts the importance of the interior action in the liturgical celebration. "The chief element of divine worship," he argues, "must be interior."[25] Giving preeminence to this interior aspect of worship serves two purposes: it prevents a dependence on external elements that can lead to formalism, and it allows the worship of the church body to be moved to union with God through contemplation—that is, it allows the church to more adequately enter into its identity as the Mystical Body of Christ. This latter aspect of interior worship has a significant role in the efficacy of the sacrament. Pius XII asserts that

> this efficacy, where there is a question of the eucharistic sacrifice and the sacraments, derives first of all and principally from the act itself (*ex opere operato*). But if one considers the part which the Immaculate Spouse of Jesus Christ takes in the action, embellishing the sacrifice and sacraments with prayer and sacred ceremonies, or if one refers to the "sacramentals" and the other rites instituted by the hierarchy of the Church, then its effectiveness is due rather to the action of the church (*ex opere operantis Ecclesiae*), inasmuch as she is holy and acts always in closest union with her Head.[26]

Not only does such an interior act help foster unity within the Body; it also mandates that a personal piety develop in conjunction with a corporate sense of the church's holiness. Thus before Pius XII even begins his formal statements regarding liturgical participation he has underscored the value of interior and exterior action in the sacraments and has related such action to an ecclesiological interpretation of the trinitarian narrative.

In the second section of the encyclical, as Pius XII begins to speak more concretely about eucharistic worship, he takes both the interior and exterior aspects of human action and applies them to the concept of participation. First, he notes that the "cooperation of the faithful is required so that sinners may be individually purified in the blood of

---

[25] Pope Pius XII, *Mediator Dei*, 24. See also AAS 39, 531: *At praecipuum divini cultus elementum internum esse debet.*

[26] *Mediator Dei*, 27. See also AAS 39, 532.

the Lamb . . . through this active and individual participation, the members of the Mystical Body not only become daily more like to their divine Head, but the life flowing from the Head is imparted to the members."[27] In this sense participation in the liturgy leads directly to the transformation of the person in grace to be more like Christ. This christocentric depiction of liturgical participation is central to the theology of Pius XII. It forms the basis not only of his sacramental theology but also of his ecclesiology.

The pope notes that participation of the faithful in the sacramental-liturgical act has two important christological-trinitarian modes within the celebration of the Eucharist. The first is in the participation with the priest who offers the sacrifice in the person of Christ. Pius XII reasserts the words of his predecessor, Innocent II, when he writes: "Not only . . . do the priests offer the sacrifice, but also all the faithful: for what the priest does personally by virtue of his ministry, the faithful do collectively by virtue of their intention."[28] The pontiff goes on to note that the liturgical texts themselves reflect the nature of the offering of the whole assembly. "The rites and prayers of the eucharistic sacrifice," he argues, "signify and show no less clearly that the oblation of the Victim is made by the priests in company with the whole people."[29] The use of "texts" in the plural number signifies for Pius XII that "the people also participate in this august sacrifice inasmuch as they offer the same."[30] He is careful to delineate that those who participate in the sacrifice do so in a way that is proper to their station in life: by the very nature of the sacrament of baptism, the faithful are incorporated into the Mystical Body of Christ and are thus appointed to give proper worship to God through participation in the sacraments, most especially the Eucharist. This participation becomes directly linked to their function within the sacramental celebration. The priest acts as the representative of Christ, the head of the Mystical Body. Thus the faithful participate in the sacramental offering in a clearly demarcated sense: "they not only offer the sacrifice by the hands of the priest, but also, to a certain extent, in union with him. It is by reason of this participation that the offering made by the people is also included

---

[27] *Mediator Dei*, 78. See also AAS 39, 551.

[28] *Mediator Dei*, 134. See also AAS, 39, 554. Pope Innocent III's words appear first in *De Sacro Altaris Mysterio*, III, 6.

[29] *Mediator Dei*, 134. See also AAS 39, 554.

[30] *Mediator Dei*, 134. See also AAS, 39, 554.

in liturgical worship."[31] By sharing in the representative offering of the priest and being united as the Mystical Body, the faithful participate in the offering of the objects of the sacrifice.

But Pius also notes that the faithful participate in the offering of themselves as victims as well, and it is through this participation that the oblation has its "full effect."[32] The offering of the self is not restricted to the liturgical act; it takes on special significance when, in the course of the sacramental action, the faithful offer themselves in union with Christ, the High Priest. Such an offering produces a likeness and similarity to Christ: "they offer themselves as a spiritual sacrifice, that each one's faith ought to become more ready to work through charity, his piety more real and fervent, and each one should consecrate himself to the furthering of the divine glory, desiring to become as like as possible to Christ in His most grievous sufferings."[33] The offering presented by the faithful *qua* victims centers not on the bread and wine presented at the altar but on the presentation of the entirety of their lives before the altar of God. For Pius XII the text and flow of the sacramental action allow the faithful to enter most fully into this offering of themselves. He asserts: "All the elements of the liturgy, then, would have us reproduce in our hearts the likeness of the divine Redeemer through the mystery of the cross."[34] For the pontiff the relationship between participation and the offering of the self as victim is crucial. He concludes this section of the encyclical with an admonition to the faithful:

> Let the faithful, therefore, consider to what a high dignity they are raised by the sacrament of baptism. They should not think it enough to participate in the eucharistic sacrifice with the general intention which befits members of Christ and children of the Church, but let them further, in keeping with the spirit of the sacred liturgy, be most closely united with the High Priest and His earthly minister, at the time the consecration of the divine Victim is enacted, and at that time especially when those solemn words are pronounced, "By Him and with Him, and in Him is to Thee, God the Father almighty, in the unity of the Holy Ghost, all honor and glory for ever and ever"; to these words in fact the people answer, "Amen." Nor should Christians forget to offer

[31] *Mediator Dei*, 135. See also AAS 39, 555–56.
[32] *Mediator Dei*, 135. See also AAS 39, 557.
[33] *Mediator Dei*, 135–36. See also AAS 39, 558.
[34] *Mediator Dei*, 136. See also AAS 39, 559.

themselves, their cares, their sorrows, their distress and their necessities in union with their divine Saviour upon the cross."[35]

The call to offer the entire self in the liturgical act reiterates Pius XII's earlier assertion that primary emphasis is to be given to the interior act of participation and that this interior act draws one more closely into likeness with Christ. Participation, within the sacrament of the Eucharist, is defined as a complete offering of the self combined with the offering of material elements made by the priest and the assembly united with him. Such an offering of both the priest and the assembly becomes identified with Christ's action within the trinitarian narrative of salvation history.

THE VARIED REACTIONS TO *MEDIATOR DEI* AND ITS CHRISTOCENTRIC THEOLOGY OF PARTICIPATION

In the decade that followed the promulgation of *Mediator Dei*, theologians, liturgists, and pastoral leaders from across the world sought to elucidate for the faithful Pius XII's teaching within the encyclical. However, the attempt to demarcate the theology of the encyclical involved myriad interpretations that crossed the breadth of the theological spectrum. There was no one universal reaction to the document. One cannot deny that *Mediator Dei* was written to address certain abuses with regard to participation in the liturgy and that some theologians took the proscriptions of the encyclical as a denunciation of the growing tide of participation in the liturgy espoused by various groups.[36] As early as 1942, Conrad Groeber, archbishop of Freiburg, warned other German bishops that the abuses of participation and the growing sense of the church as a dynamic organism were dangerous threats to church authority.[37] But Pius XII had underscored this

---

[35] *Mediator Dei*, 136. See also AAS 39, 559–60.

[36] See, for example, Eugène Flicoteaux, "Notre sanctification par la liturgie," *Vie spirituelle* 79 (1948): 99–109; Ernest B. Koenker, "Objectives and Achievements of the Liturgical Movement in the Roman Catholic Church since World War I," *Church History* 20/2 (1951): 14–27, at 23–26.

[37] See Archbishop Conrad Groeber, "Memorandum de S. E. Mgr. Groeber, Archevêque de Fribourg," *La Maison-Dieu* (1942): 97–104, at 99. Groeber's memorandum to the hierarchy of the German Church is repeatedly mentioned in European reactions to the encyclical as a way of pointing to the controversy within the German (and Austrian) church and the need for clarification from the pontiff. For a spirited Austrian reaction to his memorandum, which in its

dynamism in his encyclical *Mystici Corporis* the very next year. *Mediator Dei*, in conjunction with *Mystici Corporis*, attempts to outline the parameters of liturgical participation for the faithful while addressing those instances in which participation might go awry.[38] Despite resistance, many regarded the pontiff's repeated stress on the participation of the faithful within the liturgy as a clarion call for strengthened efforts in liturgical renewal. By the mid-1950s the theological discussion was shaped essentially not by a hard-and-fast demarcation of opposing sides on the issue, but rather by vastly varying approaches and hermeneutics used to interpret both the document and a theology of participation. In the section that follows, these various reactions have been grouped according to four central motifs that helped articulate the later notion of liturgical participation presented by the Second Vatican Council. These motifs include the Mystical Body of Christ, the theology of the laity, human suffering, and a noncommunitarian approach to participation. The first three all help situate the human person within a christological-trinitarian dynamic while the last acts as a corrective to a semi-Pelagian tendency that would make liturgical participation solely a human endeavor.

THE MYSTICAL BODY AND PARTICIPATION

For many theologians the promulgation of *Mediator Dei* had to be coupled with Pius XII's earlier encyclical, *Mystici Corporis*. The pope's articulation of the Mystical Body of Christ as the living church became the lens through which participation in the liturgy was to be evaluated. Such an interpretation was not without obvious warrant. The beginning of *Mediator Dei* establishes the relationship of the Mystical Body of Christ, the church, to the liturgy itself. Worship is seen as a continuation of the priesthood of Christ through the medium of the church. Pius XII asserts: "the divine Redeemer has so willed it that the priestly life begun with the supplication and sacrifice of His mortal body should continue without intermission down the ages in His Mystical Body which is the Church."[39] Moreover, he argues that the church

---

tone and tenor obviously points to an ongoing debate, see Theodor Cardinal Innitzer, "Response de S. Em. le Cardinal Innitzer au memorandum de S. exc. Mgr. Groeber," *La Maison-Dieu* 8 (1943): 108–15.

[38] See George Montague, "Observations on the Encyclical 'Mediator Dei,'" *Irish Ecclesiastical Record* 70 (July 1948): 577–89, at 581–84.

[39] *Mediator Dei*, 119.

"prolongs the priestly mission of Jesus Christ mainly by means of the sacred liturgy"—first at the altar itself, then through the other sacraments, and finally through the daily prayer of the church.[40] Taking this cue, theologians advocating greater participation of the faithful in the liturgy viewed the encyclical in terms quite favorable to their cause. To them, participation in the liturgy was synonymous with the Mystical Body of Christ fulfilling its mission.

For example, Dom Bernard Capelle writes extensively about the relationship between the two encyclicals and the ramifications of a relationship for the participation of the faithful. Capelle points to the pontiff's insistence on the permanent unity of the Head with its members in discussing the Mystical Body acting in the liturgy. He argues: "[t]his incessant conjunction of Christ with the Church in the liturgical mystery is absolutely fundamental for it is that which uncovers for us the most essential reason to unite always the interior homage of the heart to the visible rite."[41] For Capelle, because the people of God are always united to Christ in virtue of their baptism they must engage themselves within the liturgical act, even when that engagement is altogether interior. Participation in the liturgical act cannot be optional since it is through such participation that the human person is transformed into likeness with Christ. Moreover, the visible rite is invigorated by the invisible action of the participant. Capelle argues that this idea of participation runs throughout the entire encyclical and therefore is essential. But he is careful to note that the communal character of the celebration of the sacraments does not depend on the participation of the faithful, and while that participation, in fact, leads to sacramental transformation, it does not do so without reference to Christ as the head of the Mystical Body. The liturgical form itself suffices to ensure the communal nature of the church's liturgy. While Capelle realizes that such a public character exists in all the church's liturgical rites, especially as he encourages the faithful to participate in the Divine Office, he clearly accentuates the role of the celebration of the Eucharist itself. He maintains that "[t]he mass declares better still its ecclesiastical essence: it is celebrated in a common room; its rite assigns to each of the participants his [her] role; it is not enough that

[40] Ibid., 119–20.

[41] Bernard Capelle, "Théologie pastorale des encycliques Mystici Corporis et Mediator Dei," *La Maison-Dieu* 47-48 (1956): 65–80, at 71.

one joins it from afar; one must attend to it."[42] Capelle views the teaching of *Mediator Dei* as supporting the growing concept that a member of the faithful cannot simply stand idly by as a silent or disinterested spectator. The rite of the church itself demands participation. Capelle closes his argument by insisting on the duty to increase this communal sense of the liturgy within the faithful. He asserts:

> There seems to result, for the priests responsible for the religious behavior of the faithful, a grave duty: that of safeguarding and deepening in their hearts the sense of the community of the liturgical acts, understanding by "community," beyond the group of parishioners surrounding their pastor, the entire church, the Mystical Body linked by its chiefs with Christ. "In the liturgical action," says the encyclical, "Christ is found present with the Church."[43]

For Capelle the call to participation stems from the communal act of the liturgy itself, which by its nature reflects the Mystical Body of Christ.

In a similar vein George Montague seeks to explicate a dynamic relationship between the theology of the Mystical Body of Christ and a theology of participation for the faithful. In a series of articles in the *Irish Ecclesiastical Record,* Montague puts forward not only a synopsis of the encyclical *Mediator Dei* but also a collection of his own observations regarding the encyclical's teaching. In his opening commentary on the encyclical Montague asserts that with the growing acceptance of liturgical studies, "the faithful have thereby come to realize more clearly their duty as members of the Mystical Body of Christ to participate in the liturgical rites of the Church."[44] Thus before he even begins his detailed synopsis Montague establishes an intimate connection between the Mystical Body of Christ and the necessity of participation. The connection is made manifest when Montague articulates the pontiff's description of interior and exterior worship in the encyclical. The conjunction of exterior and interior worship occurs when the person of faith enters into the sacred rites in an imitation of Christ in prayer and

[42] Ibid., 78.

[43] Ibid., 80. Although Capelle does not cite the quotation from the encyclical, it is found in paragraph 20 of *Mediator Dei: Quapropter in omni actione liturgica una cum Ecclesia praesens adest divinus eius Conditor.*

[44] George Montague, "Recent Encyclical on the Sacred Liturgy: *Mediator Dei,*" *Irish Ecclesiastical Record* 70 (February 1948): 148–58, at 148.

sacrifice. United with Christ as Head, the Mystical Body enters into the sacramental celebration both for its own salvation and for that of the whole. Lack of interior worship belies a lack of unity with Christ. Again, the emphasis here is on participation in Christ.

Montague reiterates this dual character of worship when, in reviewing the second section of the encyclical, he speaks directly about the participation of the faithful in the Eucharist. While he is careful to say that the faithful do not participate in the sacrifice in the same manner and character as the priest presiding over the celebration, he will argue that "their prayers of praise, thanksgiving and supplication are joined with the intentions of the priest and of the Supreme High Priest and offered to the Father in the external sacerdotal oblation."[45] He goes even further to insist that "[t]his external rite of sacrifice must of its nature manifest internal worship; the Sacrifice of the New Law manifests the submission offered to God by the principal offerer, Christ, and with Him and through Him by all the members of His Mystical Body."[46] The nature of the Mystical Body as defined by Pius XII demands the participation of the faithful in the sacraments—not simply in exterior worship but in the interior recollection and unity expressed by the external rite itself. Montague envisions a highly engaged participation of the faithful under the theological backdrop of the Mystical Body of Christ and nuanced by the understanding of Christ acting as High Priest.

In a later article Montague assesses how these elements work together within the liturgical celebration. Although he writes this later article to explain the reasons why the encyclical was written and the impact it will have on the church, in making these observations he asserts his strong position on the connection between the Mystical Body and participation of the faithful and also offers certain distinctions that were not in his earlier synopsis. Montague is clear to state that he does not advocate an understanding of the Mystical Body of Christ that equates every aspect of Christ's ministry with that of the faithful—he does not wish to identify each member of the assembly with the ordained priesthood of Christ or his sacerdotal ministry. Participation of the faithful is not synonymous with the action of the ordained minister. In advocating this position he undeniably rejects the theologies put forth in the midst of the German controversy the encyclical

---

[45] Ibid., 154.
[46] Ibid.

addresses.[47] He also underscores the relationship between the daily life of the faithful and their participation in the sacramental life of the church. He argues:

> Above all, it must be kept in mind that the motive for the correct observance of the rubrics is not merely external dignity nor understanding of the ceremonies, but that careful observance of the rubrics contributes to a closer union with Christ as Priest, and so to greater sanctity . . . it is through our union with Christ in His mysteries that we are transformed into His likeness.[48]

Again, liturgical participation, an active engagement in the rites, leads to an analogous participation in Christ.

Similarly, Eugène Flicoteaux also sought to highlight the connection between the Mystical Body of Christ and the role liturgy plays in allowing the faithful to participate in the mysteries of Christ. In virtue of their baptism all the members of Christ's Body are called to become holy; however, Flicoteaux argues that that holiness is determined not simply by some sort of outward resemblance or modeling, but rather by an inner assimilation of the witness of Christ—as St. Paul asserts, "putting on Christ" (Rom 13:14; Gal 3:27; Eph 4:24; Col 3:10).[49] For Flicoteaux that inner assimilation occurs when the faithful participate in the liturgy as it cycles through the various mysteries of Christ's saving action throughout the year. In this manner, he argues, "we are penetrated by his spirit, we are united with its intimate promptings, and we have him live once again in our very selves according to the fullness of his being and according to the wealth of his holiness."[50] It is precisely through liturgical participation—an active engagement with the celebration of the rites—that the connection to Christ is made explicit. He goes on to conclude that "the celebration of the mystery is, for the Christian, all the more profitable as they participate, more

---

[47] Montague refuses to go into detail about which theologies are errant, but he does note the work of Karl Borgmann, who asserted that the participation of the faithful in the celebration of the Eucharist is "a sacerdotal act necessary for the full accomplishment of the sacrifice." See Montague, "Observations on the Encyclical 'Mediator Dei,'" 582.

[48] Ibid., 589.

[49] Flicoteaux, "Notre sanctification par la liturgie," 102.

[50] Ibid.

actively and more directly, in the liturgical prayer."[51] The corollary he draws from this statement is an admonition to ensure that the exterior elements of the ritual are substantial enough to elevate the internal spirit—namely, that the ritual itself must reflect the mysteries of Christ into which it draws its participants.[52]

PARTICIPATION AND THE THEOLOGY OF THE LAITY

Stemming from an increased understanding of the Mystical Body of Christ and its proper connection to the priesthood of Christ, a growing theology of the accurate role, function, and ministry of the laity became intertwined with the concept of participation. What appears in the years following the promulgation of *Mediator Dei* is an elevated sense of the laity within the corporate action of the church—elevated, but qualified. The latter part of the nineteenth century and the early years of the twentieth were marked by an ongoing debate regarding the role of the laity within the church, especially in the rising nationalist and liberal movements in Germany and Italy. Combined with a sense of the universal priesthood of believers growing rapidly among some Protestant denominations, the liberal movements in Germany and Italy produced a much-needed clarification of the role of the laity and their specific function in the celebration of the liturgy.[53] Moreover, the Lutheran tradition had increasingly accepted an understanding of ordained ministry as mediated by the community as a whole. While Pius XII clearly articulated the unique quality of priestly power attributed to the ordained minister as stemming from Christ alone, and not the community, he was more vague in his description of the laity's participation in the priesthood of Christ within the celebration, saying it was limited, in a different sense, according to their condition.[54] Thus

---

[51] Ibid., 107.

[52] Ibid., 109.

[53] There was certainly not a wholesale acceptance of a universal priesthood among the various German schools of theology, but the idea sparked an ever-increasing debate, especially as theologians of the Reformed movement entered into the discussion with their Catholic counterparts. See especially Johannes Brinktine, "Das Amtspriestertum und das Allegemeine Priestertum der Gläubigen," *Divus Thomas* 22 (1944): 291–308. Similar concerns were raised in the Italian peninsula the century before. See also Giovanni Perrone, SJ, *Praelectiones Theologicae* 8 (Louvain: Vanlithout & Vandenzande, 1838–1843), 255–69.

[54] See specifically *Mediator Dei* 85, 88, 92.

one of the reactions among theologians in the wake of *Mediator Dei*'s promulgation centered on clarifying the understanding of the laity's participation in the priesthood of Christ.

For instance, Gerald Ellard writes that the encyclical, "without in any least degree mitigating the sacramental distinction between priest and layman, lifts up the latter by enlisting him (in his degree) as an intelligent and active agent in helping Christ to worship God our sovereign Lord."[55] Ellard goes to great lengths to show that Pius XII has articulated a theology of the laity that is rooted in the twofold offering of the Eucharist—the first offering, by which the elements are consecrated and the presence of Christ is made manifest, is the offering of the priest alone in union with Christ the High Priest, but the second offering of the oblation itself is made *through* the hands of the priest and together *with* him. While the pontiff asserts that the oblation of the faithful takes place after the consecration, Ellard notes in analyzing the very prayers Pius XII uses to demarcate the offering of the people, namely, the *Orate fratres*, the *Memento vivorum*, the *Hanc igitur*, and the *Unde et memores*, that the first three all come before the institution narrative. These prayers point to the people's offering as the contribution of bread and wine for the sacrament and to their shared intention with Christ the High Priest and the presiding minister.[56]

Dom Lambert Beauduin, in his own summary of the encyclical, echoes this necessity for the faithful to unite their offering with the offering of Christ's priest on earth.[57] In fact, Beauduin asserts that it is precisely the proper understanding of the connection between the priest and the faithful that allows the community to come together as the Mystical Body. He states:

[55] Gerald Ellard, "At Mass with My Encyclical," *Orate Fratres* 22 (April 1948): 241–46, at 242.

[56] Ibid., 244.

[57] It should be noted that, by the time the encyclical was promulgated, Beauduin had left the Abbey of Mont César to found a new community, first at Amay and then later at Chevetogne. The Chevetogne Priory was seen as an experiment in ecumenism and would eventually include the celebration of both Latin and Eastern rites in its daily activities. In 1990 the priory was raised to the status of an abbey, and now one abbot acts as superior over both communities. Much of Beauduin's interpretation of the encyclical was influenced by his association with the community at Chevetogne.

In order for the eucharistic institution to produce all of its effects, it is indispensable to lead the faithful to participate very actively. And the encyclical devotes several paragraphs to mark the sovereign importance of this participation. It draws aside erroneous and condemned interpretations which would like to attribute sacerdotal capacities to the faithful and to distort the catholic concepts on these serious subjects.

This participation is so dear to his heart that the Sovereign Pontiff considers in detail all the means, even the most modest, which can support this union of the faithful with the priest. It is, indeed, the premier objective to reach for in view of forming a Christian community.[58]

Beauduin notes that the connection between the sacrificial offering of Christ as priest and the liturgical action is fundamental. In this sense he seeks to underscore the intimate connection between the priesthood of Christ, the liturgical action, and the formation of the Christian community.

In similar fashion Josef Jungmann asserts that the import and impact of *Mediator Dei* are due to the increased sense of the role of the laity in offering the liturgy. Looking at both the theologians of the early church and the prayers of the Mass themselves, Jungmann maintains that Christ intended "that we offer together with Him that sacrifice which He everywhere and in all times places in our midst. On the cross He offered alone; on the altar He desires to offer with His Church."[59] Jungmann notes, however, that the union of such an offering with the offering of Christ carries with it concrete implications. The more one reflects on this notion of offering, he argues, the more one sees a sacramental ethic emerge. In fact, Jungmann alludes to a sacramental ethic that derives its potency from participation in the priestly offering, an offering that calls the lay participants to give of themselves more and more completely.

This increased sense of offering on the part of the laity and its connection to how they participate liturgically provoked a significant reaction on the part of the episcopacy, especially in Europe.[60] While some

[58] Lambert Beauduin, "L'encyclique 'Mediator Dei,'" *La Maison-Dieu* 13 (1948): 7–25, at 16–17.

[59] Joseph Jungmann, "We Offer," *Orate Fratres* 24 (1949–50): 97–102, at 98.

[60] Published reports from these dioceses include those of Luçon, Nice, Laval, Strasbourg, Berlin, Bologna, and Milan, just to name a few.

bishops merely restated or summarized the content of the encyclical,[61] others went to great lengths to demarcate how the people of God were to be trained and educated in liturgical participation. In these latter cases careful attention was paid to the possibilities for engaging lay participants in the liturgical action, the interior disposition of the laity, and the necessary redefinition of the apostolate of the laity.[62]

PARTICIPATION AND HUMAN SUFFERING

Stemming from that heightened sense of self-offering in the theology of the laity, a less extensive and yet fundamentally profound interpretation of *Mediator Dei* can be seen in the relationship between participation and human suffering. Arising in some of the European countries devastated by the Second World War, this theological viewpoint attempts to make the church's liturgy a mode in which to understand the significant human suffering of the world. In his article, "The Recent Teachings of Pius XII on the Sacred Liturgy," Enrico Cattaneo espoused this intimate connection between liturgical participation and suffering. Cattaneo outlined the four sections of the encyclical after taking special note of Pius XII's introduction, quoting the opening paragraph in full.[63] While much of his synopsis is similar to the aforementioned descriptions of other theologians, Cattaneo concludes his formulation of the pontiff's theology by linking the liturgical prayer

[61] Antonio Mantiero, "La partecipazione liturgica," *Rivista liturgica* 35 (1948): 102–103. Mantiero was the bishop of Treviso in Italy.

[62] See, for example, Antoine-Marie Cazaux, "Ordonnance pour l'année de la messe," *La Maison-Dieu* 14 (1948): 129–36; Josef Calasanz Fliesser, "Allgemeine Messordnung für die volksliturgischen Messfeiern in Österreich," *Heiliger Dienst* 3 (1948): 6–11; Wilhelm Weskamm, "La participation active au cult et la vie d'une communauté," *La Maison-Dieu* 37 (1954): 25–41; and Damasus Zähringer, OSB, "Feier der heiligen Messe in Gemeinschaft," *Benediktinische Monatsschrift* 25 (1949): 476–83.

[63] Enrico Cattaneo, "I recenti insegnamenti di Pio XII sulla liturgia," *Vita e Pensiero* 36 (January 1948): 10–13, at 10. While Cattaneo quotes extensively from the encyclical in other places, this is the only place in his essay in which he allows an entire paragraph to stand alone. It is significant because here in the opening paragraph Pius XII makes explicit reference to the salvific act of Christ on the cross: the giving of himself in prayer and sacrifice. It is the "shedding of the blood of the Immaculate Lamb" that now allows each of the faithful "to set about the personal task of achieving his own sanctification." See also *Mediator Dei* 1.

and the Mystical Body to the suffering Christ. While he recognizes that the liturgical prayer united to the action is what makes the life of the Mystical Body, he argues that "what mainly strikes is the suffering Christ as Pius XII has presented (it)."[64] The liturgical act, in Cattaneo's understanding, becomes the vehicle whereby the suffering of the human person can be assuaged through participation. Cattaneo maintains: "The man who has known suffering and finds comfort in being a sharer of the redeeming passion awaiting the resurrection, as the single triumph of infinite love, repeatedly writes words of intense contemplation of the great sacrifice, of the invitation to immolation with Christ, of the most loving defense of the images that represent him aching."[65] To get away from a misrepresentation of the Mystical Body of Christ that has linked it with a glorified sense of the church he purposely highlights the sacrificial nature of the liturgical act. Participation is marked by sharing in the sacrifice, an embrace of the Crucified One rather than a denial of his crucifixion, an opportunity to empty oneself even as Jesus emptied himself on the cross, in a way proper to the nature of the faithful. Cattaneo's final remark is revelatory: "the believers, today," he argues, "more cursed because the world hates Christ, are more obliged to love the world in the way that the Redeemer has loved it: with offering, immolation, the consummation of his very self, because from the sacrifice, in this Friday of shadows, the resurrection of the Lord is rendered possible."[66] Cattaneo argues that participation in the sacrificial offering of the sacraments, especially the Eucharist, stems from the need not merely to emulate Christ but, in fact, to enter into salvation.

Ferdinand Cavallera of the Institut Catholique in Toulouse expressed a similar attention to the significance of *Mediator Dei* for a reevaluation of human suffering. In a two-part series of articles in *Revue d'Ascetique et de Mystique*, Cavallera asserts that one of the pontiff's main objectives in the encyclical is to develop a specific liturgical piety and spirituality rooted in the sacrifice and suffering of Christ. He maintains: "The collaboration of the faithful with the holy Sacrifice is the subject of particular attention and of very timely and very apt explanations to develop among the faithful an enlightened devotion

[64] Cattaneo, "I recenti insegnamenti," 13.
[65] Ibid.
[66] Ibid.

to the Holy Sacrifice of the Mass."[67] Cavallera notes that the encyclical cites very specific ways in which the faithful participate in the sacrifice of the Mass: the dissemination of the *Missale romanum*, the dialogue Mass, and participation in liturgical chant—provided these are done in accord with various decisions of the church hierarchy and are never given more value than they actually have.[68] While the majority of his first article is a mere recitation of what Pius XII had written in the encyclical, Cavalerra's second article clarifies his position on the self-offering of the faithful in the liturgical action. He asserts that the faithful participate doubly in the oblation of the liturgical celebration: communally as they are united to Christ as the Head of the Mystical Body, but also personally in the offering of their intentions and prayers together with the offering of the liturgical action.[69] That offering can take the form of the faithful's participation in the celebration of the sacrifice of Christ through the reading of the missal, the public response to the prayers of the priest, dialogue Masses, and even through private prayers that may differ in shape and form from the liturgical rite but nevertheless maintain its nature.[70]

THE NON-COMMUNITARIAN INTERPRETATION

Against these elucidations of the various nuances of the connection between the Mystical Body of Christ and the faithful there arose an interpretation of the encyclical that was wary of the modernist assumption that every human person could be baptized into an *alter Christus* or *quasi*-Christ. This concern stemmed from a fear that increased participation of the faithful would fall prey to more sociological trends of liberalism, and that a radical socialization or communization of the liturgical act could follow. Although Pius XII made it clear that such an interpretation would be fallacious, many theologians sought to ensure

---

[67] Ferdinand Cavallera, "L'encyclique 'Mediator Dei' et la spiritualité," *Revue d'ascetique et de mystique* 24 (1948): 3–30, at 13.

[68] Ibid., 15. See also, *Mediator Dei* 105–6.

[69] Ferdinand Cavallera, "L'encyclique 'Mediator Dei' et la piété liturgique," *Revue d'ascetique et de mystique* 24 (1948): 105–16, at 114.

[70] Ibid., 115. Cavallera maintains that the connection of the faithful to the cross of Christ and to the suffering-offering of Christ as victim is not achieved simply by going through the motions of a liturgical action. Rather, the liturgy demands that even internal, personal prayers and devotions are centered on the exterior action of the rite.

the high Christology of the encyclical over and against any possible distinction of the laity's connection to Christ. In these interpretations the capital grace of Christ, that is, the grace he possesses as head of the Mystical Body, was emphasized and the role of the laity in liturgical participation was minimized.

Albert Kaiser, for example, expressed the fear of an over-liberalized liturgical action in vivid terms when he asserted: "A witch's stew of liberalism, Modernism, Hegelianism and quietism spiced with pride and pharisaism cooked up two unsavory dishes, namely, the community priesthood and the unhistorical, divided, pneumatic Christ."[71] To him the encyclical was issued primarily to fight this abuse. In a two-part series of articles in *American Ecclesiastical Review*, Kaiser argued that the immediate background of the encyclical was twofold: the need to stem the socialization of the liturgy and religion in Nazi Germany (a socialization that took place in large part both because of the National Socialist movement and also as a means of resistance to it) and the excesses of the liturgical movement in Austria.[72] In the second half of that series Kaiser put forward his own understanding of participation in light of the encyclical. One cannot help but notice that he has couched much of his argument in negative terms. He briefly summarizes the concept of lay participation as such: "The laity participate *without priestly power*. They participate as co-offerers but only in a *spiritual sense*. They participate *as victims* offering themselves with the Victim on the altar. Holy Communion *of the priest* suffices to integrate the Sacrifice. The presence and the Communion of the people are not necessary to the validity or even to the public character of the Sacrifice."[73] Kaiser's emphasis on what participation *is not* expresses his desire to solidify the priesthood and the cross of Christ and their redemptive character. For Kaiser the priest cannot be seen as simply the mouthpiece of the community; rather, he is the one who acts *in persona Christi*, for it is Christ who ultimately acts in the sacraments.

[71] Albert Kaiser, "'Mediator Dei' and the Sacramental Christ," *Homiletic and Pastoral Review* 54 (1954): 1068–72, at 1068.

[72] Albert Kaiser, "The Historical Backgrounds and Theology of *Mediator Dei*. Part I: Backgrounds," *American Ecclesiastical Review* 1329 (1953): 368–78, at 374–75.

[73] Albert Kaiser, "The Historical Backgrounds and Theology of *Mediator Dei*. Part II: Philosophy and Theology," *American Ecclesiastical Review* 130 (1954): 33–45, at 35. Emphasis in original.

In a similar manner, John M. Hanssens noted that there were several exaggerations or misinterpretations by the liturgical apostolate that needed to be addressed by the encyclical. The first exaggeration Hanssens highlights is the tendency toward discrediting personal devotions during the liturgy as nonparticipatory or too subjective. He asserts that the encyclical directly opposes such a position: "without, naturally, attenuating the esteemed value of the sacred rites that must be recognized, it demonstrates that between the rites and the devotional exercises and private ascetical practices there is no opposition or loathing."[74] Instead, he maintains that such devotions and personal asceticisms can leave the faithful person, either clergy or lay, in a position to be more cooperative with the will of the Redeemer so that such actions lead one more readily into the liturgical celebration. Hanssens also notes that collective devotions (the Way of the Cross, novenas, etc.) have laudable value. Similarly, exaggerated stances on the glorified Christ in the liturgy and overly archaeological approaches to the liturgy prove problematic for Hanssens as well, since the former threaten the importance of the passion and death of Christ as central to the liturgical action and the latter lead to over-historicization and a devaluation of the church's tradition.[75]

Hanssens saves his most dramatic critique, however, for what he deems the most adverse interpretation of the liturgical action, namely, assuming that the community is the necessary intermediary between Christ and the church, on the one hand, and the priest on the other, thereby placing the community over and above the action of the priest in the liturgical celebration.[76] What is at issue here is the private celebration of the Mass and the criticism that "each sacrifice celebrated without the assistance of the people is a deviation from the primitive form of the rite; indeed, without confirmation and ratification on the part of the people no sacrifice can have strength and effectiveness."[77] Hanssens argues that such a position overemphasizes the baptismal priesthood of the faithful, noting that proponents of such an argument wish to maintain that the only priesthood spoken about in the New Testament is the priesthood of all the baptized—thus any other priest-

---

[74] John Michael Hanssens, "La liturgia nell'enciclica Mediator Dei et hominum," *La Civiltà Cattolica* (1948): 242–55, at 249.

[75] Ibid., 250–51.

[76] Ibid., 252–53.

[77] Ibid., 253.

hood receives its office and its ministerial role from the community.[78] Hanssens wants to ensure that an emphasis on the action of the Body of Christ in the liturgy does not in some manner subordinate the ministerial priesthood.

Thus the response to *Mediator Dei* by theological scholarship presents several component parts that would later help in the formulation of the conciliar definition of liturgical participation. Admittedly, *Mediator Dei*'s understanding of liturgical participation is highly Christocentric—it is the church's connection to Christ in the Mystical Body and the analogous action of Christ in the liturgical offering and celebration that provide not only the impetus for the development of a liturgical theology of participation but also the lens through which such a theology can be analyzed. The emphasis on the Mystical Body and on the need to nuance developments in the theology of the laity helped to highlight the relationship between the church and Christ in the decades that led up to the Second Vatican Council. It is precisely this relationship that became the focus of preconciliar attention to a theology of liturgical participation.

ORGANIZED REACTION TO THE CONCEPT OF PARTICIPATION

In 1953 the Third International Congress of Liturgical Studies convened in Lugano, Switzerland, marking the first international gathering of scholars and pastors on the subject of the liturgical movement that included the attendance and participation of notable Roman officials. Although the congress had convened twice before—first at Maria Laach (in the German Rhineland) in 1951 and then at Mont-Saint-Odile (Alsace, France) in 1952—both previous meetings had been strictly private and by invitation only. The first congress had gathered liturgical technicians to discuss reform proposals for the liturgy that could later be presented to Rome by various episcopates. Its discussions centered on two important areas: the canon of the Mass and the opening penitential rite. The discussions on the reform of the Mass continued at the second meeting in Mont-Saint-Odile, and again any outsiders were ejected from the proceedings. In the Lugano Congress, however, the various meetings of the liturgical technicians

---

[78] Ibid.

were coupled with open public sessions. These looked primarily at the reform of the rites of Holy Week.[79]

The *Acts* of the Lugano Congress were dedicated (but not limited) to the discussion of "Active Participation in the Liturgy." The proceedings were published in Italian almost immediately, and then within a few months in German, French, and English. Pope Pius XII asked the congress to make the entire proceedings public; hence the widespread publication of the Lugano papers in so many different languages.[80] Four keynote presentations dealt with active participation in the liturgy, and two of these are relevant to the discussion presented here: Cardinal Giacomo Lercaro's insight into the theology of Pope Pius X on the subject of participation, cited earlier, and Aimon-Marie Roguet's presentation on the "Theology of the Liturgical Assembly."[81] Roguet's analysis deserves careful attention.

As the director of the national French Centre de Pastorale Liturgique in Paris, Roguet presented a paper that articulated in detail a theology of the laity rooted in liturgical participation. In his address Roguet attempted to demarcate the various acts by which the faithful participate in the liturgy and then, with those acts as his starting point, to develop a liturgical theology of the laity. He begins by listing seven distinct actions of the assembly that mark liturgical participation: the gathering of the assembly, the bodily postures used in common, processions of

[79] For a more detailed account of the three congresses, see Botte, *From Silence to Participation*, 78–84. The fourth meeting of the congress was again private and then it did not meet at all in 1955. In 1956 the first International Congress of Pastoral Liturgy met in Assisi and was again made public.

[80] The original acts of the congress can be found in *Partecipazione attiva alla liturgia: Atti del III Convegno Internazionale di Studi Liturgici*, ed. Luigi Agustoni and Johannes Wagner (Lugano, Switzerland: Centro di Liturgia e Pastorale, 1953). French excerpts of the congress appeared in *La Maison-Dieu* 37, no. 1 (1954): 7–143; English translations in *Worship* 28, no. 3 (1954), where the entire volume is dedicated to the Lugano Congress; the German translation of presented papers appeared in *Liturgisches Jahrbuch* 4 (January 1954).

[81] The other two keynote addresses of the conference were given by Bishop Wilhelm Weskamm, who spoke on the "Essential Function of the Growth and Life of a Community of the Faithful," looking specifically at the relationship between participation and the church in Eastern Germany, and Johannes Hofinger, who spoke on "Active Participation as the Necessity and Hope for the Diffusion of the Faith in the Missions."

the faithful, chants of the assembly (which he cites as the chief form of participation), attentiveness to the liturgical rite, admiration for the liturgy, and silence.[82] The purpose of these actions reflects the very aim of participation itself and, indeed, of every liturgical action: to unite the faithful with the Mystery being celebrated. The gathered assembly epitomizes the paradox of the liturgical action. Roguet asserts:

> It is a holy and priestly people, it is a true people, a people come together from all parts, an "ecclesia," a convocation of all races, of all classes of society, of all degrees of spirituality, and not an elite, chosen and distinct, not a conventicle nor a monastery. It is because of this heterogeneity, this quality of medley, that its unity has the character of the paradoxical, of the supernatural, which is inexplicable except in terms of the gift of faith and of charity.[83]

The very gathering of the liturgical community points to an element of the divine already at work within those assembled. That such a disparate group of people unites for a common reason foreshadows the sacramental effect for which they have come together. It is because of this that Roguet asserts the participative role of the assembly or, more properly speaking, a theology surrounding their participation. He maintains that those who participate

> are not reduced to the rank of mere spectators or passive beneficiaries, but . . . they actively contribute and play a real part; and this means further that they play a part that is proper to them, that is their own, although admittedly subordinate. Their part may be limited and modest, but it is without question real, important, and often difficult of realization.[84]

Roguet underscores the demand of the sacramental action of the Eucharist that the sacrifice of the Mass be united internally with the hearts and minds of the faithful. To disavow this demand is to ignore the necessity of a proper disposition for the faithful for the fruitfulness of the sacrament. But Roguet also concedes that such a theology of the liturgical assembly in view of their participation within the sacraments

---

[82] Aimon-Marie Roguet, "The Theology of the Liturgical Assembly," *Worship* 28, no. 3 (1954): 130–34.

[83] Ibid., 135–36.

[84] Ibid., 136.

calls for catechesis. Interestingly enough, however, Roguet notes that "it would be a serious pedagogical error to maintain that active participation of the faithful should begin only after a long period of instruction. For such participation is itself educative and formative."[85] Thus it behooves the pastoral minister, in Roguet's estimation, to implement those forms of active, exterior participation that will lead the faithful "to the desired end, namely, an interior and true participation, of which external participation is merely a means and a sign."[86]

At the end of the Lugano Conference the assembled scholars and pastors put together a list of petitions (*vota*) to submit to Pope Pius XII. The original petitions were unanimously approved by the entire group of bishops present, the national organizers of the meeting, and several members of the Sacred Congregation of Rites. They were then presented to the entire assembly, where they also received unanimous support. The petitions forwarded to the pontiff included: (1) a wish to express the conference's awareness that active participation is the most efficacious source from which the assembly can be drawn into the life of Christ, (2) a request that the Scriptures used in the celebration of Mass be read in the vernacular of each region, (3) a request to allow the faithful to pray and sing in the vernacular, and (4) a word of gratitude for the restoration of the Easter Vigil rites and a request that all the ceremonies of Holy Week be considered for revision.[87] The emphasis on the use of vernacular texts is linked inextricably to the question of understanding on the part of the faithful and seeks to respond to the theology of Roguet, Lercaro, and others.

Thus, by the middle of the 1950s the concept of participation had undergone a radical transformation since its inception five decades earlier. Pius X's call for participation was tied intimately to Gregorian

[85] Ibid., 137.

[86] Ibid., 138.

[87] Godfrey Diekmann, "Conclusions of the Third Congress, Lugano, 1953," *Worship* 28, no. 3 (1954): 162–67, at 162–63. See also the editorial notes by Diekmann on p. 162. The conclusions of the congress were translated accurately by Diekmann for this edition of *Worship*, but the accompanying commentary that follows the conclusions does not adhere to the Italian text presented by Agustoni and Wagner in their edition. The commentary was part of the original *Acts* of the congress, so the added editorialized translation in the *Worship* version (which in some cases is actually additional or radically changed text) is problematic.

chant and the transformation of the faithful "to restore all things in Christ." The need to connect the liturgical action to the restoration of all things in Christ meant that the concept of liturgical participation would have to meet that end. After Pius XII's definition of the Mystical Body of Christ and the promulgation of *Mediator Dei* changed the theological understanding of the role and action of the laity in the church, the insight into what liturgical participation should mean went through a radical transformation. Participation had a pontifical mandate. With the growing amount of historical research on the liturgy and the added reform of the liturgical rites in the 1950s, liturgical participation became increasingly identified with the ability of the laity to actively understand and engage in the liturgical rites. The use of the vernacular, while still controversial to many, was seen as the means by which such understanding and engagement could be gained. Thus, on the eve of the Second Vatican Council, the concept of liturgical participation had been expanded from its original limited framing within the context of music to include both a metaphysical and a soteriological sense of participation in the aspects of the liturgical rite that were proper to the assembly. The ecclesial dimension of liturgical participation was still developing as theologians attempted to articulate the relationship between the faithful and the action of Christ in the liturgy. But much of the connection of the assembly to participation in the actual rite was based on a cognitive approach to understanding the rite—one that could be construed as flirting too heavily with a semi-Pelagian tendency to place the instigating origin of the liturgical action in the hands of the community—as a purely human construct—rather than recognizing it as a response to God's call.

ARCHBISHOP MONTINI'S PASTORAL LETTER TO THE PEOPLE OF MILAN

One important contribution to the developing theology of participation before the Second Vatican Council centers on a letter written by John Baptist Cardinal Montini to the people of Milan as a Lenten instruction in 1958. The letter is important not because of the scope of its audience, which was initially quite limited,[88] but because of its author,

---

[88] A copy of the Italian version of Montini's letter was published immediately; it was made available online through the publication office of the Archdiocese of Milan in 2003. *Worship* published an English translation of the

Montini, one of the primary architects of the decrees of the council, who would later become Pope Paul VI. It also helps to solidify a better understanding of the unity of the church and its relationship to Christ in the liturgical action. Much of what appears in Montini's pastoral letter foreshadows later formulations of the council, especially in regard to a theology of liturgical participation. The letter begins by discussing the importance and impact of *Mediator Dei* and later notes that the specific aims of the encyclical center upon "the people's participation in the sacred liturgy."[89] He then argues that the present level of participation among the faithful is not sufficient and offers (in the second half of the letter) a detailed portrait of what participation should, and could, look like within the sacramental celebration. Montini noted that, as a prerequisite for catechesis on liturgical participation, the assembly had to appropriate a communal sense of its own proper action. His words are clear and to the point:

> We cannot be content with having the church full of people, with having an amorphous crowd of individuals, a meaningless mass which assists at the sacred rite spiritually distracted or without inner unity. We must strive to give a composition to those present, an order, an awareness, so as to establish the sacred atmosphere in which the religious rite takes place. The idea is not just to require an educated behavior, such as might be required for a spectacle of some kind. *We need to infuse into all the sense of a common action, which is precisely the sense of participation.*[90]

Montini views this organic unity of the liturgical assembly as a defining characteristic of the Mystical Body of Christ. The common action of the liturgical assembly forms the most basic means by which the faithful enter into communion with Christ. Within the context of this

---

letter by Leonard Doyle with the permission of Cardinal Montini in February 1959, approximately a year after its original publication. Other translations of Montini's letter were made in French, German, Spanish, and Dutch. Although the text was "intended" for the people of Milan, its international appeal is recognized in its various extant translations. See John Baptist Cardinal Montini, "Liturgical Formation." Translation by Leonard Doyle of "Pastoral Letter to the Archdiocese of Milan for Lent 1958" (February 7, 1958), *Worship* 33, no. 3 (February 1959): 136–64. Citations are from Doyle's translation.

[89] "Liturgical Formation," 139.

[90] Ibid., 147–48. Italics in original.

communal sense, participation in liturgy plays an essential role. What remains unsaid in Montini's letter is how this actual unity is achieved. The question of the unity of the church would be a primary concern of the council.

A formula very similar to the council's description of liturgical participation also appears in Montini's pastoral letter. For him, participation has three specific characteristics: it involves seeing and hearing, it demands understanding, and it calls for action. He asserts that, for participation to involve seeing and hearing, a fullness of the senses must be used within the liturgical action. He notes especially the Thomistic axiom, "in the order of grace . . . nothing is found in the intellect which has not first passed through the senses."[91] It becomes vital, then, to appreciation and incorporation into the liturgical act to be engaged not just orally (something that was infrequent at best), but aurally and visually as well. The faithful participate in the liturgy by their reaction to the sensed experience of liturgical art, the singing of chant and carefully chosen popular song, and the visual stimulation by architecture, design, and decoration of liturgical spaces. In this sense Montini points to participation that relies on the *fullness* of the senses. But the reality of that fullness also leads the believer beyond the senses to the order of grace in recognizing what the liturgy reveals and communicates to the faithful through sense experience.

The sense experience of the liturgical act leads the faithful to a greater understanding of the mystery being celebrated and thus into a deeper participation in that mystery. Montini argues that the faithful need to understand the symbolic and signifying language of the liturgical act: "the rite is sign, the rite is language, the rite is expression of a divine truth communicated to men, and of a human truth addressed to God."[92] Liturgical education is needed to overcome what Montini views as a dual obstacle: the use of Latin in the rite and the deep symbolism and imagery of the liturgy, neither of which is comprehended easily by the faithful. The first obstacle is surmounted when the missal is translated into the vernacular so that the faithful can have prayer books that contain the liturgical prayers in their common tongue.

---

[91] Ibid., 150. Montini footnotes this line with a reference to Aquinas's *Quaestiones disputatae de veritate* 2.3.19, "*Nihil est in intellectu quod prius non fuerit in sensu.*"

[92] Ibid., 152.

The second obstacle can be overcome when the faithful have been thoroughly steeped in the liturgical life of the church. Montini asserts that "the faithful become the promoters of worship when they are associated in it."[93] It is necessary, therefore, to study the sacred liturgy in its multifaceted character—in doctrine and mystery, in song and gesture, in the very cycle of the liturgical calendar—so that the faithful may enter knowingly into what they celebrate in the sacred rituals.

Knowledge and comprehension of the liturgy are complemented when they lead to engagement in the liturgical action. Montini notes the varied roles the faithful may assume within the liturgical celebration: readers of the Sacred Scriptures, announcers of the various parts of the Mass, responding, with training, to the dialogic texts of the liturgy, singing some of the liturgical texts, and, as members of the assembly, assisting in the offertory procession.[94] Recognizing that such encouragement of the faithful to participate actively in the celebration of the sacraments would only happen gradually over time, Montini, interestingly enough, advocates using already established liturgical groups of the laity to begin the process of education, especially boys' choirs and altar servers. In these two groups he sees multilayered relationships at work between pastor and flock, parent and child, teacher and student, all becoming intertwined through liturgical participation. By resolutely pursuing the liturgical education of these young groups and moving them to active participation, Montini hopes to increase the active participation of the entire assembly exponentially.

What emerges from Montini's pastoral letter can serve as a comparative blueprint for understanding the theology of participation later adopted by the Second Vatican Council. He gave the church a definition of participation that is *full, conscious, and active.* It was precisely this kind of full, conscious, and active participation elucidated in his pastoral letter that formed the backbone of Montini's hope for renewal within the church. He saw within this augmented description

---

[93] Ibid., 154.

[94] Ibid., 157. At the time it was uncommon—in fact, rare—to find an assembly that responded to the dialogic parts of the Mass. These parts were usually recited by the server at the altar and the dialogue itself was not heard outside the sanctuary. Notable also is Montini's description of readers who would "announce" the various parts of the Mass and call people to various postures and attitudes at specific times—standing for the gospel, a sense of recollection during the eucharistic prayer.

of participation the ability to restore all things in Christ and to lead the people of God into the very mystery the church celebrates. This tripartite description of participation was schematic for the council fathers and is reiterated again and again throughout the council documents.

THE SECOND VATICAN COUNCIL CODIFIES "FULL, CONSCIOUS, AND ACTIVE PARTICIPATION"

The first constitution produced by the Second Vatican Council, *Sacrosanctum Concilium*, confirms the central importance of liturgical participation for the laity. The interpretation of this constitution, and indeed all the conciliar documents, is not without difficulties. Thus before we begin this analysis we should state in simplest terms the hermeneutical challenges of looking at the documents of the council. Unlike other councils before it, Vatican II did not produce any specifically prescriptive doctrinal statements. As Peter Hünermann points out, it is necessary to identify the specific genre of the conciliar texts if one is to interpret them adequately.[95] In this case the texts produced by the council are the result of a fundamental reflection on the life and nature of the church as it exists in the modern world. Such an introspective self-reflection seeks to underscore the foundational and ongoing narrative of the church's history. This fundamental reflection is also guided by certain principles in the life of the church that make such a reflection applicable to the lives of the faithful today and not simply a historical look at the past. Thus as the genre of this fundamental reflection manifests itself around these guiding principles it also forms the measure for the ecclesial living of the faith.[96] As constitutional texts, the documents of the Second Vatican Council differ from their more secular or state-oriented counterparts. Hünermann notes that the constitutional texts of the council are not attempting to create their own authority by their promulgation. Instead, the documents discuss how the authority of the church operates (maintaining its divine institution).[97] Moreover, the constitutions of the council go far beyond any sense of juridical or legal formulations in order to deal with every

---

[95] Peter Hünermann, "The Ignored 'Text': On the Hermeneutics of the Second Vatican Council," in *Vatican II: A Forgotten Future? Concilium* 2005/4, eds. Alberto Melloni and Christoph Theobald (London: SCM Press, 2005), 118–36, at 121–23.

[96] Ibid., 125–26.

[97] Ibid., 127–28.

aspect of social living—in this sense, as Hünermann notes, they are considered "constituent of faith."[98] One can argue, then, that the crucial role of interpretation of the conciliar documents lies in identifying the underlying narrative of the texts, what constitutes the living faith of the church to which one must return again and again in the course of both theological inquiry and the living of the Christian life. Thus every text seems to have a predominant motif as well as an underlying narrative. It might well be argued that, in the case of the Constitution on the Sacred Liturgy, the predominant motif is "active participation" but the underlying narrative is the operation of the triune God for the salvation of the world.

What is perhaps also interesting to note at this juncture is the drastically different way in which theologians and scholars comment on this constitution as compared to the encyclical *Mediator Dei*. The encyclical produced a flurry of activity in the academic arena and myriad interpretations. This is not the case with the constitution—reactions to its promulgation are much more formalized, often appearing as commentaries on the text. For this reason the treatment of the constitution presented here will be interspersed with the various insights made in the subsequent theological commentaries.

The promotion of active participation in the original schema of the Constitution on the Sacred Liturgy was received well by the council fathers.[99] But one could also argue that it became the "chorus" or *leitmotif* of the document, that is, the central place that it holds within the constitution became the measure and the comparative rule for the development of the text.[100] In conjunction with this normative position of the phrase *actuosa participatio* one has to consider also that the nature of the liturgical action is presented somewhat differently than it was in *Mediator Dei*. Here, the subject of the liturgical action clearly includes

[98] Ibid., 128.

[99] Mathijs Lamberigts, "The Liturgy Debate," in *History of Vatican II*. Vol. 2: *The Formation of the Council's Identity, First Period and Intersession, October 1962–September 1963*, trans. Matthew J. O'Connell; ed. Guiseppe Alberigo and Joseph Komonchak (Maryknoll, NY: Orbis, 1977), 107–68, at 113.

[100] The notion of the phrase *actuosa participatio* as the "chorus" of the document comes from Herman Schmidt. See his *Die Konstitution über die heilige Liturgie: Text, Vorgeschichte, Kommentar* (Freiburg: Herder, 1965), 80, and "Il popolo cristiano al centro del rinnovamento liturgico," *La Civiltà Cattolica* 115, no. 1 (1964): 120–32, at 123.

the church as an organic unit. The Constitution on the Sacred Liturgy stresses repeatedly the vital role of participation in the liturgy for fostering a real transformation in Christ. In fact, the opening paragraphs of the constitution (1–8) establish a theology that makes the participation of the assembly an integral part of any liturgical celebration. Reiterating the themes of *Mystici Corporis* and *Mediator Dei* that preceded it, the constitution speaks of the liturgical action as the "chief means through which the faithful may express in their lives and demonstrate to others the mystery which is Christ and the real nature of the true Church" (SC 2). The subject of the liturgical action is clearly seen as the people of God, united to their head, Christ, through the ministerial priesthood of the bishop/priest, and gathered into one assembly by the power of the Holy Spirit.[101] Two things must be highlighted from this statement. First, the operation of the people of God as the church is not clearly defined until the promulgation of the Dogmatic Constitution on the Church, *Lumen Gentium*. Thus references to the activity of the church, the faithful, the body of believers, etc., gain further elucidation only later.[102] Second, liturgy is seen as an activity that is both constitutive of the believing assembly and also creedal: it defines who the gathered assembly is and helps articulate the assembly's beliefs in and before the world. In this sense the council begins by depicting the liturgy as a uniquely communal act of faith and kerygma. It charges pastors to realize that the celebration of the liturgy is not simply about following rubrics. Rather, they must take care "to ensure that the faithful may participate knowingly, actively and fruitfully in it" (SC 11).[103]

[101] The phrase "the subject of the liturgical action" was made popular by Yves M.-J. Congar, OP, in 1967 with the publication of an essay in the *Unam Sanctam* series. Congar looks to an understanding of the Mystical Body of Christ to underscore the fullest dimension of the acting subject. See Yves M.-J. Congar, "L'Ecclesia' ou communauté chrétienne, sujet intégral de l'action liturgique," in *Unam Sanctam, 66: La Liturgie après Vatican II, Bilans, etudes, prospective,* ed. Jean-Pierre Jossua and Yves M.-J. Congar (Paris: Cerf, 1967), 241–82.

[102] In one sense this simple fact points to the inability to interpret any of the conciliar documents in isolation from the others. Each of the documents has a canonical significance in the sense of its relationship to the rest of the canon of conciliar constitutions and decrees.

[103] See also Jozef Lamberts, "Active Participation as the Gateway Towards an Ecclesial Liturgy," in *Omnes Circumadstantes: Contributions Towards a History of the People in the Liturgy Presented to Herman Wegman,* ed. Charles Caspers and

In doing so they assist the faithful in the very aim of the liturgy: that the church might become both subject and object of the message of salvation. Hence, the "burden" of active participation lies in some sense in the formation of both clergy and laity.[104]

The participation to which the faithful are called is also rooted in the union with God given to them at their baptism. The council fathers assert:

> Mother Church strongly desires that all the faithful should be led to that full, conscious and active participation in liturgical celebrations which is demanded by the very nature of the liturgy. Such participation by the Christian people as "a chosen race, a royal priesthood, a holy nation, a people he has claimed for his own," is their right and duty by virtue of their baptism. (SC 14)

Annibale Bugnini notes in his history of the reform of the liturgy that *"by virtue of their baptism"* was an added amendment to the original text, which had allowed the participation of the faithful to be viewed simply as an ecclesial concession to the laity.[105] The addition was first mentioned by Archbishop Francis Grimshaw from Birmingham, England, clarified in a later *relatio*, and then passed by a significant majority of the council fathers.[106] The importance of this addition cannot be overstated. By asserting that the mandate for participation is a

---

Marc Schneiders (Kampen: Kok, 1990), 234–361, at 252–53. Lamberts offers a detailed explication of how the council fathers establish this fundamental relationship between the liturgy and the essential character of participation.

[104] Jungmann alludes to this in his commentary on the constitution, maintaining that the council fathers went immediately from speaking about "active participation" into a discussion of how to form clergy properly so that they could secure such participation for the people. See Joseph Jungmann, "Einleitung und Kommentar von Univ.-Prof Dr. Josef Andreas Jungmann, SJ, Innsbruck," in *Das Zweite Vatikanische Konzil, Dokumente und Kommentare,* ed. Heinrich Susa Brechter (Freiburg: Herder, 1966), 28. For a similar stance, see also Louis Bouyer, *The Liturgy Revived: A Doctrinal Commentary on the Conciliar Constitution on the Liturgy* (Notre Dame, IN: Notre Dame University Press, 1964), 100–102.

[105] Annibale Bugnini, *The Reform of the Liturgy: 1948–1975,* trans. Matthew J. O'Connell (Collegeville, MN: Liturgical Press, 1990), 34.

[106] See AS I/4, 167. Grimshaw's elucidations can be found on 170–71. The vote was dramatically in favor of the addition: "for"—2051, "against"—52, and "invalid"—6. See also AS I/4, 213.

character resulting from baptism, the council fathers prevented such participation from ever being relegated to the status of an accidental element within the liturgy. If baptism is viewed as the fundamental initiation sacrament, culminating in the celebration of the Eucharist, then participation in the sacramental action comes "in virtue of their baptism." The baptismal mandate is also rooted in the nature of the church itself. In his commentary on the constitution Reiner Kaczynski notes that this passage maintains that the essential character of the church is its gathering, the εκκλεσια that is initiated by baptism and vivified in the liturgy.[107] But the inclusion of the baptismal origin of the call for participation also provides a vital link to the operation of the Holy Spirit within the life of the faithful and the sanctification of the human person through grace. William Baraúna, a *peritus* of the council, argues that the insertion of the baptismal phrase makes participation more than a simple recommendation. He maintains that

> by virtue of baptism, every member of the faithful becomes a true and responsible member of the Mystical Body, acquiring thereby rights and duties which are the heritage of all, becoming a participant in the gifts of the Holy Spirit, and of the same grace which constitutes the vivifying principle for all—a grace which comes from the liturgy as its primary font.[108]

So important is this connection to baptism that the principle of full, conscious, and active participation becomes "the aim to be considered above all else" in the reform and renewal of the liturgy that the constitution proposes (SC 14).

Liturgical participation takes on special significance as the council fathers move to a more detailed discussion of the mystery of the eucharistic celebration. In speaking of that celebration the constitution clearly seeks to "prevent Christian believers from attending this

[107] Reiner Kaczynski, "Theologischer Kommentar zur Konstitution über die heilige Liturgie (*Sacrosanctum Concilium*)," in *Herders Theologischer Kommentar zum Zweiten Vatikanischen Konzil*, ed. Peter Hünermann and Bernd Jochen Hilberath (Freiburg: Herder, 2004), 1–228, at 80.

[108] William Baraúna, "Active Participation, the Inspiring and Directive Principle of the Constitution," in *The Liturgy of Vatican II*, ed. William Baraúna, English edition ed. Jovian Lang (Chicago: Franciscan Herald Press, 1966), 131–93, at 139.

mystery of faith as though they were outsiders or silent onlookers"
(SC 48). Instead, having been instructed in the mystery and possessing
a decent understanding (*bene intellegentes*) of it, they should actively
and piously participate in the sacred action (48). Salvatore Marsili, in
his analysis of the text, compares the mystery of Christ in the Eucharist
to a "passover, a *passing* from the world to the Father, a *sacrifice*, a *consecration* of himself and his followers (Jn 17:19)."[109] Thus the mystery of
Christ in the eucharistic celebration implies some sort of inner movement of the human person in conjunction with Christ—a passing, a
sacrifice, a consecration. Marsili maintains that "this interior movement, which is a separation from oneself and an adhering to God, is
the natural requisite for the eucharistic 'mystery of worship,' and at
the same time a justification for that external action of the Christian assembly which is being rightly called 'active participation.' "[110]

It is important to realize that while the constitution refers to "full,
conscious, and active participation" in its original statement, the
phrase appears truncated to "active participation" (*actuosa participatio*)
in nearly every subsequent mention of the concept. Within the course
of the document the phrase *actuosa participatio*,[111] or other forms of its
Latin declension, appears twelve more times: in relation to a more
noble expression of the sacred rites (27, 41, 113), in describing the relationship between music and participation (30, 114, 121), in relation to
the dual character of participation as both internal and external (19), in
the differentiation of ministerial roles that accompanies participation
(26), in the concept of participation as the guiding norm for revision

[109] Salvatore Marsili, "The Mass, Paschal Mystery and Mystery of the
Church," in *The Liturgy of Vatican II*, 4–25, at 15. Italics in original.

[110] Ibid.

[111] The phrase that was used in the Latin text of *Tra le sollecitudini* (1903) was
"*actuosa communicatio*," even though the original Italian used the phrase "*attiva
partecipazione*." Whereas modern Italian only uses one word for the concept of
"active," the Latin retains two: *activus*, meaning simply active, and *actuosus*,
meaning full of life, energetic, active—the latter implies a much more vigorous
activity and engagement. In the encyclical *Mediator Dei* (1947), Pope Pius XII
uses "*actuosa participatio*" to refer to *active participation*. This phraseology is retained in the council documents and is distinct from the concept of *communicatio*, which in the council documents typically refers to participation or sharing
between two distinct bodies. The verbal form, *communicare*, often connotes the
sharing of spiritual realities or divine life, stressing the divine action necessary
in such a sharing.

(14, 40), and in expressing the need for other elements of the liturgy and devotion to promote intelligent and active participation (79, 124). In this way the Constitution on the Sacred Liturgy has taken nearly every previous magisterial document that spoke of liturgical participation of the faithful and incorporated those texts within its own formulation, but in doing so it has erased any question of whether that participation could be optional.

The primary importance of this theology of participation not only for the renewal of the liturgy but indeed for the entire scope of the council itself cannot be overestimated. The phrase *actuosa participatio* echoes throughout the conciliar teachings and appears directly in seven other documents, most notably in *Lumen Gentium*, where participation in the sacred mysteries of the church is linked to participation in the one priesthood of Christ.[112] Within the Constitution on the Church the council fathers repeatedly speak of the significance of the common priesthood of the faithful acting in the church, especially with regard to sacramental action. *Lumen Gentium* states succinctly, "The common priesthood of the faithful and the ministerial or hierarchical priesthood, although they differ essentially and not simply in degree, are nevertheless interrelated: each in its own particular way participates in the one priesthood of Christ" (LG 10). This sharing in the mission of Christ is heralded throughout the constitution's discussion of the intimate relationship between and among the bishop, the priest, and the faithful, especially in the mediation of salvation in the liturgical life of the church. Here the mystery of Christian liturgy is intimately connected with the council's understanding of the mystery of the church itself. The opening chapter of *Lumen Gentium* goes to great lengths to articulate the salvific nature of the church constituted by Christ through the power of the Holy Spirit. Here the lack of reference to the Holy Spirit, once lamented in the formulation of the Constitution on the Sacred Liturgy, is rectified.[113] Both Marsili and Bouyer point to the "mystery of the church" as a qualitative lens for appreciating the council's earlier statements on participation. Marsili, for example, maintains that the "sacramental sign of bread and wine is not merely an appeal to read, so to say, an appeal to unity in it, but rather the

---

[112] See *Apostolicam Actuositatem* 4, 10; *Ad Gentes* 5; *Christus Dominus* 30.2; *Gravissimum Educationis* 4; *Lumen Gentium* 28, 42; *Optatum Totius* 8; *Presbyterorum Ordinis* 5.

[113] Lamberigts, "The Liturgy Debate," 116–17.

Church lives within this unity and realizes it in the mutual harmony and charity of its members, and in the sacrament offers its own continual sacrifice."[114] In a sense Marsili points to the mystery of the church itself that is being offered in the celebration of the Eucharist. Similarly, Bouyer presents a detailed analysis of the ramifications of maintaining the link between the mystery of worship and the mystery of the church: "the Mystery of worship can be called with equal accuracy, the Mystery of the Church. Here again we mean first the Mystery which is to be found in the Church, but only to be later discerned as the Mystery of the Church herself: the Mystery of her life, of her progressive building in history."[115] One can assert that the mystery of the church, "of her life, of her progressive building," is safeguarded and maintained by the operation and work of the Holy Spirit. Introducing the Spirit into the dynamic—that is, indicating that the common priesthood stems from the Spirit's gifts given at baptism—diminishes the concern that the laity might act on their own accord (something we saw earlier in Kaiser's and Hanssens' reactions to *Mediator Dei*). Lay participation is sanctioned by the presence of the Spirit within the individual and the gathered community. In discussing the universal call to holiness, the council fathers aver that "frequent participation in the sacraments, especially the Eucharist, and in the sacred liturgy" helps foster the life of charity within the soul (LG 42). In this way the council has placed liturgical participation squarely in the center of the renewal of the entire church, for it is this participation that helps lead to transformation in Christ through the power of the Spirit.

The other occurrences of the phrase "full, conscious, and active participation" (or a corollary form) in the council documents are worthy of note here. In the Decree on the Pastoral Office of Bishops, *Christus Dominus*, the council fathers assert that in carrying out the work of sanctification the parish priest, linked to the bishop, must "make a special effort so that the faithful receive spiritual nourishment through devout and frequent reception of the sacraments and through conscious and active participation in the liturgy" (CD 30, 2). The description of participation and its intimate link with the priesthood of Christ as stated in *Lumen Gentium* is echoed here. In a similar vein, *Optatum Totius*, the Decree on Priestly Formation, also relates participation in

[114] Marsili, "The Mass, Paschal Mystery and Mystery of the Church," 17.
[115] Bouyer, *The Liturgy Revived*, 52.

the sacred mysteries to the proper formation of seminarians as a way of seeking Christ (OT 8).[116] This same union with Christ through active participation in the sacred mysteries is seen in the Decree on the Laity, *Apostolicam Actuositatem*, in which the council fathers assert that "[t]he life of intimate union with Christ in the Church is fed by spiritual aids which are common to all the faithful, especially active participation in the sacred liturgy" (AA 4). That same participation, argues the decree, leads to a concern that the laity also take part in the apostolic work of the church. Because the laity are sharers (*participes*) in the priestly, prophetic, and kingly office of Christ, they must also share (*laici suas partes active habent*) in his work. Liturgical participation leads to this realization (AA 10). This duty of the church is echoed in the Decree on Missionary Activity, *Ad Gentes*, when the council fathers state that the primary aim of all church activity is to "open up for all a free and reliable way to full participation in the mystery of Christ" (AG 5). Sacramental participation is seen as a vehicle for participation in Christ and thus in the mystery of the Trinity itself.

The two remaining uses of "active participation" in the council documents both refer to the crucial need for catechesis. *Gravissimum Educationis*, the Decree on Christian Education, highlights the vital role of catechetical instruction, noting that such instruction "illuminates and strengthens faith, nourishes a life in accord with the spirit of Christ, leads to a conscious and active participation in the liturgical mystery, and prompts to apostolic action" (GE 4). Similarly, the Decree on Priestly Life, *Presbyterorum Ordinis*, asserts that the parish priest is called to teach the faithful "to participate in the celebrations of the liturgy" in a way that leads to deeper personal prayer and the offering of their lives (PO 5).

THE TRINITARIAN NARRATIVE AND SACRAMENTAL PARTICIPATION IN THE SECOND VATICAN COUNCIL

While the recurring *leitmotif* of *actuosa participatio* pulses through the Constitution on the Sacred Liturgy and echoes in various other documents of the council, the underlying narrative that propels the vision

---

[116] The document states: *Christum quaerere edoceantur in verbi Dei fideli meditatione, in actuosa cum sacrosanctis ecclesiae mysteriis communicatione, imprimis in eucharistia et in officio divino.* It is important to note that *"communicatio"* is used here because the referent is Christ.

of the council forward is decidedly trinitarian in nature. The operative assumption in developing a theology of liturgical participation that leads to participation in the divine life of the Trinity rests in the understanding that such a transformation is accomplished by a divine action of the Trinity itself. Since no human action, in and of itself, could produce a participation in the divine life, a trinitarian action must be at work to achieve this end.[117] Inevitably one returns to a question of causality in determining the agent by whose action sacramental or sanctifying grace is effected. It is important, then, at this juncture, to outline the church's teaching on trinitarian action in the sacramental-liturgical act, especially in light of its teaching on "full, conscious, and active participation" in the Second Vatican Council. We have already seen how the council and earlier documents have linked liturgical participation to participation in the priesthood of Christ and to an intimate union with him. Now that link will be extended to the action of the Trinity as well by an increased understanding of the nature of the ecclesial union of the church.

The text of *Sacrosanctum Concilium* envisions a highly Christocentric theology of divine sacramental action.[118] After discussing the fourfold

---

[117] For a comprehensive look at the Western idea of participation in the divine life, see, for example, Rudi A. TeVelde, *Participation and Substantiality in Thomas Aquinas* (New York: Brill, 1995), and Alan J. Torrance, *Persons in Communion: An Essay in Trinitarian Description and Human Participation* (Edinburgh: T & T Clark, 1996). For a contemporary non-Catholic approach to the same idea, see especially Samuel M. Powell, *Participating in God: Creation and Trinity* (Minneapolis: Fortress Press, 2003), 4–57. Powell comes from the Methodist-Holiness tradition and the Church of the Nazarene, but much of his work on trinitarian participation is based on Aquinas and the systematic theology of Paul Tillich.

[118] While there is an overt reference to the trinitarian dynamic of salvation history (God the Father, sends his Son to the world, the Son redeems the world through his suffering and death, and the Holy Spirit is sent out into the church so that it might proclaim the good works of the Son) in the opening paragraphs of the document, primary attention is given to the saving works of Christ and the priesthood of Christ that is operative in each liturgy. This seems to be indicative of the development of sacramental theology in the West prior to the Second Vatican Council: an admission of trinitarian activity in sacraments followed by an extensive look at the action of Christ in the sacramental event. For magisterial documentation of this methodology, see the Fourth Lateran Council's *De fide catholica* in Norman P. Tanner, ed., *Decrees of the*

reality of Christ's presence in the liturgy (in the proclaimed Word, the presiding minister, the gathered assembly, and the eucharistic species), the council goes on to say that the liturgy "is rightly seen as an exercise of the priestly office of Jesus Christ" (SC 7). Christ's presence is defined as real and active in the liturgical-sacramental event. Such an active presence of Christ is depicted following the model presented by Pope Pius XII in his encyclicals, *Mystici Corporis* and *Mediator Dei*: "in it [the liturgy] full public worship is performed by the Mystical Body of Jesus Christ, that is, by the Head and his members" (SC 7).[119] Christ's presence animates the Mystical Body; joined with the church as head to members, Christ then acts in every liturgical event and sacrament. This action of Christ and the church has special significance. The council asserts that "in the earthly liturgy we take part in a foretaste of that heavenly liturgy which is celebrated in the Holy City of Jerusalem toward which we journey as pilgrims" (SC 8). Implicit in this reference is the divinization of the human person through union with God, a union effected by participation (*participamus*) in a heavenly reality made possible by the action of Christ and the church in the earthly liturgy. As the central activity of the church, the liturgy provides this crucial link in the human person's potential to participate in the divine life. But the council notes: "in order that the liturgy may be able to produce its full effects, it is necessary that the faithful come to it with proper dispositions, that their minds should be attuned to their voices, and that they cooperate with heavenly grace lest they receive it in vain" (SC 11). The fruitfulness of liturgical participation is presented as directly related to its fullness, its consciousness, and the extent to which it constitutes active cooperation. If that is the case, then "full, conscious, and active participation" has a direct correlation to participation in the action of Christ in the liturgy. *Sacrosanctum Concilium* maintains that one participates in the presence of Christ and

Ecumenical Councils. Vol. 1: *Nicaea I to Lateran V* (Washington, DC: Georgetown University Press, 1990), 230. For theological works roughly contemporaneous with the Fourth Lateran Council, see St. Thomas Aquinas, ST III, q. 64, a. 3; St. Bonaventure, *Breviloquium* VI, 1.1–2.4; and Hugh of St. Victor, *De Sacramentis*, Book II, Parts I–XV. For a twentieth-century equivalent, see François Taymans d'Eypernon, *The Blessed Trinity and the Sacraments* (Westminster, MD: Newman Press, 1961).

[119] See also Pope Pius XII, *Mediator Dei* and *Mystici Corporis*, AAS 35 (1943): 193–248.

in his sacrifice. The constitution asserts that "all who are made sons of God by faith and baptism should come together to praise God in the midst of his Church, to take part in the Sacrifice and to eat the Lord's Supper" (SC 10). This liturgical activity—praising God, participating in sacrifice, and eating the Lord's Supper—is always "an action of Christ the Priest and of his Body" (SC 7). It is precisely in this liturgical activity and especially in the sacraments that the community of believers is brought into the trinitarian dynamic and mystery being celebrated. The constitution points out that this is how through "Baptism men are grafted into the paschal mystery of Christ; they die with him, are buried with him and rise with him. They receive the spirit of adoption as sons, 'in which we cry, Abba, Father' (Rm 8:15), and thus become true adorers such as the Father seeks" (SC 6). The constitution makes it clear, then, that through baptism one participates in Christ and through participation in him one is brought into the life of the Trinity. This dynamic continues in the Trinity's self-communication: the bestowal of grace that is participation in the divine life itself. In the constitution's assessment the sacramental-liturgical act begins through the Father's initiative, is made present through the priestly action of Christ, and is animated in the church by the power and activity of the Holy Spirit.

In subsequent decrees and constitutions from the council this dynamic view of trinitarian action in the sacraments and in the world is expanded and augmented to provide a descriptive explication of the action of the Trinity within human history.[120] The rationale for such an explication centers on the nature of divine revelation (the self-communication of God to humankind) and its purpose within salvation history (to redeem humankind through grace). The bestowal of grace had been firmly established well before the council as the means by which humanity is able to participate in the divine nature. For instance, in the previous century Pope Leo XIII had maintained that "no one can express the greatness of this work of divine grace in the souls of men. Wherefore, both in sacred scripture and in the writings of the

---

[120] In fact, each of the constitutions promulgated by the council begins with a trinitarian formulation of the interrelation between revelation and salvation history. See also LG 2–4, GS 1–3, DV 2–4. References to the self-communication of the Trinity or the communication of divine life or spiritual realities occur also in *Ad Gentes, Presbyterorum Ordinis, Apostolicam Actuositatem*, and *Gravissimum Educationis*.

fathers, men are called in splendid fashion regenerated, new creatures, partakers of the Divine Nature, children of God, god-like, and similar praises."[121] Leo echoes the Second Letter of Peter, which encourages the community to hold fast to what they have received from God so that they "may become sharers in the divine nature" (2 Pet 1:4).[122] Moreover, this communication of grace is ultimately rooted in a trinitarian dynamism. The pontiff demonstrates that the Spirit is sent forth from the mutual love of Father and Son and that the indwelling that results in the human person is not simply that of the Spirit but rather "the presence of the whole Blessed Trinity."[123] This same concept is at work when the council articulates its theology of the communication of grace (*communicatio*) as participation (*participatio*) in divine life. For example, *Dei Verbum* asserts that "God wished to manifest and communicate (*communicare*) both himself and the eternal decrees of his will concerning the salvation of mankind. He wished, in other words, 'to share (*participanda*) with us divine benefits which entirely surpass the human mind to understand'" (DV 6).[124] Communication of the divine life through grace and participation in that divine life are intimately connected. Of the sixty-two references made to *communicare/communicatio* in the council documents, nearly half denote a sharing or participation in spiritual realities: communion with Christ (AG 39; GS 68), communion with others through the Holy Spirit (LG 13, 52; PO 12), participation in God's power or work (LG 26, 36; GS 50), sharing spiritual gifts or realities (LG 13, 50, 51; DV 7, 25; GS 48; AA 6; PO 4,

---

[121] Pope Leo XIII, *Divinum Illud Munus*, ASS 29 (1896–1897), 644–58, at 651–52. Leo's use of the word *consortes* is somewhat problematic, since the term often implies partnership and equality that would necessarily be inapplicable when referring to human sharing in the divine nature.

[122] The Greek of the letter refers to "sharers" as κοινωνόι, from the Greek root κοινωνία, loosely translated as "fellowship, community, sharing, or participation." See 2 Pet 1:4: "δι᾽ ὧν τὰ τίμια καὶ μέγιστα ἡμῖν ἐπαγγέλματα δεδώρηταί ἵνα διὰ τούτων γένησθε φείας κοινωνοὶ φύσεως ἀποφυγοντες τῆς ἐν τῷ κόσμῳ ἐν ἐπιθυμίᾳ φύσεὼς." For a more comprehensive look at the New Testament usage of κοινωνία see also J. Y. Campbell, "KOINΩNIA and Its Cognates in the New Testament," *Journal of Biblical Literature* 51 (1932): 352–80; H. W. Ford, "The New Testament Conception of Fellowship," *Shane Quarterly* 6 (1945): 188–215; G.V. Jourdan, "Κοινωνια in 1 Cor 10:16," *Journal of Biblical Literature* 67 (1948): 111–24.

[123] Pope Leo XIII, *Divinum Illud Munus*, 653.

[124] The internal quotation is taken from Vatican Council I's declaration on revelation.

49

21); the specific sharing of divine charity (PO 13; LG 33, 49; AA 3; GS 93); participation in divine life or the fruits of salvation (LG 7, 8; GS 40; GE 3; AG 2); and sharing in the death and resurrection of Christ (AG 13).[125] In each of these examples sanctifying grace is viewed as a communication of or participation in the divine life.

For instance, *Lumen Gentium* describes that participation in terms of the communication of the Spirit of Christ to believers. The Constitution on the Church asserts that the Mystical Body of Christ, the church, is formed by this communication of the Spirit (LG 7). In the sacraments that Spirit is poured forth among the faithful in such a way as to unite them to Christ, for it is in the Mystical Body formed by the Spirit that "the life of Christ is communicated to believers" (LG 7). That same Spirit acts to unite the faithful even as they are dispersed throughout the world. The constitution adds that the faithful everywhere are in communion with, or participate in, all the other faithful in the Holy Spirit (LG 13).[126] Through the sacraments of initiation all believers are brought into this dynamism of the Holy Spirit's unifying and vivifying action; they participate in the action of Christ as high priest inasmuch as they are united to him in the Mystical Body formed by the Spirit.

In similar fashion *Ad Gentes*, the Decree on the Missionary Activity of the Church, asserts that the central aim of the Father's action in the world is the communication of the divine life. The decree maintains that the Father "in his great and merciful kindness freely creates us, and moreover, graciously calls us to share (*communicandum*) in his life and glory" (AG 2). This is reiterated in the description of the mission of the Son, who "entered the world by means of a true incarnation that

---

[125] The correlative noun form of *communicare*, *communicatio*, appears 45 times, but it applies much less frequently to the communication of grace or sacred realities (only three times, to be exact: LG 49, participation in spiritual benefits; SC 6, referring to the sharing in the breaking of the bread; and OT 8, where the phrase *actuosa communicatio* is used to refer to active participation in the sacred mysteries). Normally, within the council documents *communicatio* is used to express an agreement or communication between two established bodies, as demonstrated in the phrases *communicatio in sacris* (worship in common) and *instrumenta communicationis socialis* (instruments of social communication).

[126] *Cuncti enim per orbem sparsi fideles cum ceteris in Spiritu sancto communicant.* Here the council uses *communicare* as a synonym for *participare*.

he might make men sharers in the divine nature" (AG 3).[127] This is accomplished in his preaching and in the sacrifice he offered once for all. The Spirit, in turn, through the activity of the church, communicates the mystery of the death and resurrection of Jesus (AG 4, 13).

The conciliar documents consistently refer to the communication of grace and other spiritual realities (the theological virtue of charity, for example) that are linked to the sacraments and the actions of the triune God. For example, *Apostolicam Actuositatem*, the Decree on the Apostolate of the Laity, asserts that charity, as the soul of the whole apostolate, is communicated to the faithful through the sacraments, especially the Eucharist. Moreover, this communication happens through the action of the Holy Spirit who pours such virtue into the hearts of the faithful (AA 3). Similarly, *Gravissimum Educationis*, the Declaration on Christian Education, notes that the church, constituted as such by Christ in the Spirit, takes on the responsibility "to provide for its children an education by virtue of which their whole lives may be inspired by the spirit of Christ" (GE 3). Interestingly, *Gravissimum Educationis* goes on to assert that catechetical instruction links a life in harmony with the spirit of Christ and active participation in the liturgical mysteries.

What emerges from the council, then, cannot be regarded simply as a highly Christocentric view of sacramental action like that typified by the neo-scholastics of the early twentieth century. Only a cursory glance at *Sacrosanctum Concilium* might yield such a declaration. Rather, when one traces the interrelationship between *communicare* and *participare* throughout the conciliar documents one can determine that a true broadening of sacramental theology is envisioned by the council, a theology that includes a trinitarian understanding of participation and self-communication. Within the liturgical activity of the church a trinitarian action unfolds—the Father calls the faithful to share in the divine life, the Son offers himself as the way to participation, and the Spirit vivifies the church that it might follow in the path of the Son. It is an action based on the self-communication of the triune God and the bestowal of grace as participation in the divine life. In the decades that follow the council, then, we begin to see real attempts to expand sacramental theology in trinitarian terms.

---

[127] This is one of only two instances in which the council makes reference specifically to sharing or participating in the divine nature (the other is LG 40). The more typical phraseology for the council is the "participation in divine life or glory" seen in the earlier citation from *Ad Gentes*.

Chapter 2

Attempts at Creating
a Trinitarian Approach to Participation I

Cipriano Vagaggini

If the decades leading up to the Second Vatican Council formed a logical progression of thought and theological insight culminating in a theoretical embrace of a trinitarian approach to a sacramental worldview, the decades afterward showed an increased determination to articulate this trinitarian theology of participation in more concrete terms. One could argue that the multiple statements about participation in the divine life that the council seemed to favor were, in fact, divorced from a common understanding of the meaning of such a participation. Moreover, as noted earlier, even though many of the conciliar documents began with an articulation of the prominence of the trinitarian narrative in the life of the faithful, especially in the communication of grace, most of the lived expressions of the faithful still saw grace within a productionist schema, as something most people received like coins in a child's piggy bank. The personalist theology of the human-divine encounter and engagement articulated by Edward Schillebeeckx was still relatively new. Most people had difficulty translating the reception of grace into a participation in the divine life itself.

Within this milieu several theologians attempted to demarcate possible ways for the faithful to appropriate a greater understanding of a trinitarian theology of liturgical participation. The development of such methodologies was neither consistent nor facile. Two of the more significant approaches were those of Cipriano Vagaggini, who began his work a little before the council, and Edward Kilmartin, who came to the foreground in the succeeding decades. Both theologians provide a systematic approach by which the faithful could more easily appropriate a theology of liturgical participation rooted in the divine life of the Trinity. A detailed look at what these two theologians bring to the table can perhaps provide some insight into the more recent attempts to articulate a trinitarian theology of participation in the last decade. This chapter will focus on the work of Cipriano Vagaggini; chapter 5 will treat that of Edward Kilmartin.

CIPRIANO VAGAGGINI: LITURGICAL PARTICIPATION AS "TUNING IN" TO THE SACRAMENTAL SIGNS

Cipriano Vagaggini contributed significantly to Catholic thought in liturgy and worship throughout his lifetime. He entered the Benedictine Monastery of St. Andrew's in Belgium at the age of twelve and was solemnly professed by the time he was nineteen. He pursued both philosophical and theological degrees while studying in Rome and eventually earned three doctorates, two from Sant' Anselmo (1931, 1938) and a third in the theology of the Eastern Churches from the Pontificio Istituto Orientale (1940). Having served as a professor of theology and vice rector of Sant' Anselmo, Vagaggini was asked to be a member of the preparatory commission on the liturgy for the Second Vatican Council. He would, in turn, be nominated by Pope John XXIII as *peritus* to the council and later was named as *peritus* to the *concilium* for the reform of the liturgy. In 1961 the Pontificio Istituto Liturgico was founded at Sant' Anselmo by the Sacred Congregation of Seminaries and Universities. Because of his expertise in the area of sacramental theology and liturgy, Vagaggini was asked to give the inaugural address for the school. That discourse, "Liturgia e Pensiero Teologico Recente," not only set the tenor for the Pontifical Institute but also helped shape methodology for many in liturgical studies in the succeeding decades.[1] He was instrumental in the drafting of the Constitution on the Sacred Liturgy, helped formulate the eucharistic prayers added to the Roman Missal after Vatican II (1968), and gave substantial assistance in the development of the new rites for Mass, the formulation of the Lectionary, and the revision of the rites for the other sacraments.[2] After the council he became a professor of theology in Milan (1967–1971) and then rector of Sant' Anselmo (1974–1978).

[1] Published as *Liturgia e pensiero teologico recente* (Rome: Pontificio Ateneo Anselmiano, 1961), 31–32.

[2] For a detailed list of commissions and subcommissions on which Vagaggini served and a listing of the various appointments he received before and during the council, see Annibale Bugnini, *The Reform of the Liturgy: 1948–1975*, trans. Matthew J. O'Connell (Collegeville, MN: Liturgical Press, 1990).

He was named to the International Theological Commission in 1969 and stayed in that position for eleven years.[3] Several of his numerous books and articles were translated into other languages, most notably *Il senso teologico della liturgia,* which by its fourth edition had been translated into English, French, Spanish, and German, no small feat since it contained approximately 750 pages of text.[4]

The text of *Il senso teologico della liturgia* provides a viable framework within which to analyze Vagaggini's extended theology and methodology on the sacraments, liturgical participation, and trinitarian action. His theological discourse, however, was not limited to the publication of *Il senso teologico,* even in its several revisions.[5] The many articles and

---

[3] For a list of dates and events in the life of Cipriano Vagaggini, see "Data Biografici e Attiva di Don Cipriano Vagaggini" in Gerardo J. Békés and Giustino Farnedi, eds., *Lex Orandi, Lex Credendi: Miscellanea in Onore di P. Cipriano Vagaggini* (Rome: Editrice Anselmiana, 1980), 7.

[4] The bibliography included in the Békés edition cited above briefly mentions English, French, Spanish, and German editions of Vagaggini's tome. The actual translations are: *Theological Dimensions of the Liturgy,* trans. Leonard J. Doyle and W. A. Jurgens (Collegeville, MN: Liturgical Press, 1976), based on the 4th Italian edition; *Initiation théologique a la liturgie,* 2 vols., trans. Philippe Rouillard and Robert Gantoy (Paris: Société Liturgique, 1959–1963); *El sentido teologico de la liturgia,* trans. Manuel Garrido Bonaño (Madrid: Biblioteca de Autores Cristianos, 1959); *Theologie der Liturgie,* trans. August Berz (Einseideln: Benzinger, 1959); the French, Spanish, and German translations were all based on the second Italian edition. A first volume of the English language edition, based on the second Italian edition, had also been published in 1959, but the second projected volume was never published. Instead, the American publishers decided to translate the augmented fourth Italian edition, which included the additions made by the author in light of the Second Vatican Council. The English translation of the fourth edition, however, presents some concerns to this author. The original translator, Leonard J. Doyle, died before he completed the work, and his successor, W. A. Jurgens, admits changing Vagaggini's text to have it concur with the liturgical reforms in place by 1976 rather than at its original publication in 1965, and his word choice for translating the text does not always match that of his predecessor. For that reason all translations of Vagaggini's writings in this book are this author's own.

[5] Vagaggini's work, *Il senso teologico della liturgia,* was revised three times from its first edition in 1957. Within a year the second edition was published to correct typographical errors and formatting, with little to no change to the vast majority of the text. In 1962 the third edition was published, strictly as a

other books he published in the same arena augment and refine the discussions he presents in his mammoth work. Thus in what follows we will use the framework of Vagaggini's discussion presented in *Il senso teologico* (including its significant revisions) while also noting the various other sources and articles that elucidate the development of his thought.

Certain themes characterized Vagaggini's methodology for liturgical study, as evidenced in his inaugural lecture for the Pontifical Institute in 1961. First, he points to a convergence of method with respect to revelation between the resurgence of biblical scholarship, the writings of the Greek and Latin fathers, and the more recent liturgical movement of the twentieth century. He posits an intimate connection among the three: "they not only consider and propose the same revelation, but, moreover, they make it one substantially identical perspective."[6] That identical perspective allows each of the grand questions of human inquiry to fall under the auspices of salvation history—God acting in human history in order to save us. Moreover, Vagaggini maintained that the liturgy plays a crucial role in this perspective since it presents not only a premier locus for understanding divine action and the unfolding of the plan of salvation but also a vantage point from which the faithful can examine how they live in accord with that plan.[7]

Second, Vagaggini asserted that the liturgical movement has produced an organic sense of liturgical theology that had not been present before, a theology that recognized that an appreciation of the spiritual value of the Bible and the fathers depended on their being read within the action of the liturgy. But such a reading at the same time forces a renewed look at the liturgical action and the theology that follows from it.[8] It produces a never-ending cycle of spiritual and theological growth. Thus the three areas—liturgical studies, scriptural studies, and patristic studies—feed into each other, opening new insights into the other disciplines and then having those discoveries re-impact the

---

reprint of the second. In 1965 the fourth edition was published; it included significant changes in the text, accommodating not only the Constitution on the Sacred Liturgy (1963) but also Vagaggini's developing liturgical theology.

[6] Vagaggini, *Liturgia e pensiero teologico recente*, 41.

[7] Ibid.

[8] Ibid., 74.

original discipline. This interconnectedness can be witnessed in many of Vagaggini's writings.[9]

Finally, Vagaggini proposed that liturgy bridges the gap between the theology of academia and the everyday struggle of the believer. He wrote: "The contribution of the liturgy to recent theological thought can be summarized in the affirmation of the following general methodological rule: that no integral consideration of any dogma is had if this does not also include the perspective of its practical realization in the liturgy."[10] Such an assertion boldly proposes a less ambiguous interpretation of the axiom *lex orandi, lex credendi* (the law of prayer determines the law of belief). On the basis of his firm belief that liturgical theology can shape every other branch of the discipline, Vagaggini concluded:

> I believe that day will be realized on the terrain of the liturgy, never separated from the field of biblical scholarship, a remarkable progress toward that deep unity between speculative theology, the Bible, the Fathers, and the spiritual and pastoral life that we all wish. It will be a leap ahead in the theological field, toward that just equilibrium between metaphysics and life, abstract and concrete, that is, basically, the legitimate and nagging worry of modern thought.[11]

In this sense the field of liturgical studies, for Vagaggini, was not simply another theological discipline among many, but rather the arena through which all other disciplines are made sensible. Thus a comprehension and understanding of the multivalent images and signs of the liturgy become a necessary step for both theologian and believer.

Vagaggini's Starting Point: The Network of Signs

Originally published before the convening of the Second Vatican Council, Vagaggini's *Il senso teologico* served not only as a recapitulation of the efforts of the liturgical movement through the first half of the century but also as a future blueprint for theological discussion in

---

[9] As will be seen later, Vagaggini frequently assesses a theological point by viewing it from the position of the Scriptures, the fathers, and then the liturgy. This is true for much of his work in *Il senso teologico* but most especially in his depiction of the Trinity and its action in the liturgy.

[10] Vagaggini, *Liturgia e pensiero teologico recente*, 75–76.

[11] Ibid., 76.

the area of sacramental theology. In the text of the first edition Vagaggini systematically detailed an understanding of liturgical participation dependent on: (a) the network of signs used in the liturgy, (b) the action of Christ and the church within the liturgical action, and (c) the recapturing of a trinitarian understanding of liturgical texts and action. These three elements were then developed further in the fourth edition of the work, after the Second Vatican Council had clearly emphasized elements of revelation and liturgical participation. Nowhere was this development more profound than in the starting point Vagaggini used for his work in discussing the relationship of the history of salvation to liturgical action, that is, emanation from and return to God as seen in the complexus of signs that is the liturgy.

One of the underlying motifs in Vagaggini's writings is his depiction of the movement of salvation history through three specific stages: in heaven, on earth, and then back to heaven.[12] Following a Thomistic strain of thought,[13] he notes that all history emanates from God and has God as its directed end. In this sense the whole of salvation history becomes the context in which to view the unfolding of the liturgy. The primary direction of his argument is derived from Pope Pius XII's depiction of the liturgy in *Mediator Dei*, where the whole of the liturgy is seen as the extension of the priestly office of Christ as the mediator of grace throughout human history.[14] While Vagaggini's first edition of *Il senso teologico* notes this motif succinctly ("the liturgy cannot be understood unless it is viewed with the background of salvation history, the mystery—mystery of Christ and mystery of the Church"), his postconciliar edition augments this notion substantially.[15] He repeatedly

---

[12] Cipriano Vagaggini, *Il senso teologico della liturgia: saggio di liturgia teologica generale* (Rome: Edizioni Paoline, 1957), 23–24. Vagaggini details three distinct temporal phases, from "eternitá" to "tempo" back to "eternitá." The second phase on earth is divided into two subphases: one in relation to Adam and creation and the other in relation to Christ as the new creation.

[13] Thomas Aquinas structures his *Summa theologiae* in a Neoplatonic *exitus-reditus* framework, beginning with God the Creator and ending with the sacramental life of the church brought together in Christ. Joseph Cardinal Ratzinger, now Pope Benedict XVI, uses this same starting point in his book *The Spirit of the Liturgy* (Joseph Cardinal Ratzinger, *The Spirit of the Liturgy*, trans. John Saward [San Francisco: Ignatius Press, 2000]).

[14] See especially *Mediator Dei*, 1–3.

[15] Vagaggini, *Il senso teologico* (1965), 32.

points to the validation of this motif by the conciliar fathers. Citing both *Sacrosanctum Concilium* and *Lumen Gentium*, Vagaggini notes that the terms *sacred history* (or *salvation history*), *mystery*, *mystery of Christ*, and *mystery of the church* form a unique concept of a unified expression with various shades of meaning.[16] He is also clear about distinguishing himself from the definition of Odo Casel's sense of "worship-mystery" as presented in Casel's article "Mysteriengegenwart."[17] Casel advocates a re-presentation of the redemptive acts of Christ in their numeric individuality, that is, that the singular historic acts of Christ in his passion are made present in the liturgy. Vagaggini maintains that such a conviction would imply that the bloody torture and crucifixion of Christ that happened once in history (in its numeric individuality) is re-presented in the liturgical act. Instead, he asserts that such a specification of the mystery-presence of Christ cannot be identified with the concept of *mysterion* as it is presented in the New Testament. Moreover, Vagaggini notes that Casel's position overemphasizes the significance of the pagan mystery cults and wrongly identifies them with the early church; he argues that such a numerical re-presentation of Christ's mystery within Christian worship was never a part of the early liturgies or of patristic usage.[18] Christ's historical actions are manifestations of a permanent divine disposition made present through the instrumentality of Christ's humanity. While the central focus of Christ's redemptive action is found on the cross, Vagaggini maintains that the permanent disposition of Christ can be seen in his entire life, teachings, death, resurrection, and ascension. He argues: "All of this is true because all of the phases of the Lord's historical and metahistorical life, up to and including his second coming, are so closely united that they form only one great mystery: the mystery of Christ the Redeemer."[19] Vagaggini's disapproval of Casel's position is somewhat muted in his first edition, but in the years after the council

---

[16] Ibid., 31–32. Vagaggini notes specifically SC 2, 5, 35.2 and LG 1–8 (Chapter I: The Mystery of the Church).

[17] *Il senso teologico* (1965), 42–43. See Vagaggini's extended n. 19. See also Odo Casel, "Mysteriengegenwart," *Jahrbuch für Liturgiewissenschaft* 8 (1928): 10–224, at 145, 212. Casel offers a definition of the liturgy as the "mystery cult of Christ and of the church" (212). Vagaggini critiques the lack of intelligibility in the terms Casel employs.

[18] *Il senso teologico* (1965), 115–19.

[19] Ibid., 122.

it became clear that when he spoke of the presence of the mystery of Christ and the efficacy of the sacraments he wished to distinguish himself unequivocally from Casel.[20] Thus, for Vagaggini, to speak of the liturgy as the manifestation of the mystery of Christ is to speak of it also in relation to salvation history and the self-communication of God in the world through the mystery of the church. The sanctification and worship engendered in the liturgy then become the demonstrable signs of God's action in salvation history and the human response. Vagaggini asserts (referring to *Mediator Dei*) that this "double movement of the liturgy, that of God which descends to man and that of man which goes up to God, is much more clearly marked in the Council's notion of the liturgy than when it occurs in the encyclical."[21] However, he also laments that while many might recognize the overarching influence of salvation history in theological study and the truth of an *exitus-reditus* schema within Christian doctrine, most do not heed or understand it, much less live their lives effectively by it. Nor do they recognize the central role of liturgical action as the lived expression of the life of faith.[22] For him it is a question of praxis, not theory. Vagaggini's belief underscores all the more his intentional purpose in framing his work within this schema and attempting to provide a liturgical-pastoral ethic by which to live.

It is precisely within this framework of salvation history and the double movement of the liturgy that Vagaggini posits both his

---

[20] The first edition of *Il senso teologico* points to Casel as one who has unearthed the terms *sacramentum* and *mysterion* for modern scholarship. There is a slight admonition in Vagaggini's tone when he advises that one should not dispute the terms simply because one disagrees with the theories of Casel. Rather, the notion of *sacramentum* and *mysterion* has a historical basis rooted in the patristic tradition and in the liturgy. Later in the text Vagaggini proffers a short summary and critique of Casel's position (see pp. 89–92). In the 1965 edition this exposition is far more developed and much more incisive (see pp. 115–19). See Vagaggini, *Il senso teologico* (1957), 38 n. 18. For Casel's approach, see Odo Casel, "Das Mysteriengedächtnis der Messliturgie im Lichte der Tradition," *Jahrbuch für Liturgiewissenschaft* 6 (1926): 8–204; idem, *Die Liturgie Als Mysterienfeier*, ed. Ildefons Herwegen, Ecclesia Orans: Zur Einführung in den Geist der Liturgie, 9 (Freiburg: Herder, 1923).

[21] *Il senso teologico* (1965), 35. See also idem, "Riflessioni sul senso teologico del mistero pasquale," *Rivista di Pastorale Liturgica* 2 (1964): 102–12, at 103–4.

[22] *Il senso teologico* (1965), 40.

nuanced definition of a sacrament and the explanation for the complexus of signs that makes up the liturgy. Early in his discussion of sacraments in general he succinctly states the classical definition of sacraments given by Saint Thomas: sensible signs effecting (*ex opere operato*) the grace they signify.[23] But in his reformulation of sign theory Vagaggini wishes to extend the classical definition of a sacramental sign in two essential ways. First, among "efficacious signs" he wishes to include those signs that work not only *ex opere operato* but also *ex opere operantis Ecclesiae*. Second, in sensible signs Vagaggini seeks to include not simply those that signify and produce grace directly, and only indirectly the worship the church seeks to give to God, but also those that directly signify human worship and only indirectly the grace through which God sanctifies humankind.[24] What is unique to Vagaggini's notion of the complexus of signs that makes up the liturgy is this broadening of the concept of sacrament to include the entire liturgical arena. At its root stands the patristic understanding of *sacramentum* and *mysterion* that was restricted by the scholastics. His aim is not simply historical; rather, he seeks to rediscover "that 'sacramentality' does not apply exclusively to the seven major rites which we today call precisely sacraments, as if to say sacraments *par excellence*; rather, except that which is proper to those seven rites especially as far as regards divine institution and the particular efficacy *ex opere operato*, sacramentality is common to the whole liturgy."[25] Vagaggini does not go as far as Karl Rahner would in his depiction of the world as sacramentally graced, but most assuredly he attempts to redefine the understanding of what could be classed as sacrament in relation to all liturgical action. This extended notion of sacrament fits directly into his *exitus-reditus* theme of salvation history. Vagaggini avers that the whole liturgy is the point at which the church "appears most aptly as the pure and sensible instrument which the divine life uses to

---

[23] Although Vagaggini makes the claim that this definition was created by Aquinas, the Angelic Doctor never actually uses the exact formulation Vagaggini posits. In fact, in his most developed sacramental treatise in the *Summa theologiae* Aquinas foregoes the use of the phrase *ex opere operato*. Instead, a more detailed and nuanced approach is made to explain instrumental efficient causality in the sacraments. See *Summa theologiae*, IIIa, q. 62, a. 1: . . . *sacramenta novae legis non solum significant, sed causant gratiam.*

[24] *Il senso teologico* (1965), 42–43.

[25] Ibid., 44–45.

manifest and transmit itself to men properly disposed."[26] In this sense he posits that the complexus of signs that makes up the liturgical action becomes the nexus for believers' participation in salvation history and the movement of the Trinity through that history.

Within this rather large spectrum of the liturgical action Vagaggini sees two fundamental bases for Christian exemplarism—the metaphysics of participation (including sign and image) and revelation itself. It is through these two aspects that the human person is able to participate in the divine life of God. Thus at the outset Vagaggini maintains both a metaphysical and a soteriological understanding of participation. The metaphysical component of Christian exemplarism for Vagaggini can be summarized easily: "in every effect of efficient causality, there is always an exemplary causality at work as well. This means that there is always in the effect a participation of the form of the agent, who is first of all God himself."[27] Because of this, all things are necessarily actual signs or images of God: "they truly participate in Him, and He is truly present in them."[28] The other basis for Christian exemplarism, that of revelation, helps to unfold the mystery behind salvation history, namely, that the human being, a unity of matter and spirit, is destined for a reality in union with the Godhead made possible by the incarnation of Christ, the exemplar of the human person. Vagaggini posits the "law of incarnation" to explain the relationship between revelation and liturgy. He asserts that the law of incarnation has two distinct aspects: "first of all, it signifies that God communicates the divine life to man through and under the veil of sensible things, in such a way that man should pass through these sensible things in order to receive that divine life. Secondly, it signifies that the result of that communication is an elevation of man to a divine way of being and acting."[29] This elevation is not simply in the moral order but takes place on the ontological level of the human person. The liturgical world becomes the nexus where such an elevation happens because that liturgical realm is "the world of the incarnation prolonged, made present, and participated in by men in the sanctification that God

[26] Ibid., 45.

[27] Ibid., 55.

[28] Ibid. Vagaggini is careful to note that the knowledge of the exemplar (of the divine reality) is neither arbitrary nor subjective.

[29] Ibid., 290.

makes happen in the church and in the worship that the church renders to God."[30]

Thus Vagaggini positions his sacramental theology across the rather broad spectrum of his introductory themes: the trajectory of salvation history emanating from God and returning to God, the broadening of the concept of sacrament and mystery, and the dual aspects of participation in light of both metaphysics and revelation. Such a positioning produces a vast complex of signs operating within the liturgical celebration—speech, gestures and movements, earthly elements, art, and even persons—signs that act as sensible realities to express those very themes in the overarching communication of God's grace within the sacramental act.[31] The liturgy, however, also recognizes that these signs are efficacious in their signifying, and for that reason Vagaggini wishes to distinguish within his complex of signs those that have their efficacy because they are instituted by God (*ex opere operato*) and those that are instituted by the believing church (*ex opere operantis Ecclesiae*).[32] As mentioned earlier, Vagaggini sought to elucidate the definition of sacrament to include both notions of efficacious signs. He realizes that one must determine the context in which a sign gains or acquires its signifying value because the supernatural reality that is signified is not readily or automatically perceptible to the human person within the natural order. He argues, "The immersion in water and the emersion from water is a disappearance and a reappearance, but it does not naturally signify death to sin and the resurrection to supernatural life in Christ. The ablution with water certainly does signify natural physical purification, but not also the purification from sin."[33] While liturgical signs may have certain analogous connotations in nature or through human convention, they are chosen to carry specific supernatural signification and that sign value is determined either by God or by the church. In the latter instance the church itself acts as a sign, that is, Vagaggini envisions the church as an instrumental sign of Christ through the work and activity of the Holy Spirit. He describes the church itself in the same terms, as a sacramental sign. Vagaggini

---

[30] Ibid., 294.

[31] For Vagaggini's explication of each one of these various signs, see ibid., pp. 60–74.

[32] *Il senso teologico* (1965), 109–10. See also Vagaggini, "Lo spirito della Costituzione sulla liturgia," *Rivista Liturgica* 51 (1964): 5–49, at 46–47.

[33] *Il senso teologico* (1965), 57.

asserts: "By the Spirit which he communicates to her, Christ gives life inwardly to the church, so that she can be compared in this respect to a body; for the body is the visible expression of the invisible soul which intrinsically gives it life, it is the soul's complete and concrete sphere of vital outward action."[34] While Vagaggini clarifies the nature of the church and its own sign value, it should be noted that his insistence on the contextual determination of the nature of signs raises questions of cognitive understanding and viability he does not answer. In order to answer those questions he places that contextual determination firmly within an ecclesiological understanding of participation.

With respect to efficacious signs operating in virtue of their ecclesial institution, it should be noted that the signs employed are primarily communitarian; it is the church that gives worship to God through these signs, not any one individual. The worship of the individual is necessarily dependent on the worship of the church. The individual cannot determine the meaning and existence of liturgical signs. Vagaggini asserts repeatedly that the existence and precise sense of individual signs in the liturgy "depend essentially on the positive free will of God and of the church."[35] Thus even the very structure and identification of liturgical signs is dependent on the action of the Christ—both the person of Christ and the Mystical Body of Christ in the church—a point that cannot be neglected in analyzing the performance and efficacy of those sacramental signs.

Given the objective nature of the signs used in the liturgy of the church, it is imperative for the individual believer to acquire the frame of reference needed to interpret sensible signs as spiritual realities. Aquinas states that such a determinate reference is given by God in the sacraments.[36] In the revision of his text Vagaggini takes note of Aquinas's position and proposes that "for the individual to render true and personal worship to God in Christ in the liturgy involves necessarily making his own those signs of the church and those realities the church expresses through those signs—it involves tuning in to those signs and those realities."[37] Elsewhere Vagaggini writes that this

[34] Ibid., 30.
[35] Ibid., 58.
[36] ST IIIa, q. 60, a. 5.
[37] Il senso teologico (1965), 58. It is perhaps important to note that Vagaggini's concept of theological "syntonization" or tuning appears only in the revised editions of his text of Il senso teologico. Vagaggini found it increasingly

internal tuning of the soul (*la sintonia d'animo interna*) is different from the internal act of contemplation outside of the liturgy.[38] The internal tuning of the soul to the liturgical signs and actions of the church more fully unites the individual to Christ through the church. But even the purely private act of contemplation can be offered to God and can be seen as an intimately personal act of the individual—that is, from the human person to the divine Person (*di persona a Persona*)—when

> this intimate and also personal action is none other than the internal tuning of the soul connaturally corresponding—at least in its general and profound sense—to the completion of and also the external participation in the liturgical act (for example: Mass, recitation and singing of the psalms); it is not at all purely the private act of the person who completes it, but it is also an action of the church as such that, in intimate union with its divine Head, in this person and through this person, completes the liturgical act and offers it to God.[39]

Thus through this inner tuning of the soul the human person is able to engage him- or herself more intimately and more fully in the liturgical action of the church.

This internal tuning is also necessary in the realm of meaning—as a way of understanding the vast network of liturgical signs the church employs. Vagaggini argues that the very existence of liturgical signs themselves is dependent on the free choice of God and the church. The positive will of God can only be known through revelation and is made manifest through theological exercise, as in establishing the matter and form of the sacraments.[40] The will of the church, however, and the meaning it assigns to liturgical rites and symbols, is determined through ritual evidence—through the rite itself and its history.

---

important to explicate the manner in which liturgical participation could be made more complete as the preparatory commission for the liturgy was drafting the constitution for the council in 1962.

[38] Vagaggini, "Contemplazione nella Liturgia e Contemplazione fuori della Liturgia," *Rivista di ascetica e mistica* 7 (1962): 8–35, at 15–16. Vagaggini's discussion here places primary emphasis on contemplation in the liturgical act over the purely private act of contemplation that takes place outside of the liturgy. Part of his rationale is that liturgical contemplation, through its *sintonia d'animo*, also participates in the liturgical act of the church.

[39] Ibid., 17.

[40] *Il senso teologico* (1965), 58.

Vagaggini asserts that the church makes its intention clear through the words that accompany a particular liturgical sign, words that are meant to give a precise meaning to the liturgical action.[41] But he also avers that the exact symbolic meaning of a liturgical rite can be unintelligible or at least greatly obscured by the present form of a given liturgy and thus a historical consciousness is necessary in order to ascertain the liturgical and theological meaning of the symbolic act. This happens when the current texts no longer explain the meaning of the rite or when the rite itself has been reduced to a point at which it becomes difficult at best to approach its symbolic value. Vagaggini cites a few examples he finds wanting: "the fact that the priest in the administration of penance at the moment of absolution raises his hands slightly toward the penitent; the full symbolism of the baptismal rite, recognized with difficulty in the present common rite in which a little water is poured over the head of the baptized; the same may be said about the full symbolism of the table in many of our present altars."[42] In the wake of such examples Vagaggini makes a forceful statement about determining the church's will when the rites themselves are unclear: "the historical study of the origin and development of the rites is indispensable."[43] This clear call for historical study of the development of the rites and the texts becomes even more important as Vagaggini unfolds his own work on the meaning of the sacramental action and the participation of the human person in both worship and sanctification.

Worship and the Sanctification of the Body

As we have seen earlier, Vagaggini defines "sacrament" so as to include acts that are efficacious *ex opere operato* and *ex opere operantis Ecclesiae*. These two dimensions assist him in creating a definition of

[41] Ibid., 58–59. It is significant that the words to which Vagaggini refers do not include those that would be considered the form of a sacrament. Rather, he cites in particular the words for the commingling of water and wine, the former prayer of incensation, the prayer of Ash Wednesday, and the prayer for the procession of palms on Palm Sunday.

[42] Ibid., 59. It should be noted that in this text "leggermente" could have a dual meaning—either slightly or thoughtlessly—and both would seem to apply.

[43] Ibid. In the text Vagaggini sets these words in italics to highlight their importance.

liturgy that arrives at its essential core: "The liturgy is a complex of the sensible, efficacious signs of the church's sanctification and of her worship."[44] The church's sanctification is carried out by the action of God toward the church (*ex opere operato*), while the worship of the church becomes its demonstrable action toward God (*ex opere operantis Ecclesiae*). Vagaggini seeks to situate liturgical participation within these two spheres of worship and sanctification.

Vagaggini asserts, in keeping with the tradition of the church, that the sanctification of the human person that takes place in the liturgical act occurs through participation in Christ. In discussing the metaphysical causality associated with Christ's historical actions by Aquinas and other scholastics, Vagaggini asserts that these actions "are also the exemplary cause of our sanctification and of our worship. In fact, in us, sanctification and worship are nothing but a participation in Christ's sanctity, of which those actions were the fruit. And our liturgical worship is but a continuation of the worship that Christ rendered to God in those actions."[45] Christ's saving acts become the merit by which the human person is sanctified, and Christ's worship of the Father through the sacrifice of his life becomes the example *par excellence* of all human worship. In the celebration of the sacraments, believers participate in the redemptive actions of Christ made present in the rite. Vagaggini explains: "The salvific actions of Christ, even in their numerical individuality by now past and not reproducible, are rendered truly present in the liturgical rite in such a way that the living image makes present the prototype that represents and re-presents because that image truly participates in it."[46] This rendering of the redemptive actions of Christ is not viewed as merely a memorial of past events; rather, those events, by being rendered present, are complete together with their ontological effects—namely, the outpouring of sanctifying grace, the gifts of the Spirit, the sanctification of believers.

Coupled with participation in Christ's sanctity as a means for our sanctification, Vagaggini positions the worship enacted by the liturgical rite as a participation in the worship of Christ as well. While sanctification occurs in the sacraments *ex opere operato*, the worship believers offer to God and the reception of grace are both dependent

---

[44] Ibid., 40.
[45] Ibid., 120.
[46] Ibid.

on the moral disposition of the person. For Vagaggini this creates a sacramental ethic—one that underscores the entire development of his treatise throughout his works—namely, "the disposition of the soul in which internal worship consists is not conceivable without the commitment, at least implicit, to live in the future as it demands—that in worship we recognize God's pre-eminence and we profess our submission to him."[47] In this sense the faithful who are gathered in the name of Christ are required to put themselves in a kenotic state of acceptance by the very nature of the sacrament being celebrated. In the liturgical act, and especially in the sacramental liturgical act, the individual is caught up in something much bigger than either himself or herself. Vagaggini asserts in *Il senso teologico*: "The worship of the church is nothing other than the worship Christ renders to God by means of the church, making the church participate in his worship. Thus the church's spiritual dispositions are an instrument Christ uses and are a participation in the spiritual dispositions of Christ."[48] Within Vagaggini's framework, liturgical worship is always viewed as an act of the corporate body of the faithful acting in the church. Central to his discussion of participation is the individual's relationship to the corporate body of the church especially when the church acts liturgically in worship toward God (*ex opere operantis Ecclesiae*). This concept of the *opus operantis Ecclesiae* seems to pervade nearly all of Vagaggini's writings. In order to understand it fully one must first look at his explication of the interrelationship between the body (flesh) of Christ, the Body of Christ (as church), and the human person acting in the church's worship and seeking sanctification.

In his 1966 work, "Caro salutis est cardo,"[49] Vagaggini sets out to demarcate the essential character of the body in the role of salvation; as the axiom he uses for the title suggests, the flesh is the instrument of salvation.[50] Tracing the role of corporeity throughout the development

[47] Ibid., 84.

[48] Ibid.

[49] Vagaggini, "Caro salutis est cardo. Corporeità, Eucharistia e Liturgia," in *Miscellanea Liturgica in onore di sua eminenza Il Cardinale Giacomo Lercaro* (Rome: Descleé, 1966), 73–210. The original work was written as a long article in the above edition but it was quickly reprinted by the same publisher in the same year as a separate volume.

[50] Vagaggini borrows this phrase from Tertullian, who in his *De resurrectionis mortuorum* wrote "*adeo caro salutis est cardo.*" In his analysis Vagaggini

of Catholic theology, Vagaggini attempts to explicate the interdependence of the Body of Christ, salvation, and the sacraments, especially the Eucharist. "The entire Christian life," he argues, "is nothing other than a participation by single individuals in the divine realities that came to pass in Christ, in his flesh—a participation that has its effect in configuring the individuals to the model itself."[51] Thus the individual instance of Christ becoming flesh and offering himself to the Father in the redemptive act of the cross becomes the means through which the Body of Christ as the church is formed and in that church's worship the human person has the opportunity to be modeled in similitude to the offering of Christ. In this sense Vagaggini sees a vital link between faith and sacraments as the means by which that saving grace is brought to life within individual believers through the flesh of Christ. Again, following Aquinas, he posits that the contact of salvation must have both a spiritual and bodily dimension since the one who is saved, the human person, is both body and spirit. He argues: "Our contact with what He did and suffered in his flesh must be made in the soul,

---

reproduces the entire text from chapter 8, 2-3 of Tertullian's text. That text follows here: *Etsi sufficeret illi, quod nulla omnino anima salutem possit adipisci nisi dum [est] in carne crediderit: adeo caro salutis cardo. De qua cum anima a deo allegatur, ipsa est, quae efficit, ut anima allegi possit a deo. Sed et caro abluitur, ut anima emaculetur; caro unguitur, ut anima consecretur; caro signatur, ut et anima muniatur; caro manus inpositione adumbratur, ut et anima spiritu inluminetur; caro corpore et sanguine Christi vescitur, ut et anima de deo saginetur. Non possunt ergo separari in mercede quas opera conjungit.* (It might be sufficient then to realize that absolutely no soul is able to obtain salvation unless it believes that it is in the flesh: truly, the flesh is the pivotal point of salvation. When the soul is subjected by God, it is the flesh itself which makes it possible that the soul is able to be subjected by God. Therefore the flesh is washed that the soul may be purified; the flesh is anointed so that the soul may be consecrated; the flesh is signed so that the soul may be fortified; the flesh is overshadowed by the imposition of hands so that the soul may be illuminated by the Spirit; the flesh is nourished with the Body and Blood of Christ so that the soul may be fed lavishly by God. Therefore those that are united in work cannot be separated in the reward.) Tertullian, *De resurrectione mortuorum* 8, 2-3, in CC, vol. 2. Vagaggini's translation into Italian points to the fact that he may have been working with a slightly different version of Tertullian's work—the *incipit* differs and some phraseology is altered, but the overarching meaning of the passage remains identical.

[51] Vagaggini, "Caro salutis est cardo,"165.

which is realized in faith (hope and charity), and in the body, which is accomplished through the sacraments of the faith: rites that are also sensible and external in which the body is also involved."[52]

The nature of this involvement is clarified by the church's adherence to the principle that Christ's humanity serves as the instrumental cause of the justification of the believer. Quoting Aquinas, Vagaggini asserts that such a cause "is applied to us spiritually by means of faith, and corporeally by means of the sacraments, because Christ's humanity is both spirit and body."[53] But such a stance also points to the corporeity of the church itself acting as the instrumental cause of the sacrament— that through and in the faith of the church the sacraments are enacted and lived out. Here lies the crux of Vagaggini's conclusions with regard to the body: if Christ's body is seen as the pivotal point of salvation according to the tradition of the fathers and the medieval scholastics like Aquinas, then the living Body of Christ, the church, must be inextricably linked with and caught up in the work of salvation. The church, however, is viewed not as some ethereal cosmic entity that exists only in its institutional or juridical reality, but in the bodies of believers that make up that church united to Christ as Head—in the interplay of ministers and assembly in sacramental action, in the handing on of faith to believers and nonbelievers through the hierarchy of the church and its magisterium, in the effort to live a life in accord with the faith the sacraments profess, all in union with Christ as Head.

In the concluding chapter of "Caro salutis est cardo" Vagaggini demarcates precisely this relationship between the corporeity of Christ and the church (the body) and the liturgy (the instrument of salvation). Returning to the law of incarnation he posits in his larger work, *Il senso teologico*, he proposes a more nuanced version of this law within his conclusion. The "law of sacramentality," as a particular representation of the law of incarnation, reflects the fittingness of the communication of divine life through the sacraments. If the law of incarnation suggests that God communicates divine life to the human person through sensible things in accord with human nature so as to divinize the human person, then the law of sacramentality demonstrates where the divine and human come together. Vagaggini positions his argument succinctly:

[52] Ibid., 166.
[53] Ibid., 167. See also, Aquinas, *De veritate* 27a, 4c.

A connatural means for divinizing an incarnate being is itself incarnate: in which it happens that the divine is present in the human, including the senses, and operates through the human, including the senses, in order to elevate [the human], even in the sphere of the senses, to a divine level of being and acting.

These means are called exactly, in the most general sense, sacraments: human and sensible means that, as instruments of divine virtue, contain and communicate this divine reality to those who are well disposed.

Thus this communication of divine life through the sacraments defined as such is the law of the relationships between God and [humanity].[54]

When the eucharistic mystery is viewed in light of Tertullian's phrase, *caro salutis est cardo*, it necessarily becomes the "center, apex and source of the economy of salvation."[55] The Eucharist is that moment when the believer can most fully participate in the saving work of Christ. That participation is done not merely individually but in recognition that the sacrifice of Christ is also the sacrifice of the church, united in worship for the sanctification of its members. Thus, for Vagaggini, the liturgy, and especially the Eucharist, becomes the new pivotal point of salvation—where the flesh of Christ sanctifies the living body of the church.

The preceding discussion of corporeity was necessary in order to explain the nuances of Vagaggini's understanding of the notion of *opus operantis Ecclesiae*. Within *Il senso teologico* he carefully delineates how this concept is to be interpreted, especially in the sense of the liturgical rites as efficacious *ex opere operantis Ecclesiae*. He begins his discussion by pointing to Pius XII's use of the phrase in the encyclical *Mediator Dei*.[56] As mentioned earlier, the pontiff asserts that the efficacy of those liturgical signs instituted by the church "is due rather to the action of the church (*ex opere operantis Ecclesiae*), inasmuch as she is holy and

---

[54] Ibid., 187.

[55] Ibid., 203.

[56] While Aquinas uses the phrase repeatedly in the *Tertia pars* of the *Summa theologiae*, Vagaggini notes that as far as he can discern, the promulgation of *Mediator Dei* marks the first time that *ex opere operantis Ecclesiae* was included in an official document of the church. See also the discussion in Vagaggini, *Il senso teologico* (1965), 123–24.

acts always in closest union with her Head."[57] Those signs are defined by the pontiff as the part the church takes in the sacramental action, "embellishing the Eucharistic Sacrifice and the sacraments with prayer and sacred ceremonies, or if one refers to the 'sacramentals' and the other rites instituted by the hierarchy of the church."[58] In this sense they are not the actions of the church or ministers that produce the form of the sacrament (e.g., the pouring of water and the trinitarian formula in baptism, the exchange of vows in marriage, or the anointing of the forehead with the invocation of the Spirit in confirmation—all of which effect grace *ex opere operato*) but everything else that surrounds it.

Vagaggini delves uniquely into the concept of *ex opere operantis Ecclesiae* in order to unpack both its richness and its implications for sacramental worship.[59] He attempts such a foray to highlight the proper activity of the church body and to demarcate the distinction between liturgy and devotion. The liturgy that effects grace *ex opere operantis Ecclesiae* has a special role over and above personal or even communal devotions. In creating this exposition Vagaggini hopes to counter the overly simplistic notion that any ritual could effect grace *ex opere operantis*, because that would imply that the effect of grace is dependent on the moral disposition of the minister or recipient. Rather, he attempts to position sacraments within the liturgical milieu in which they are performed and through which they operate. He asserts: "The spiritual effect of the *opus operantis* is not simply the fruit of human effort or dignity alone, but is an effect produced by God that transcends human power."[60] In this sense God produces within the subject a grace variable in nature and degree in response to the prayer that finds its expression in the liturgical action brought to life by those engaged in the sacramental celebration. He willingly admits that there are differing types of liturgical signs and actions instituted by the church and differing degrees to which grace is made manifest. Here the earlier discussion of corporeity plays a significant role. While Vagaggini readily acknowledges the general distinction between the *opus operantis* of the

---

[57] *Mediator Dei* 27. See previous reference in this text, chap. 1, p. 12.

[58] *Mediator Dei* 27.

[59] In the preface to the fourth edition of *Il senso teologico*, Vagaggini states that this concept of the *opus operantis Ecclesiae* is one of the primary revisions of the new text. See *Il senso teologico* (1965), 13.

[60] Ibid., 124.

minister or member of the faithful and the *opus operantis* of the church, he divides the latter into liturgical (which is public in nature and officially regulated and formed by church hierarchy) and nonliturgical (which may be public, but is not official), while maintaining the corporeity of the liturgical act.[61] When the action of the faithful is, properly speaking, liturgical, that is, prayer offered to God through the official means of the church, that action, according to Vagaggini,

> is the direct action of Christ himself, head of his members, who works through his special visible representatives and agents, to whom he gave a special investiture for that end, which the rest of the faithful do not have. Therefore Christ himself considers such action in a very special way his own action, which, through his visible hierarchical agents, he fulfills before God as head of his members, that is, as head of his church. . . . With good reason therefore, the liturgists, in order to distinguish the much greater spiritual efficacy such an action has before God from the private action of the faithful, even though the private action be done in union with Christ and with the church, have recourse to the concept of *opus operantis Ecclesiae*.[62]

The complex of signs that makes up the liturgy and in turn is viewed as the vehicle both for worship and for sanctification is always the action of the entire church, rooted in Christ. The guarantor of the moral disposition of the church is Christ himself as its head and, as Vagaggini would argue, the Spirit that is poured forth into the church in the wake of the paschal mystery.

Vagaggini uses this concept of efficacy *ex opere operantis Ecclesiae* throughout his various writings on the liturgy and the life of the church. In defending the practice of concelebration and its inherent sign value he writes that the liturgy is redefined by the council as "the exercise of the priestly function of Jesus Christ, in which, by means of sensible signs, the sanctification of the human being comes to be signified and realized in everyone in its own way, and at the same time the public and integral worship of the Mystical Body, that is of Jesus Christ and of his members, is exercised."[63] Concelebration serves

---

[61] Ibid.

[62] Ibid., 126.

[63] Vagaggini, "Il valore teologico e spirituale della messa concelebrata," *Rivista Liturgica* 52 (1965): 189–218, at 203.

to enhance the signifying action of the liturgy as the work of Christ united to his Mystical Body.

Similarly, Vagaggini uses this same motif in discussing the very identity of the church in Christ. Citing the central sacramental reality that the "Eucharist makes the church," he explains the relationship of Eucharist to liturgy and the formation of the church in his article, "La Chiesa si ritrova nella liturgia."[64] He asserts that "the eucharistic mystery is the quintessence of the liturgy; all the sacraments are ordained to it and they prepare for it, having, to this purpose, a most special efficacy *ex opere operato*. To this mystery is ordained, with greater reason, all the liturgy of ecclesiastical institution, which has, to the same purpose, a special force *ex opere operantis Ecclesiae*."[65] It is the "special power" granted *ex opere operantis Ecclesiae* that helps the church become fully manifest in the world and essentially helps create its identity. Vagaggini goes on to assert:

> That is why, to have better understood that the invisible aspect of community and the community of the divine life in the church is the determined end with respect to its juridical structure, it has sought to discover with a clarity that has never before happened that the liturgy, principally in the full celebration of the eucharistic mystery, is the apex of the life of the church to which all tends, the source from which it derives every virtue, the principal manifestation of its very self.[66]

Speaking of the grace effected *ex opere operantis Ecclesiae* in the liturgy consistently underscores the formative aspect of the liturgical rite on the self-recognition of believers as the Mystical Body of Christ *qua* church. The Second Vatican Council, Vagaggini notes, echoes this hallmark of the liturgy as the principal manifestation of the church.[67]

In another instance Vagaggini uses the notion of *ex opere operantis Ecclesiae* to highlight what he sees as a postconciliar emphasis on the profound union between sacrifice and sacrament.[68] Tracing the various

---

[64] Vagaggini, "La Chiesa si ritrova nella liturgia," *Rivista Liturgica* 51 (1964): 343–54, at 348. Here he begins a section of his article on the principle: "l'Eucharistia fa la Chiesa."

[65] Ibid., 350.

[66] Ibid.

[67] See SC 41.

[68] In his article, "La messa, sacremento del sacrificio pasquale di Cristo e della Chiesa," *Rivista Liturgica* 56 (1969): 179–93, Vagaggini asserts that one of

expressions of Christ's sacrifice in the Scriptures—in the sacrifice of the Last Supper, of the cross, and of the heavenly sacrifice—he posits how the church is intimately tied to Christ's sacrifice by linking the liturgical act of offering to the offering of Christ in the paschal mystery. Here the term "sacrifice" is used primarily in terms of an outpouring or giving of oneself. Vagaggini avers: "The church offers the sacrifice in awareness of this fact (namely, that it is united to Christ as Head), accepting it with joy and thus offering Christ as victim to the Father and offering itself at the same time with Christ in the union with the offering Christ makes of himself and of us and in continuation of what he did at Golgotha and throughout his life."[69] But this offering of the church is made manifest in the entirety of the liturgical act and not simply in the actions that are constitutive of the sacrament. Rather, the entirety of the eucharistic prayers has meaning for those who wish to join their sacrifice to the sacrifice of Christ. Thus Vagaggini rightly argues that a special emphasis should be placed on the liturgy in catechesis and in the explication of the prayers of the canon so that the interior act of the faithful (as offering) can be more fully realized in the liturgical signs instituted by the church.[70]

The importance of the concept of *ex opere operantis Ecclesiae* for Vagaggini is also intimately tied to the relationship between grace and liturgical participation. He notes that through the sanctifying grace received in the sacrament *ex opere operato* there is a "true participation in the divine nature, although this participation is accidental and mysterious."[71] There exists also a "participation in the Incarnation and a conformity to Christ that comes about in us through the indwelling of the divine persons and has as its end the glory of the beatific vision, which is its connatural fulfillment."[72] This grace is given by God in every enactment of the sacramental rite. But Vagaggini asserts that there is a qualifier attached to this simple maxim: that when the rites instituted by the church (those that act *ex opere operantis Ecclesiae*) obtain actual graces for the believer, then, insofar as the rites are

---

the new elements of postconciliar theology following from the sign value of the complex of the liturgy is this union of sacrifice and sacrament in the Mass, which post-Tridentine theology was less inclined to admit.

[69] Ibid., 191.

[70] Ibid., 193.

[71] *Il senso teologico* (1965), 137.

[72] Ibid.

sanctifying rites, those actual graces "are directed to the recovery and augmentation of sanctifying grace in us."[73] Thus the graces received through the action of the church are directly linked to the graces of the sacrament itself. The Eucharist, which unites sacrament and sacrifice, also unites the graces received from both. Through liturgical participation, through the offering of themselves in the official and public prayer of the church, believers are more fully disposed to receive the sacramental grace that, in turn, allows them to participate in the divine life of the Trinity. But one cannot ignore the action of the Trinity in such a model. If liturgical participation is nuanced to include the grace-activity that comes from God's self-communication, then every liturgical celebration of the church must mirror that reality, that is, the acceptance of the offer of grace has to be inculcated in the rite itself. Vagaggini believes that this tenet is so central to Christian liturgy and worship that every liturgical action and prayer is molded by a trinitarian motif—that God who communicates himself through grace sacramentally as the triune God invites the believer through liturgical participation to enter most fully into that divine life.

The Trinity in the Liturgical Action

Out of the rather intricate network of signs he distinguishes within the sacramental-liturgical act, Vagaggini formulates a highly nuanced, well-developed sense of the christological-trinitarian dimension of liturgy. The overt reinsertion of a trinitarian motif within Western sacramental theology would seem to many to be a natural consequence of both the twentieth century's liturgical movement and the reforms heralded by the Second Vatican Council. Vagaggini, however, wrote much of his trinitarian thought before the council was even convoked. The inclusion within sacramental theology of a trinitarian perspective coupled to the christological emphasis of the West articulated for him what is central to the liturgy itself: the self-communication of the triune God. Moreover, he links his trinitarian motif to the fundamental basis for liturgical participation: that liturgy forms the vehicle by which the "return to God" is made complete. He demarcates a method whereby liturgical participation becomes not only advantageous but necessary for the believer to enter into the divine life of the Trinity most fully. Following from his starting point that one must "tune in"

[73] Ibid.

to the complex of signs in the liturgy, Vagaggini now turns *sintonia d'animo* toward the trinitarian dimension of the liturgy itself.

Vagaggini begins his discussion of the Trinity and liturgy by returning to the same starting point that helped him form his concept of the complex of signs in the liturgy: the emanation and return of creation to God. For Vagaggini revelation teaches two things to the human person: first, that the God from whom we come and to whom we return is a Trinity of persons; second, that there is a "cycle of relations" between the trinitarian God and each human person that illumines the human person's reason for existence.[74] This cycle is defined in simple terms: "Every good thing comes from the Father, through the medium of his incarnate Son, Jesus Christ, in the presence of the Holy Spirit (in us), and thus it is in the presence of the Holy Spirit, through the medium of the incarnate Son, Jesus Christ, that everything must return to the Father and be reunited with its end, the most blessed Trinity."[75] Here the *exitus-reditus* theme of his previous chapters is made explicit in trinitarian terms.[76]

However, in the earliest edition of his work Vagaggini describes this christological-trinitarian cycle as "dialectic," even though he is not speaking of two opposing terms being resolved into one central truth.[77] Such a characterization is problematic since the activity described primarily centers on the relation between God and the human person, which cannot be construed as the reconciliation of opposing forces. By the time of the fourth edition Vagaggini had rid himself of the Hegelian term and described the cycle simply as a movement or

[74] Ibid., 196.

[75] Ibid.

[76] Vagaggini cites this same description in his inaugural address to the Pontifical Liturgical Institute in 1961 when he states, "The same constitutionality of the divine Persons should not make us forget the association between them, or the fact that every good thing comes from the Father, through the mediation of his Son Jesus Christ, in the presence in us of the Holy Spirit and thus, in the same presence, through the mediation of Jesus Christ, all returns to the Father." See Vagaggini, *Liturgia e pensiero teologico recente*, 46.

[77] He uses this characterization only in the opening paragraph of his chapter on the trinitarian dimension of the liturgy, arguing that "it is the christological-trinitarian dialectic of sacred history and of salvation, of the economy of God in the world. Every structure of the liturgy presupposes this dialectic, without which it is incomprehensible." See *Il senso teologico* (1957), 157.

activity (*movimento*).[78] This depiction appears more amenable to his discussion of the cycle of relations seen in the emanation from and return to God in the economy of salvation.[79] By designating the cycle as a movement rather than a dialectic Vagaggini can also much more easily describe the action of the Trinity itself. This movement or activity is viewed as the communication of God to the created world. Moreover, it is this christological-trinitarian movement, in Vagaggini's vision, that "effectively saturates the entire liturgy"[80] and forms the basis for the communication of grace.

In order to explicate his understanding of this christological-trinitarian perspective within the liturgy, Vagaggini necessarily retraces the varied ways in which both theologians and the faithful might reflect upon the revelation of the Trinity. The mystery of the Trinity, he argues, lies in trying to reconcile the two terms of the dogma surrounding it: that there is both a unity of nature and three distinct persons. Because those two terms are in seeming tension one can approach the mystery of the Trinity by two equally valid paths, with either the unity of nature or the three distinct persons as the starting point.[81] In the West it became customary after the time of Augustine to use the unity of the divine nature as the point of departure for theological reflection on the Trinity and then move, in a second mental act, to the reality of the three distinct persons. Vagaggini asserts that "the psychological danger that threatens anyone who considers the mystery of the Trinity in this way is that he may not take seriously enough the real distinctions of the three persons in God from a vital point of view, and, when considering God, may take refuge in a psychology of the philosopher, or one common

[78] *Il senso teologico* (1965), 196. In this fourth edition Vagaggini keeps the same sentences in the text but substitutes the word "*movimento*" for "*dialettica*."

[79] One possible explanation for this appears in Vagaggini's article on the "history of salvation," in which he cites the Second Vatican Council's preoccupation with and need to respond to the supposedly Christianized version of Marxism in theologies of liberation and human development. See especially Cipriano Vagaggini, "Storia della salvezza," in *Nuovo dizionario di teologia*, ed. Giuseppe Barbaglio and Severino Dianich (Rome: Edizioni Paoline, 1977), 1559–83, at 1573–74.

[80] *Il senso teologico* (1965), 196.

[81] Ibid., 197. Vagaggini notes that while both ways of viewing are equally valid, each presents diverse ways in which the mystery of the Trinity is approached and appropriated.

to the Jew, so much so that Father, Son, and Holy Spirit, especially the Father and Holy Spirit, may not be a sufficiently living reality in his religious psychology."[82] He does not deny the validity of such an approach, but simply points out its shortcomings and potential problems. He adds a rather interesting footnote in regard to his earlier declaration:

> For as regards the Son, he will always be able to maintain a living reality in religious psychology considering he is the incarnate Son, the Christ. But the awareness of the Father and the Holy Spirit, as distinct persons, will be at times very tenuous. Practically speaking, in the religious psychology of the faithful, God will dominate—the God of the philosophers, or, at best, the God of the Old Testament—and Christ. In theology there will be a tract *On the One God*, often, indeed, whatever anyone might say, strongly resembling a philosophical theodicy illustrated with texts from the Scriptures and the Fathers—and a Christology, while the importance of the tract on the Trinity will necessarily be very clouded over.[83]

Despite the number of treatises on the Trinity stemming from this mode of approach, the problem still remains how to move from "one" to "three," and the reality of the Trinity, that of three distinct persons, remains shrouded.

Vagaggini notes, however, the advantages and disadvantages of following the inverse process—of beginning with the Trinity and moving to the unity of the one God. The distinction of the three persons of the Trinity is moved to a foundational level of understanding in this approach and the conception of God is one that is uniquely Christian—of Father, Son, and Holy Spirit as revealed in the incarnation. The danger, though, lies in maintaining their equality with regard to the divine nature. Vagaggini asserts that a problem arises from such a firm insistence on the real distinction of the three persons, one of "leaving the unity of nature too much in the shadow of one's consciousness and of effectively forgetting their absolute equality in respect to eternity,

---

[82] Ibid., 198.

[83] Ibid. See also Vagaggini, "La hantise des *rationes necessariae* de St. Anselme dans la théologie des processions de S. Thomas," *Spicilegium Beccense* 1 (1959): 103–39. In this article he goes into great detail about the influence of Anselm on Aquinas and the "personalist" view Aquinas takes of the intratrinitarian life.

power, knowledge, wisdom, etc."[84] Thus one has to be careful not to fall into some sort of subordinationism with respect to the three persons of the Trinity, or a form of Arianism in which Christ is so distinct from the Father that he loses his divinity. For this reason Vagaggini admonishes believers and theologians to constant vigilance in reaffirming the opposite term from which one starts so as not to appear to leave it behind. Such a stance is necessary because the "Trinity is a mystery having two antithetical terms, through which, whatever point of view one chooses in his consideration of the Trinity, one always and necessarily arrives at the mystery."[85]

Despite the obvious limitations of either approach, Vagaggini is not without a preference for one over the other. He argues that the "Trinitarian awareness is more vivid psychologically" in those who choose to begin with the three distinct persons.[86] But more convincing for him is the evidence that "in Scripture, in the Greek Fathers and in the Latin Fathers before Augustine, in the liturgy, in the Roman liturgy especially, the second mode of considering the Trinity prevails by far."[87] For Vagaggini this second mode offers a much greater possibility for theological reflection. It was in this mode that the communication of God's self as Trinity was first made known to believers. The first mode, on the other hand, developed out of an apologetic need to defend the unity of the divine nature.[88] Vagaggini warns the Pontifical Liturgical Institute to be consistent in seeking this complementary approach to the Christocentrism of the West, lest the Trinity become "with due cause, nothing else but a formidable enigma without any real weight in our life or in our preaching."[89]

Vagaggini also notes that there is another axis around which trinitarian reflection revolves, namely, whether one wishes to speak about the

[84] *Il senso teologico* (1965), 199.

[85] Ibid., 200.

[86] Ibid.

[87] Ibid.

[88] Ibid. In the concluding paragraphs of this section Vagaggini refers to the second mode of approaching the Trinity as "più primigenio e irenico," that is, "more original and peaceful." While *original* advantage makes sense, *peaceful* status requires more thought. Perhaps Vagaggini is pointing to a facility of using the second mode over the first that requires less rupture with established trinitarian language in liturgy and early sources.

[89] Vagaggini, *Liturgia e pensiero teologico recente*, 47.

inner life of the Trinity in its ontological structure or about the relationship of the Trinity to the world, that is, how God acts in the world. Vagaggini asserts that the texts of Scripture are primarily concerned with the latter. He argues:

> on the subject of the Trinity, Scripture not only considers the distinct Persons, Father, Son, and Holy Spirit, always *in recto*, but more than that, it considers these same Persons not with the primary concern of coming to know what they are ontologically in themselves, and not even with another concern for their intratrinitarian life, but much more with a concern for coming to see what is signified practically for us, [and thus] what their real importance is and their specific role in the history of the relations of God with the world and even of our personal relations with God.[90]

Thus the primary thrust of the scriptural evidence regarding the Trinity is *ad extra*, and this external concern becomes the basis for Vagaggini's understanding of the trinitarian cycle found not only in the Scriptures but in the fathers and in the liturgy as well. Such a stance has severe limitations we will address in the fifth chapter.

Vagaggini asserts that, within the New Testament, whenever the scope of salvation history is discussed in relation to the divine persons a certain formulaic schema is used. This schema is the source of his trinitarian cycle of relations mentioned earlier, and that he repeats again in this section: "Every good thing comes from the Father, through the medium of his incarnate Son, Jesus Christ, in the presence of the Holy Spirit (in us), and thus it is in the presence of the Holy Spirit, through the medium of the incarnate Son, Jesus Christ, that everything returns to the Father."[91] The textual schema, which he gives in Latin, is simply *a Patre, per Filium eius, Iesum Christum, in Spiritu Sancto, ad Patrem* (from the Father, through his Son, Jesus Christ, in the Holy Spirit, to the Father). Vagaggini explains the significance of this formulaic depiction of the Trinity in reference to the action of God in creation, asserting that in this formula a relationship unfolds:

> There the mystery of the Trinity is presented above all from the real distinction of persons, and these same persons are considered first of all in their relationships with the world, in the movement descending

---

[90] *Il senso teologico* (1965), 201.
[91] Ibid., 202–3.

from God to the world, through which every being and every good thing derives from God, and in the ascending movement of the return of the creature to God. In this grand perspective of salvation history of the *exitus a Deo* and the *reditus ad Deum*, the Father appears primarily as the one *a quo* and *ad quem*, the Son as the one *per quem*, and the Holy Spirit as the one *in quo*.[92]

But Vagaggini is also careful to note that the presence of the formula *a . . . per . . . in . . . ad* in the New Testament is not literally re-presented every time salvation history is discussed by Paul or John. In fact, he readily cites numbers of examples in which one or more of the components of the formula is/are missing. Despite the missing formulaic elements, Vagaggini avers, the christological-trinitarian perspective remains, at times incidental and without explanation, not because of its insignificance but because of its common acceptance—a point especially seen in the early kerygmatic statements of believers in the Acts of the Apostles:[93] "The God of our ancestors raised Jesus, though you had him killed by hanging him on a tree. God exalted him at his right hand as leader and savior to grant Israel repentance and forgiveness of sins. We are witnesses of these things, as is the Holy Spirit that God has given to those who obey him" (Acts 5:30-32).[94]

Vagaggini asserts that the *a . . . per . . . in . . . ad* formula in the New Testament provides a framework for understanding not only the Trinity but also the impact of the trinitarian God on the lives of the faithful. In speaking of the religious life of believers he argues that "it is this grand christological-trinitarian perspective *a Patre, per Filium eius, Iesum Christum, in Spiritu Sancto, ad Patrem* that animates their faith, hope, and charity. . . . [T]his view is indeed the inexhaustible source of their adoration, admiration and gratitude to God."[95] Within the Pauline letters (especially the first three chapters of the letter to the Ephesians) Vagaggini notes a fundamental framework for Christian prayer based on this perspective.[96] In the early Christian communities of the New Testament the prayer of thanksgiving offered by believers is "to the Father through his Son, Jesus Christ, with the consciousness

---

[92] Ibid., 203.

[93] Ibid., 204. His list of places where the omission occurs includes, but is not limited to, Col 3:16-17; 1 Tim 2:5; 1 Cor 8:4-6; and Rom 1:8-10.

[94] Other examples in Acts include 2:32-33 and 15:7-11.

[95] *Il senso teologico* (1965), 205.

[96] Eph 1:3-14; 2:11-21; 3:1-21.

that it is not possible to do this without the active presence in us of the Holy Spirit."[97] Moreover, Vagaggini sees within the Pauline corpus repeated use of this formula to provide motivation and meaning to the Christian way of life: determining moral conduct in the attempt to do the good, defining the obligation of living in accord with the Gospel of Christ, showing kindness and mercy. Thus, while the christological-trinitarian perspective still embraces the mystery of the Trinity itself, it in no way prevents the early Christian, at least from the evidence of the New Testament, from forming a consciousness of the relations within this perspective in order to shed light on the demands of Christian life.[98]

As further evidence of the dominance of the *a . . . per . . . in . . . ad* perspective in the early church Vagaggini points to the frequent recurrence of this motif in the writings of the Latin and Greek fathers. Citing Clement of Rome, Ignatius of Antioch, Polycarp, and Irenaeus, Vagaggini shows how the "christological-trinitarian consciousness in the scriptural view of the formula *a, per, in, ad* operated efficaciously in the religious psychology of the first Christian generations."[99] Vagaggini notes that the fathers' use of the formula is not simply idle repetition of a scriptural example but rather a way of perceiving the world and their role within it. Their object was to return to the Father, whether through martyrdom or by graced holiness. In the later fourth and fifth centuries the formula became more and more necessary for

---

[97] *Il senso teologico* (1965), 205.

[98] Ibid., 205–6. In these pages Vagaggini makes several references to the Scriptures in which the christological-trinitarian perspective is at work. See especially n. 13 in Vagaggini's text and the multiple references cited within the body of the text.

[99] Ibid., 206–9. Vagaggini's references to the Fathers here are illustrative and poignant. In speaking of Ignatius of Antioch's letter to the Ephesians he depicts the trinitarian cycle in terms of a deliberate construction: "You are the stones of the temple of the Father, prepared in order to be constructed as an edifice by God the Father (*ad Patrem*), hoisted to the heights by the means of the machine (crane) of Jesus Christ, which is the Cross (*per Christum*), with the rope of the Holy Spirit (*in Spiritu*). Your faith then is the lever that raises you, and love is the road that leads you to God (*ad Patrem*)." Similarly, Irenaeus of Lyons formulates his law of universal return according to the scriptural motif Vagaggini has described: "This is the order and the plan for those who are saved . . . they advance by these steps: through the Holy Spirit they arrive at the Son and through the Son they rise to the Father (pp. 207–8)."

use against the Arians. The scriptural perspective on the Trinity that had become part of the psychology of the early Christian genera-tions could now be used apologetically to defend the divinity of the Holy Spirit who, within us, accomplishes the deification of ourselves: "our participation in the divine nature could not be accomplished by any created being."[100] The insistence on the divinity of the Holy Spirit by Athanasius, Gregory of Nyssa, and others safeguards both the scriptural formula of the trinitarian cycle and the early Christian understanding of the relationship between the created world and the persons of the Trinity: it is through the Triune God, through partici-pation in the divine, that the creature is redeemed and sanctified.[101] Vagaggini notes that when, in these early stages of the church, the ancient tradition expresses the extratrinitarian relations of the Trinity through the *a . . . per . . . in . . . ad* formula, this represents a simple statement of belief from the scriptural evidence. Only later will that same formula be used to translate a perception of the intratrinitarian life.

After looking at this perspective within both Scripture and the works of the Greek and Latin fathers, Vagaggini examines how the christological-trinitarian cycle is operative in the liturgy itself. He be-gins by noting simply that the God made manifest within the liturgical celebration is a "specifically Christian God, the God-Trinity."[102] The liturgical texts and the movement of the liturgical action repeatedly refer to three persons (Father, Son, and Spirit), and the interpretation of texts is always from a point of reference to the triune God, even when those texts are from the Old Testament "before," if you will, the revelation of the incarnation of the Godhead in Christ. The liturgy, "like the most ancient patristic tradition, simply adopts the viewpoint that consists in placing the real distinction of persons on the first level of the attention and the consciousness, and in affirming their unity of nature only in a second psychological moment."[103] This extratrinitarian direction of the liturgy was mitigated in light of the Arian controversy,

---

[100] Ibid., 208.

[101] Vagaggini makes explicit reference to Athanasius's "Four Letters to Sera-pion." The English translation of the fourth edition is somewhat problematic here in that the translator/editor has included within the main text parts of Athanasius's letters that Vagaggini never cites.

[102] *Il senso teologico* (1965), 209.

[103] Ibid.

when Vagaggini sees a subtle shift in liturgical texts, especially doxologies, in which the equality of the divine persons is upheld.

In order to demarcate his assessment of the trinitarian emphasis of the liturgy, Vagaggini delves into three distinct textual elements of the early Christian liturgy: the orations, the doxologies, and the anaphoras. A brief look at his analysis of each of these elements can prove helpful.

In the orations of the early church the schema *a . . . per . . . in . . . ad* dominates through most of the textual structure of the prayers. Vagaggini asserts that the "general rule quite well noted in the ancient tradition is that the liturgical orations are directed to the Father through the mediation of Jesus Christ, who is our supreme mediator."[104] At this juncture it should be noted that the rule alluded to above, which stemmed from the Council of Hippo, referred originally to the Preface prayers of the early church. Following the lead of Jungmann, Vagaggini now applies this rule to a specific group of orations (collect, secret, postcommunion).[105] Typically the initial address of the prayer (Father, God, Lord God, etc.) is modified by either attributes of the one being addressed or recognition of the work or action the addressee has done on behalf of the people of God (Almighty, Eternal, who sent us Your Son). This attribution, Vagaggini notes, underscores the fact that "the *Deus* to whom, without additional trinitarian indications, so many of the Roman liturgical orations are addressed, whether ancient—as nearly all of those in the Leonine Sacramentary, along with many of the Gelasian—or modern, with the simple conclusion *per Christum Dominum nostrum*, is in fact the Father, the First Person of the Trinity."[106] Similarly, the body of the collect will often express some form of thanksgiving, adoration, or petition, and in so doing will make reference to the Son and Spirit. Vagaggini writes: "thanksgiving is made to the Father for the good things which he has done for us, most frequently with the explicit mention of the fact that he has done them through the mediation of Jesus Christ, or by sending us the Spirit . . . in all this, the christological-trin-

---

[104] Ibid., 212. Vagaggini argues that the rule to direct the collect to the Father was so normative that it became a practical decree of the Council of Hippo in 393 CE.

[105] Here Vagaggini clearly follows Jungmann's lead. See specifically Joseph Jungmann, *The Place of Christ in Liturgical Prayer*, trans. A. J. Peeler, 2d rev. ed. (Staten Island, NY: Alba House, 1965), 114.

[106] *Il senso teologico* (1965), 214.

itarian perspective always predominates, with its consideration of the Persons *ad extra* in the schema *a, per, in, ad.*"[107] The ending of the collects, while maintaining the christological-trinitarian dynamic, is somewhat more problematic. Vagaggini asserts that in the East the ending of the collect is almost always doxological, emphasizing the trinitarian formula; in the West, however, this is not universal and quite frequently the prayer ends simply with *per Christum Dominum nostrum.*[108] Vagaggini's assertion here is somewhat problematic. Jungmann notes that the address to Christ as mediator (*per Christum Dominum nostrum*) stems from the earlier rule dictated by the Council of Hippo. He tersely notes: "This rule is not once broken in the *Leonanium*. Hundreds of *orationes* show the same end-note *per*. The formula itself is nowhere written out in full."[109] If, indeed, the prayers end simply with the abbreviated *per* there is no way to determine when that *per* represents the simple formula *per Christum Dominum nostrum* and when it represents a longer formula inclusive of the Holy Spirit's power.[110]

The mediation of Christ, however, prevails in both traditions, and Vagaggini acknowledges that because of this reality a certain dynamism becomes inherent in the collects. He asserts that

> one sees, however, that up until the present the orations that have this conclusion, even without the mention of the Holy Spirit, are always in the christological-trinitarian line on account of it (*per Christum Dominum nostrum*). . . . They are all based on the consideration of the Father as the origin *a quo* and the end *ad quem* of the *ad extra* economy, and of the incarnate Son, now glorious beside the Father as the *per quem* of the same economy.[111]

[107] Ibid., 215.

[108] Ibid.

[109] Jungmann, *The Place of Christ in Liturgical Prayer*, 114.

[110] Paul Bradshaw, "God, Christ, and the Holy Spirit in Early Christian Praying," in *The Place of Christ in Liturgical Prayer: Trinity, Christology, and Liturgical Theology*, ed. Brian D. Spinks, 51–64 (Collegeville, MN: Liturgical Press, 2008), at 55–56. According to Bradshaw, "So far as we can tell, there were no standardized prayer conclusions among the conventions of the first few centuries, and it was only in the Christological and pneumatological debates of the fourth century that the choice of prepositions assumed major doctrinal significance."

[111] *Il senso teologico* (1965), 216.

It is only later in the development of the prayers, often in reaction to Arian controversies, that the Holy Spirit is added as an amplification of the ancient way of concluding the prayer *per Christum Dominum nostrum*. This addition, Vagaggini notes, causes only a slight shift in the attention and focus of the prayer on the intratrinitarian dynamic.[112]

After finishing this analysis of the ancient orations Vagaggini turns his attention to the doxologies of the early liturgy. These, while abundant in the tradition of the Greek liturgy (practically every liturgical prayer concluded, and concludes, with a doxology), appeared less frequently in the Roman tradition. Vagaggini argues that in the East the formula *a . . . per . . . in . . . ad* was firmly established even before the Arian controversy, but because of that polemic the formula was muted by the early fourth century.[113] In the West, however, no such tradition of concluding every liturgical prayer with a doxology existed. Instead, it "retained those doxologies universally used for ending the canon of the Mass, and it has adopted a certain number of doxologies created separately from the Greek tradition—especially the *Gloria Patri*, the *Gloria in excelsis*, the *Te decet laus*—to which one can also add the *Te Deum*, of Western origin, and it ended its hymns with its own doxologies."[114] These doxologies in the West were often modified to present more specifically anti-Arian qualities. However, Vagaggini notes that the text of the *Per ipsum*, the final doxology of the Roman Canon, maintains the character and flavor of the ancient tradition and perspective of the christological-trinitarian scheme: "the Father is considered the source of all good things . . . Christ, our Lord, is considered the great Mediator through whom the Father accomplishes everything . . . it is Christ through whom, together with whom, and in union with whom, as our Head . . . we return all glory

---

[112] Ibid., 216–18. Vagaggini maintains that the dominant character of the prayers remains rooted in the christological-trinitarian perspective of salvation history. He does, however, note the many exceptions that occur the further a collect is removed from the ancient tradition. The first known deviation from the rule of address to the Father comes in the late fourth and early fifth centuries in the *Apostolic Consitutions*.

[113] Ibid., 221–23. Vaggaggini makes special note of the work of Basil, *On the Holy Spirit*, which frequently references the trinitarian formulas of the doxologies in the East.

[114] *Il senso teologico* (1965), 219.

to the Father."[115] While the phrase "in the unity of the Holy Spirit" is typically understood as an anti-Arian development, Vagaggini appeals to the work of Josef Jungmann in *The Place of Christ in Liturgical Prayer* to assert that this unity is more a reference to an activity of the third person of the Trinity (the coming forth or presence of the Spirit as a result of unity) than a belief statement about the oneness of God.[116] In this sense the fullness of the christological-trinitarian schema can be seen in one of the most ancient of doxologies.

In the investigation of the ancient and more recent anaphoras, Vagaggini similarly concludes that the structure of the prayer maintains the trinitarian *ad extra* scheme. He characterizes the textual witness of the anaphoras succinctly:

> The Father appears there as the *principium a quo* and the *terminus ad quem* of the eucharistic action. The incarnate Son, Christ, appears there as the High Priest, through whom, by means of which, we perform the same action. The Holy Spirit appears there as the *in quo*, that is to say, in whose presence this same action is completed *hic et nunc*. Essentially it is always the vision of salvation history in relationship to the divine persons.[117]

---

[115] Ibid., 223. The editor of the English edition has made changes to Vagaggini's text here, and in subsequent pages, in order to account for the changes in the canon of the Mass after Vagaggini finished writing. However, analyzing the fittingness of the Roman Canon in comparison to the more contemporary anaphoras completely misses the simple fact that Vagaggini helped formulate the newer anaphoras. Those revised anapahoras would, of course, fit more succinctly and tidily into his model of the eucharistic prayer. For instance, see the parenthetical comments of the English editor in Cipriano Vagaggini, *Theological Dimensions of the Liturgy: A General Treatise on the Theology of the Liturgy*, trans. Leonard J. Doyle and W. A. Jurgens (Collegeville, MN: Liturgical Press, 1976), 222, where he compares the Roman Canon with the newer Eucharistic Prayers III and IV. No such references or comparisons occur in the fourth Italian edition. For Vagaggini's assessment of the problems and defects of the Roman Canon, see also Cipriano Vagaggini, *Il canone delle messa e la riforma liturgica: probleme e progetti* (Turin: Leuman, 1966), 63–98.

[116] *Il senso teologico* (1965), 223. See also Joseph Jungmann, *Die Stellung Christi im liturgischen Gebet*, Liturgiewissenschaftliche Quellen und Forschungen 19/20 (Münster: Aschendorf, 1962), xvii.

[117] *Il senso teologico* (1965), 224. Vagaggini argues in the footnote here that the completion of the sacrifice by the presence of the Spirit has a biblical origin (Rom 15:15-19 and Heb 9:14).

Within the analysis he presents, Vagaggini investigates the canon of Hippolytus (early third century) and the Roman Canon (as it existed in the mid-twentieth century) with brief references to several other anaphoras, notably the anaphora of Serapion (fourth century), the Aposotolic Constitutions (end of the fourth century), and the anaphora of St. Basil (end of the fourth century).[118] The essential structure he outlines is one rooted in anamnesis and epiclesis. In the memorial of the eucharistic prayer the saving works of Christ are remembered to the Father, and indeed it is Christ, as mediator, who makes that prayer of thanksgiving to the Father. The invocation of the Holy Spirit comes not only to ensure the oblation of the church but also to transform the believers and unite them more intimately to the Christ as Head of the Body. For Vagaggini this motif of anamnesis and epiclesis, of remembrance and invocation, helps undergird the christological-trinitarian perspective not only in the prayers of the sacrifice of the Mass but also in the liturgy of the other sacraments.[119] For him the overarching predominance of the christological-trinitarian perspective in the liturgy forms the basis for understanding why we enter into the sacraments in the first place, why we participate in the liturgy. Citing Cyril of Alexandria, Vagaggini concludes his section on the christological-trinitarian perspective with these words:

> To sanctify has (in Scripture) the customary meaning of consecrating and of offering; and thus we say that the Son sanctifies Himself for us (cf. John 17:19). Indeed, that sacrifice and that holy victim is offered to God and Father, reconciling the world to Him and recalling to His friendship those who had lost it, that is, the human race. "He, indeed, is our peace," as we find written. Our return to God, which is made through Christ the Savior, takes place only through the participation and sanctification of the Holy Spirit. The one who joins us and, so to speak, unites us to God is the Spirit. In receiving the Spirit we become participants and sharers in the divine nature; we receive Him through the Son, and in the Son, we receive the Father. . . . The liturgy, if we know how to understand it and live it, better than any other means can make us penetrate these marvelous realities and keep us attuned to them.[120]

[118] Ibid., 224–28.

[119] Ibid., 229–36.

[120] Ibid., 241–42. See also *Commentarium in Joannis Evangelium* 11, 10 (PG 74, 544–45) for Cyril's orginal text.

Liturgical participation and sanctification, that is, participation in grace and in the life of the Trinity, are intimately linked. Moreover, that link is provided in the very unfolding of the history of salvation. The *a . . . per . . . in . . . ad* schema Vagaggini sees in Scripture, the fathers, and the liturgy necessarily forms the key schema for understanding participation in the divine life as well. Vagaggini laments a basic lack of awareness on the part of the faithful, who fail to see this christological-trinitarian perspective in their liturgical celebration when, in fact, for him it is the very action of the liturgy that allows us to participate in that dynamic. He now moves from analyzing the christological-trinitarian perspective within the liturgy and sacraments to explaining the necessity of "tuning in" to it: understanding and living it.

Understanding the Paschal Mystery and the Role of the Kyrios

In order to achieve this *"sintonia d'animo"* toward the christological-trinitarian perspective within the liturgy Vagaggini highlights the intimate connection between the paschal mystery[121] and the resurrected Christ, the *Kyrios*, and the need to take the *Kyrios* as the starting point for understanding and living in the image of the triune God.[122] Vagaggini posits that, from the evidence of the Scriptures and the fathers, it was precisely the resurrection of Christ that was most significant in the early church: "a single Christ: Jesus, who yes, was born, lived, suffered, and died in Palestine, but is now for all time resurrected and glorified at the right hand of the Father, in full exercise, even as man, of the limitless lordship of creation: the *Kyrios*."[123] The later writings of

---

[121] Vagaggini employs a definition of the term "paschal mystery" that is simultaneously complex and yet convincingly simple—namely, that the paschal mystery is the entire economy of salvation, passing from death to life, that is only completely fulfilled in the heavenly Jerusalem. It implies not only the passage of the Son, who directs the way for others, but also that of the church as a whole, that of individuals, and indeed that of the entire world. See Vagaggini, "Riflessioni sul senso teologico del mistero pasquale," *Rivista di Pastorale Liturgica* 2 (1964): 102–12, at 103–4.

[122] Vagaggini, *Il senso teologico* (1965), 245. Interestingly, Vagaggini's description of the importance of the *Kyrios* does not appear in the first editions of *Il senso teologico*. While he does speak of the heavenly priesthood of Christ in the earlier editions, the notion of the *Kyrios* he presents in the fourth edition originates in the inaugural lecture he gave at the *Orientale* in 1961. See also Vagaggini, *Liturgia e pensiero teologico recente*, 52–53.

[123] *Liturgia e pensiero teologico recente*, 52.

the New Testament consistently refer to the Christ who once was dead but now has been resurrected; because of that resurrection people are called to belief. Vagaggini asserts that this *Kyrios*, the resurrected one, forms the key to understanding the paschal mystery and its significance in the liturgical action, since every earthly action of Jesus points to his eternal existence as the *Kyrios*: "it is to this state of the Lord in glory that all the episodes and sentiments of this earthly life reach out with all their might, and from it alone do they take their full significance."[124]

In this sense the paschal mystery and the risen Christ, the *Kyrios*, are connected by a common purpose. The primary intention behind the paschal mystery is to communicate the divine life of the Trinity as the means of redemption for humanity. This communication of the divine life is the proper action of the *Kyrios*: "he communicates to us the divine life with which [the *Kyrios*] is not only full but even resplendent, the sole dispenser of divine life, in order to allow us, primarily in the liturgy—and not only us but in some way the whole world—to pass more and more from spiritual and physical death to total life in God."[125] Thus at the heart of the paschal mystery is the activity of the *Kyrios*, *hic et nunc*, in the world. In this sense Vagaggini highlights the corporeality inherent in the unfolding of the paschal mystery and its fulfillment in the action of Christ. The human body and nature of Christ have a central role within the paschal mystery and the history of salvation. Vagaggini maintains that without a body there is no death and resurrection, and that the death and resurrection of Christ are vital to the transmission of divine life through the sacramental celebration.[126]

The communication of the divine life occurs when Christ, in his resurrected and glorified state at the right hand of the Father, enters into his role as High Priest and Mediator. Christ's presence and action are overarching in the liturgical celebration; thus there is "but one liturgist, Christ, and but one liturgy, that of Christ."[127] Pointing to the scriptural evidence from the letter to the Hebrews, Vagaggini surmises that the priesthood of Christ forms the nexus for understanding the

---

[124] *Il senso teologico* (1965), 245. See also "Riflessioni sul senso teologico del mistero pasquale," 112.

[125] *Il senso teologico* (1965), 246.

[126] "Riflessioni sul senso teologico del mistero pasquale," 110–11.

[127] *Il senso teologico* (1965), 249.

connection between salvation history and Christian life. The author of Hebrews presents a heavenly liturgy that, as it unfolds, centers all sanctification and worship in the *Kyrios*, acting as High Priest and Mediator before the Father. This is the heart of the christological-trinitarian perspective of the liturgy—namely, that Christ initiates a pilgrimage of the faithful to return to the Father that is rooted in his own life, death, and resurrection. The phrase *per Christum Dominum nostrum* demonstrates the mediation of the *Kyrios* in the heavenly liturgy.

But how does one make the connection between the heavenly liturgy depicted in the letter to the Hebrews and the earthly liturgy that is the mode of liturgical participation for the faithful? Certainly the priesthood of Christ, the *Kyrios*, allows the faithful to draw near to the heavenly sanctuary. Vagaggini explains:

> This has been made possible and remains possible for them, thanks to the High Priest, the Mediator of the new covenant, Jesus. He it is who, having sprinkled them with his blood, and by thus purifying them of their sins, has introduced them, in a real way even now, into the sanctuary of the holy Zion. He has truly united them even now to the liturgical assembly of the angels and of the just, in which he is the eternal High Priest at the right hand of the Father, the liturgist of the sanctuary and of the true tabernacle, living always to intercede on behalf of those who are his own.[128]

That intercession takes place in the earthly liturgy, where Christ uses the instrumentality of the church to allow the faithful to participate in the divine life. In the earthly liturgy there is still only one liturgist, Christ, and one liturgy, the one he offers. This is the only way that the earthly liturgy could be truly efficacious for human sanctification—only a divine action could communicate grace.[129] The *ex opere operato* efficacy of the sacraments derives from the action of Christ within the sacramental event and the Thomistic notion that every act of "sanctification that God works in human beings is now made through the humanity of Christ as the physical instrument of his divinity."[130] The earthly liturgy is then seen as the instrument the *Kyrios* uses; the

---

[128] Ibid., 253.

[129] Ibid., 255.

[130] Ibid., 258. See also David Bourke, ed., *Summa theologiae*, vol. 56: *The Sacraments* (New York: Cambridge University Press, 1975), IIIa, q. 48, a. 6; IIIa, q. 56, a. 1, ad. 3; IIIa, q. 78, a. 5.

earthly and heavenly liturgies are the same act of Christ. Vagaggini writes that the earthly liturgy is "the manifestation on earth of the heavenly liturgy, enclosed in an earthly wrapping."[131]

Vagaggini asserts that even when the church acts in the sacraments it is, indeed, Christ acting through his Mystical Body: the one action in the heavenly liturgy is imaged in the earthly one. This Christ-centered liturgy is enacted through the Holy Spirit; in this, the action of Christ and that of the Spirit are not seen as competing or diverse realities. Following the biblical tradition, Vagaggini notes that everything Christ does in the world is done through (or in) the power of the Holy Spirit, the same Spirit he himself sends to the church to allow it to participate in his action as the High Priest and Mediator.[132]

The appropriation of the christological-trinitarian perspective in the liturgy, then, is rooted in the appropriation of the paschal mystery through the intercession of and union with the *Kyrios*. Vagaggini ends his discussion of the *Kyrios* by returning to the phrase in the trinitarian motif that prompted his discussion: *per Christum Dominum nostrum*. He speaks of "the reality of the dead and risen *Kyrios*, one priest, one mediator, one liturgist who continually carries out the one liturgy, the paschal liturgy, existing in the world to tear the world away from death and to communicate to it the divine life with which he is filled: *per ipsum cum ipso et in ipso*."[133] Vagaggini sees that, through Christ, the events of the paschal mystery can be celebrated in us by our participation in the liturgical-sacramental event. He then turns his attention to exploring the relationship between liturgical participation of the faithful and participation in the divine life of the Trinity.

Liturgical Participation and Participation in the Divine Life

Vagaggini's approach to liturgical participation revolves around dual axes: on the one hand participation stems from the communitarian nature of the liturgical action, and on the other such

---

[131] *Il senso teologico* (1965), 255.

[132] Ibid., 257. Vagaggini differs with Dom Gregory Dix, whom he cites as critical of an action of the Holy Spirit as somehow taking away from the central act of Christ in the liturgy. Dix asserts that to argue for the role of the Holy Spirit in the Eucharist and still maintain that it is Christ "who Himself offers, Himself prays, Himself consecrates" is a "happy illogicality." See also Gregory Dix, *The Shape of the Liturgy* (Westminster [London]: Dacre, 1945), 292.

[133] *Il senso teologico* (1965), 264.

participation must also appropriate and be rooted in the christological-trinitarian perspective that saturates the liturgy. In order to fully explain Vagaggini's assessment of liturgical participation we will look not only at these two axes but also at the background against which he presents his argument on participation: the "liturgical pastoral."[134]

The "liturgical pastoral" arena in which Vagaggini begins to delve most deeply into the concept of liturgical participation establishes certain parameters that help to demonstrate both the communitarian nature of the liturgy and the need to enter into the trinitarian action within it. First of all, the proper object of the art of the pastoral is the people of God.[135] Vagaggini clarifies this simple declarative statement by making a qualification with regard to both the individual and the community. While affirming that salvation most certainly contains a rather intimate individual character, he reiterates his earlier discussion of the social character of liturgical signs and the law of salvation in community. Regarding the social value of liturgical signs he maintains that "anyone who has discovered the value of the communitarian aspect of religion and Christian piety not only does not fear liturgical symbolism but indeed is at ease with it, because he connaturally intuits the social value of the liturgical sign."[136] While Vagaggini is speaking here of the communitarian nature of the recognition of signs and their meaning, he also points to the importance of the intimate connection between the body of believers as the Body of Christ and their Head, Christ the High Priest. In explaining the Catholic perspective on the sacraments and the law of salvation in community he makes a series of profound statements that bear repeating here:

---

[134] To the English speaker or listener "liturgical pastoral" seems to be an adjectival phrase in need of a noun subject. While this phrase is awkward in translation, it points to a nuanced distinction that Vagaggini argues came about through the decades-long work of the liturgical movement. In his use of the term he defines "pastoral" as the "art of leading and conducting the people to Christ" (*l'arte di condurre e conservare il popolo a Cristo* [*Il senso teologico* (1965), 754]), something that is not a momentary exercise but one that is realized and maintained (hence his use of the word *conservare*). Here too, his use of the curious word *inveramento* that we noted earlier now becomes clear. The pastoral is the art of practical realization (*inveramento*) of unity with Christ and the Trinity.

[135] *Il senso teologico* (1965), 757.

[136] Ibid., 80. See also Jean C.-M. Travers, *Valeur sociale de la liturgie d'aprés S. Thomas d'Aquin* (Paris: Cerf, 1946), 313–17.

When it is said that God sanctifies a man, what is meant is that He actually works a real and physical transformation in his being, allowing him in fact to participate in the mode of being and of acting proper to the Divinity. This transformation, however, does not take place without the sacraments, *in re*, or *in voto*. . . . All the sacraments are ordered toward the sacrifice. The sacrifice itself does not take place without a sacramental, hierarchical priesthood. This priesthood, then, is a real and physical participation in the priesthood of Christ, which really and physically empowers the hierarchical priest to be his instrument through which He actualizes his sacrifice for us in a real but unbloody manner, and thereby really and physically sanctifies human beings. The hierarchical priesthood is a cause that formally constitutes a group of individuals into a community, that is, the church.[137]

Thus what is presented here in his opening discussion of the meaning of *pastoral* and its application is a recapitulation of the law of salvation in community: "the individual reality of salvation not only moves toward an understanding that cannot exist outside the community, much less run counter to the community, but rather within the structure of the community and through the community."[138] Thus the pastoral approach recognizes the fullness of its scope above and beyond the individual. This becomes all the more clear when one considers the pastoral's proper end.

As noted earlier, Vagaggini defines the pastoral as the "art of leading and conducting the people to Christ." This union with Christ is not separated from the trinitarian reality of Christ united with Father and Holy Spirit. Thus the pastoral's final end is, indeed, linked to the participation of the faithful in the divine life of the Trinity through union with Christ. Vagaggini describes this action in terms of the encounter with Christ and the effect of grace:

the encounter happens when the people receive the sanctification of God in Christ and respond as they must to this action of God in Christ. Since, however, this sanctification and this response are able to have varying degrees, pastoral tries to achieve the most perfect degree possible. Thus it seeks not only to pull the people away from mortal sin so that they will live in the state of grace, but also to lead them to the fullest possible development of this grace.[139]

---

[137] *Il senso teologico* (1965), 268.
[138] Ibid., 756–57.
[139] Ibid., 754.

As we have made clear, it is this grace, received through the liturgical action, that allows the believer to participate in the divine life of the Trinity.[140]

Vagaggini takes his cue from *Sacrosanctum Concilium* to discuss the significance of liturgical participation in the lives of the faithful.[141] Interestingly, he focuses on the goals of the reform of the texts and rites of the liturgy which (here he cites article 21 of SC) are meant to accomplish the expression of the mysteries in such a way that "the Christian people, as far as possible, are able to understand them with ease and to take part in the rites fully, actively, and as befits a community."[142] Thus in his revision of *Il senso teologico* Vagaggini understands liturgical participation as full (*plenaria*), active (*attiva*), and communitarian (*communitaria*),[143] with the caveat that the rites must be easily understood, that is, that there is a psychological component as well whereby the liturgical action can be appropriated by the faithful.[144]

For Vagaggini, full liturgical participation is both external and internal. It is external in that the believer is engaged physically in the rite

---

[140] See nn. 74-76 in this chapter.

[141] This, of course, was not the case when he wrote his first version of the text of *Il senso teologico*, in which his argument was centered primarily on Pius XII and his theology in *Mediator Dei* and on the writings of the pontiffs who immediately preceded him. This section of the book, along with the entire chapter on the principles of the liturgical pastoral, was significantly adapted and modified not only to highlight the tenets of the Constitution on the Sacred Liturgy but also to undergird Vagaggini's argument for full, active, and communitarian participation.

[142] SC 21.

[143] *Il senso teologico* (1965), 784–87. This demarcation of liturgical participation is slightly different in the first and second ediitons of *Il senso teologico*. In the first edition participation is cited as first material/external and spiritual/internal, and then as active, living, conscious, and heartfelt (*attiva, viva, conscia, sentita*, pp. 664–65). The communitarian aspect is also included. In the second edition Vagaggini drops the notion of participation as *sentita* for a more cognitive-psychological approach (pp. 648–51).

[144] Vagaggini's insistence here on the psychological efficacy of the rites stems from his theological method discussed earlier. His gnostic-sapiential method of theology views the rites as those acts that lead the believer further and further into the mystery being celebrated, not simply in an empiric or historic appreciation of the rites but by experiential knowledge of God gained through grace by "tuning in" to the rites and the action of the Trinity within them.

by his or her presence in the church and in the gestures, movements, and responses that may be requested. But he cautions that "any sort of presence or any sort of participation in the liturgical action does not suffice."[145] The liturgical participation he desires must also be internal, creating in the believer "an internal moral attunement with the liturgical reality as sanctification in Christ and worship of God in Christ."[146] Here, Vagaggini brings his earlier notion of *sintonia d'animo* to bear on the concept of liturgical participation. It is not enough simply to appropriate the signs and symbols within the liturgical action; rather, one must also be attuned to the actual realities they signify, that is, be connected to the paschal mystery of the self-communicating triune God. Thus the full (*plenaria*) liturgical participation he describes goes beyond the external actions and internal dispositions of the believer and points to the possibility of entrance into divine life. He asserts that "the goal, therefore, is plenary participation, that is to say, a participation in which the Christian, responding with perfect attunement to the given objective of the celebration, displays in full the possibilities of the supernatural actions included in his supernatural being as a man appointed to the worship of God in Christ."[147] What Vagaggini envisions is not simply a "tuning in" to the complexus of signs in the liturgy but rather a "tuning in" to the Trinity itself, which that complexus signifies. Such a "sintonation" begins with the recognition of the *Kyrios* and his central role in the liturgy. Access to the Trinity is gained through Christ (*per Christum*). Following the scriptural foundation of the christological-trinitarian perspective on salvation history, the early liturgical texts place this signification at the forefront of the liturgical action. Moreover, the trinitarian motif is meant to be inculcated in the heart of the believer.

For Vagaggini, active liturgical participation is the natural counterpart to full participation that is both external and internal. "The liturgy," asserts Vagaggini, "is, in fact, according to its nature, an action not only of the priest but of each of the faithful present, although in a way that is properly their own, which is not that of the priest and hence without an equalization or a confusion of roles."[148] Moreover,

---

145 *Il senso teologico* (1965), 784.
146 Ibid.
147 Ibid.
148 Ibid., 784–85.

the activity of the believer in the liturgical action is made his or her own duty by virtue of the sacrament of baptism, which initiated them into the believing community and, perhaps more important, brought them into the life-changing experience of the divine life. Vagaggini argues succinctly that "the intrinsic nature of the liturgy as action and the intrinsic nature of the Christian, who has been vested, through his own baptism, with the 'royal priesthood' that deputes him to make that liturgical action his own, are such that it is not perfect participation in the liturgy if he does not render a participation that is not only internal as well as external but also active, vital, and conscious."[149] Thus once the believer has "tuned in" to the complexus of signs within the liturgy—and the attunement to the divine life of the Trinity that implies—he or she must also enter into the performance of the liturgical act. Here Vagaggini's understanding of the gnostic-sapiential method of theology comes into play. He asserts that "without active participation, the liturgy's principal characteristic—being a concrete vital instruction by means of the action itself—ceases, or at least is much diminished, from the didactic educative point of view in which the vital posture is transmitted not so much from concepts and from reasonings as from living and realizing a sacred situation with the whole person at the very moment."[150] For him, active participation implies an entrance into the paschal mystery through the enactment of the rites and the offering of one's self in those rites.

Finally, Vagaggini asserts that liturgical participation must also be necessarily communitarian. Because the liturgical action is, indeed, the action of the entire Mystical Body united to Christ, it intrinsically points to its communitarian character. Vagaggini points out that

> to participate perfectly and actively in the liturgical action therefore necessarily signifies participating actively in the action that is by right the action of the entire community in the act of worship, of the whole assembly of the children of God as *ekklesia* in Jesus Christ, in the presence of the Holy Spirit, the one who gathers each of the dispersed. Active participation, even externally communitarian, is but the expression, also extrinsic, of this communitarian requirement, ontologically intrinsic to the liturgy.[151]

[149] Ibid., 785.
[150] Ibid.
[151] Ibid.

At this juncture several of Vagaggini's earlier themes must come to the foreground again if we are to understand the full implications of his statement. First of all, the assembly as the Mystical Body of Christ is intimately connected to Christ as Head. Christ's personal action in the sacraments and in the liturgy becomes the action of the entire church. Second, in virtue of that personal action of Christ, which is itself infused with charity, the efficacy of the sacraments *ex opere operato* demands a liturgical action that is, in fact, *ex opere operantis Ecclesiae*. The efficacy derived from the liturgical action *ex opere operantis Ecclesiae*—that is, by the gift of self-offering rooted in the love of Christ, performed by the church through Christ, in the presence of the Spirit who unites it, and directed to the Father—becomes the means by which the fullness of grace is received in the sacraments.[152] For Vagaggini this communitarian dimension to liturgical participation is perhaps the most significant aspect of the theology of the Second Vatican Council, for here the implication of the action of the *Kyrios* is brought to full significance: the resurrected Christ united with the community of the church intercedes for it and works through it in the celebration of the liturgy.[153]

The full, active, and communitarian participation in the liturgy espoused by Vagaggini thus manifests a necessary requirement for the full reception of grace in the sacraments: it is precisely that reception of grace that leads to and effects participation in the divine life of the Trinity. The christological-trinitarian dimension of the liturgical act, a perspective rooted in the relationships posited by the formula *a . . . per . . . in . . . ad*, provides the framework for understanding how liturgical participation becomes more than a fortunate byproduct of the liturgical action of the church. Moreover, in his later works Vagaggini argues that the communion ecclesiology that develops from the writings of the conciliar fathers (as compared to a more juridical notion of ecclesiology) is inherently connected to the transmission of divine life in the sacraments, especially the Eucharist. He maintains that it is this

---

[152] Ibid., 765–66.

[153] Vagaggini returns to this point again and again in his writings. See, for example, "L'Eucharistia come centro della vita liturgica e l'insegnamento della teologia," *Seminarium* 8 (1968): 49–67, at 63–66; "La Chiesa si ritrova nella liturgia," 346–47; "La messa, sacramento del sacrificio pasquale di Cristo e della Chiesa," *Rivista Liturgica* 56 (1969): 179–93, at 191–92; "Lo spirito della Costituzione sulla liturgia," 8–16.

"invisible, divine aspect—of grace, of the communion of the divine life, of the transmission of this life, of spiritual unity—that results in the unity of men with the Father, by means of the incarnate Son, in the outpouring and presence of the Holy Spirit and in spiritual unity of [human beings] among themselves."[154] This reality is made manifest again and again in the liturgical action, especially that of the Eucharist. Full, active, and communitarian participation in the liturgy opens the way to the perfect reception of sacramental grace, which is nothing less than a participation in the divine life, to which that believer has been called by baptism.

[154] "L'Eucharistia come centro della vita liturgica e l'insegnamento della teologia," 64.

Chapter 3

Attempts at Creating
a Trinitarian Approach to Participation II

Edward Kilmartin

EDWARD KILMARTIN AND THE TRINITARIAN
DYNAMIC OF THE LITURGY

When Edward Kilmartin died of myeloma in June 1994 he left a legacy of insight and influence that is still unfolding even today. Born nearly seventy-one years earlier in Portland, Maine, he had been educated by the Jesuits during his high school years and sought entrance to the Society at the age of eighteen. Early in his scholastic formation within the Society his superiors noted his intellectual aptitude and rather hearty constitution and decided that he could best serve the Society and the church by ministering in the Jesuit missions in Baghdad, Iraq. With this in mind he studied physical chemistry and completed a master of science degree at Holy Cross College in 1950. After a brief teaching position (chemistry and mathematics) at Fairfield College Preparatory School in Connecticut and a one-year study at the Massachusetts Institute of Technology, Kilmartin began his formal training in theology and his preparation for ordination to the priesthood. From 1956 to 1958 he pursued graduate studies in dogmatic theology at the Gregorian University in Rome. Although his dissertation centered more on the ecumenical work of the World Council of Churches, it was during these years that he was first influenced by the sacramental theologian William A. van Roo, SJ, who in turn encouraged him to study the writings and theology of Karl Rahner.[1]

---

[1] Michael A. Fahey, "In Memoriam: Edward Kilmartin, SJ (1923–1994),"
Orientalia Christiana Periodica 61 (1995): 5–35, at 5–6. Fahey's article provides an excellent account of Kilmartin's life and influence as well as a detailed bibliography of his works. All information in these opening paragraphs regarding Kilmartin's life is taken from this source unless otherwise noted.

In 1958, when Louis Sullivan, SJ, became ill at Weston College, Kilmartin was asked by the provincial of the New England Province of Jesuits to begin teaching sacramental theology. What was to be a temporary assignment until he could begin teaching in Baghdad became instead the beginning of a fruitful career as a preeminent sacramental and liturgical theologian. During the years he taught at Weston— nineteen to be exact, obviously no longer a "temporary assignment" at all—Kilmartin also served as dean of the school (1960–1961), participated in the informal meetings of Orthodox and Catholic theologians in New York, worked as an editor for *New Testament Abstracts*, and studied at the universities of Würzburg and Tübingen. At Würzburg he continued his study of the writings of Johannes Betz, especially in relation to the latter's work on the history and development of the Eucharist among the early Greek fathers; at Tübingen he concentrated primarily on a study of contemporary theological approaches to the Eucharist, which he later published.[2] His early years at Weston were marked by his attempt to replace the theology of the manuals, characteristic of seminary formation at the time, with his own copious notes on biblical and patristic sources. As his term at Weston progressed Kilmartin increasingly found himself teaching in university settings during the summer months, including Marquette University, the University of San Francisco, and Creighton University. In 1975 he agreed to teach as a visiting professor at the University of Notre Dame, but two years later that position became permanent. He served there as a tenured professor until 1984. He taught extensively in those years and eventually came to direct the doctoral program in liturgical studies. A year after he left Notre Dame, Kilmartin was asked to teach sacramental theology at the *Pontificio Istituto Orientale* in Rome and was appointed an ordinary professor of liturgical theology. His years in Rome (1985–1994) were extremely productive. During this time Kilmartin published the first volume of what was to be considered his *magnum*

---

[2] See Edward J. Kilmartin, "Sacramental Theology: The Eucharist in Recent Literature," *Theological Studies* 32 (1971): 233–77. Kilmartin's research here is extensive. The article is presented thematically with elements ranging from the notion of eucharistic sacrifice to ecumenism, eucharistic ministry, and trinitarian life, just to name a few. Kilmartin cites more than fifty different contemporary theologians in the text.

opus, Christian Liturgy: Theology and Practice.[3] In 1994, shortly before his death, he was recognized by the North American Academy of Liturgy with its annual Berakah award for a lifetime of distinguished contributions to liturgical theology.

Early in his career Kilmartin was influenced by Odo Casel and Karl Rahner. Later he gained much from the works of Cesare Giraudo, Heribert Mühlen, and David Coffey. Much of his research and time were spent in discussing the role of Christ and the Holy Spirit in the sacraments, and especially adapting the Eastern concept of the proper mission of the Spirit to the Western theologian's sensibility.

Kilmartin's Starting Point:
The Content and Structure of the Early Eucharistic Prayers

In the course of his long tenure as professor, priest, and liturgist Kilmartin sought to develop fully a trinitarian theology of liturgical participation that would furnish the underpinnings for two fundamental aspects of his early sacramental theology: a theology of the Holy Spirit's mission and the faithful's response to God's initiative. To accomplish this task he first looks at the theological bases for the early church's celebration of the Eucharist. In the decade following the council Kilmartin repeatedly wrote on the early anaphoras and their theological significance for the church.[4] Part of his rationale, it

---

[3] There is evidence in Kilmartin's papers that he actually intended to publish three separate volumes of this work. The first was *Theology and Practice.* The second was published posthumously as *The Eucharist in the West.* Kilmartin mentions his intention to work on the third volume in a letter to the rector of the *Orientale* dated February 2, 1994. In this letter he speaks of not returning to Rome permanently to teach because of his failing health, but he also mentions his desire to return there briefly to gather up his papers, which contained the research he had conducted for the third volume. The bulk of those papers, now residing under the care of Robert Daly, SJ, at Boston College, consists primarily of notes and lectures he had gathered on two central topics: communion ecclesiology and the action of the Holy Spirit. Kilmartin died in June 1994, never having made that return trip to Rome.

[4] During this decade Kilmartin wrote one book and three major articles on this subject. The last article, "*Sacrificium Laudis*: Content and Function of Early Eucharistic Prayers," *Theological Studies* 35 (1974): 268–87, is his most thorough assessment of the postapostolic celebration of the Eucharist. See also Edward J. Kilmartin, *The Eucharist in the Primitive Church* (Englewood Cliffs, NJ: Prentice-Hall, 1965), idem, "The Eucharistic Prayer: Content and Function in Some

seems, in doing such detailed work on the anaphoras stemmed from his earlier work on the patristic interpretations of sacramental theology. By looking at these anaphoras one by one he clearly articulated how the sacramental celebration of the Eucharist in the first centuries expresses a trinitarian dynamic that includes the participation of the worshiping assembly. What he determined was that the early eucharistic prayers all show that the sacramental celebration points to a sole purpose: effecting a covenantal relationship with God through participation in a sacrificial meal. Moreover, it was precisely Kilmartin's assessment of the literary-theological structure of the eucharistic prayers that formed the springboard for his understanding of participation as being present to and in the saving acts of Christ's sacrifice. His studies revealed that there exists a trinitarian dynamic to the content and structure of the early eucharistic prayers that places the sacramental action within the trajectory of salvation history.

In *The Eucharist in the Primitive Church*, Kilmartin emphasizes the fundamental differences between Jewish table prayers and the early Christian eucharistic anaphoras.[5] He began his analysis with the various accounts of the Last Supper and demonstrated the historic religious and cultic significance of the eucharistic words and gestures presented by Christ. Clearly, the sharing of the body and blood of Christ signifies an intimate union of the apostles with Christ that goes beyond the unity of normal table fellowship in the Jewish milieu. Kilmartin argued that "the act of eating bread at the beginning of a meal was considered by the Jews as establishing table-fellowship, and it was a sign of union among the participants."[6] But because Jesus identifies the bread he offers with his own body, the meaning and significance of the "sharing of the body" is altogether new. Kilmartin explained this newness in detail:

Early Eucharistic Prayers," in *Word in the World*, ed. Richard J. Clifford and George MacRae (Cambridge, MA: Weston, 1973), 117–34; idem, "The Last Supper and Earliest Eucharists of the Church," in *The Breaking of Bread. Concilium* 40, ed. Pierre Benoit, Roland Murphy, and Bas van Iersel (New York: Paulist Press, 1969), 35–47.

[5] This is not to imply that the two did not share vast similarities. But in noting the similarities between the two, Kilmartin also showed how their differences highlight the particular function and meaning of the eucharistic prayers.

[6] *The Eucharist in the Primitive Church*, 65.

The Apostles could understand the symbolism of the sharing of food and drink as a sign of union among the participants of a banquet. They could understand the sharing of food and drink of a liturgical banquet as a sign of union with Yahweh. But the food was not considered to be a symbol of the participants of the feast or of Yahweh. At the Last Supper, on the contrary, the bread is interpreted as Jesus' person.[7]

Similarly, because Jesus identifies the cup with his own blood, the action of drinking the cup as the blood of Jesus would have seemed sacrilegious to practicing Jews. But now the drinking of the blood Jesus offers becomes the vehicle by which the apostles enter into union with him. Interestingly, Kilmartin would eventually limit this conception of actually eating the body and blood of Christ in the Eucharist to the time period of the primitive church. In his later works he noted that many of the fathers of the church, especially Augustine, viewed the eucharistic species as the sacrament of the body and blood of Christ, pointing to a spiritual reality made present by the sign of bread and wine.[8]

Second, Kilmartin asserts that the "sharing of the body and blood signifies the redemptive act."[9] The eating of the eucharistic bread and the drinking of the eucharistic wine entail far more than just unity. The words of Jesus in the institution narrative imply a covenantal relationship that is also redemptive. As Kilmartin noted, "Participation in this food signifies the bestowal of redemption on the participants."[10] Moreover, he continues, "this whole action (the words and gestures of Jesus), in turn, manifests the offering which Jesus makes of His life for men and the acceptance by the Father which makes the gift possible."[11] That action becomes paradigmatic for all believers.

Last, Kilmartin notes that the memorial of the Last Supper is to be distinguished from other Jewish memorials and rituals in that the redemptive act being memorialized and the redeemer are both made present in the ritual. In the prayers surrounding the presentation of the gifts of bread and wine at the Last Supper, Jesus "manifests the offering of obedience and love which is present in His soul: the essence

[7] Ibid., 65–66.

[8] Edward J. Kilmartin, *The Eucharist in the West*, ed. Robert J. Daly (Collegeville, MN: Liturgical Press, 1998), 24–28.

[9] *The Eucharist in the Primitive Church*, 66.

[10] Ibid., 67.

[11] Ibid. See also "The Last Supper and Earliest Eucharists of the Church," 36–42.

of the redemptive act."[12] In this sense the Last Supper takes on a sacramental character because it effects what it signifies. Kilmartin asserts that Jesus' action at the Last Supper "is the efficacious anticipation in ritual form of the redemptive event which will have its historical fulfillment in the actual death and Resurrection of Jesus. Sacramentally Jesus is already the Christ at the Last Supper."[13] Such an anticipatory understanding would not be alien to the mind-set of the Jewish believer at the time of Christ. Rather, the Last Supper unfolds in the context of a Jewish understanding whereby the words and gestures of someone who is known to be a valid and genuine representative of God become efficacious with their pronouncement and enactment. Kilmartin shows how the actions and words of Jesus would probably have been interpreted by those gathered around him. He maintains that "by this bread and wine, now identified with his body and blood, Jesus mediates to the disciples not merely a share in the table blessing but more properly a share in the blessings derived from his 'given body' and 'shed blood': freedom from the power of sin and a new covenant with God."[14] What is being memorialized and signified by Jesus' words becomes truly present with the sign of the Last Supper— redeemer and redemption are made present to the apostles.[15] That presence is made manifest in the beginning of a new covenant in Jesus, as Christ, who implores the apostles to share in his body and blood until he comes again. With this, Kilmartin asserted that the "ritual act by which the Apostles were given a participation in the establishment of the covenant remains in the church. The covenant of the New Law is re-presented each time the Eucharist is celebrated, and thereby Christians are given the opportunity of manifesting their membership in the covenant and deepening their participation in it."[16]

[12] *The Eucharist in the Primitive Church*, 67.

[13] Ibid., 68. This section of his treatise echoes the work of Odo Casel in his description of the Last Supper. See also Odo Casel, *The Mystery of Christian Worship and Other Writings*, ed. Burkhard Neunheuser, OSB (Westminster, MD: Newman Press, 1962), 22–25. It should also be noted that the capitalization of the term "resurrection" in the above quotation is Kilmartin's, but its significance is uncertain; perhaps he is merely distinguishing the resurrection as an action of God as opposed to the death of Christ, which is of human origin.

[14] "The Last Supper and Earliest Eucharists of the Church," 41.

[15] *The Eucharist in the Primitive Church*, 68–69.

[16] Ibid., 73.

In looking at the various accounts of the institution narrative in both the Synoptics and the letters of Paul, Kilmartin concluded that "despite obvious differences between the accounts, there is an essential kernel displaying a uniform relational system which must be found in all celebrations claiming to be conformed to the tradition of the night of betrayal."[17] He defined that kernel as twofold: (a) the community of life among the participants is centered on their relationship to the God who has established a covenant with them, and (b) the union between Jesus and the disciples is grounded in their common union with the Father, a union not rooted in the old covenant but in Christ, as it stems from the personal attachment of the disciples to Jesus.[18] Moreover, Kilmartin agreed that this union has a decidedly redemptive quality to it. The unity between Jesus and the disciples expressed in the institution accounts is "based on their participation in his new relation to the Father sealed by his obedience 'unto death, even death on a cross' (Phil 2:8)."[19] Thus the unity of the disciples and Christ is linked intimately with the paschal mystery itself, which at the same time creates a link to and unity with the Father because of it. In turn, the eucharistic feast is oriented toward the mission of Christ as servant of the Father. In this sense the words of the prayer of Jesus serve a simple purpose: "ordering the meal to the mission of Jesus."[20] Those who participate in the sacrament, because of their consequent unity with Christ and the Father, are expected to participate in the saving works of Christ in the world. In a Pauline sense the Eucharist becomes an extension of the mission and work of Jesus within human history. Thus the prayer of thanksgiving that marks Jesus' action in the Last Supper and the consequent reference to the sacrifice of praise by the early church provide the fundamental basis for comprehending the transformative significance of the "sharing of the body and blood." In this sacrifice of praise the one eternal sacrifice is made present to the believers.

Kilmartin noted that in the decades and centuries that followed the apostles the eucharistic anaphoras began to develop a theology that augments this fundamental understanding of the significance of the

[17] "Sacrificium Laudis," 268.

[18] Ibid., 269.

[19] Ibid., 270.

[20] "The Eucharistic Prayer: Content and Function," 118. See also "The Last Supper and Earliest Eucharists of the Church," 44–45.

Last Supper and the establishment of a new covenantal relationship with Christ. In the second century "the Lord's Supper took on the form of ritual sacrifice and a clear distinction emerged between the offering of the sacrifice of praise and the communion of the holy food."[21] In his analysis of the fragmented eucharistic texts of the *Didache*, Kilmartin asserts that the *Didache* community viewed the celebration of the Eucharist as an incarnational event, "[an] anticipated eschatological meal, providing the gifts of the primordial epoch."[22] The prayer refers to Jesus as the fulfillment of Wisdom, and the *Didache* community seems to take its understanding of Wisdom from Genesis's depictions of the trees of life and knowledge: "We thank you, Father, for the life and knowledge which you have made known to us through your Son Jesus."[23] Kilmartin asserts: "In Gen 2:9, life and knowledge are presented as actual food provided by the trees of life and knowledge. The fact that 'immortality' is provided by the tree of life in Gen 3:19, and is linked together with the 'knowledge and faith' as fruit of the meal in *Did. 10.2*, supports the opinion that the Eucharistic food is recognized as the renewal of the gifts of paradise."[24] It seems clear then that the paradisiacal gifts of immortality and knowledge are linked to the sharing of the eucharistic elements: redemption is mediated through consecrated bread and wine.

Kilmartin notes that the commentaries of Justin Martyr also provide some insight into the eucharistic prayers of the second century. In his *First Apology* and the *Dialogue with Trypho*, Justin consistently references the celebration of the Eucharist in terms of a prayer of

---

[21] Ibid., 275.

[22] "The Eucharistic Prayer: Content and Function," 128.

[23] See Ronald C. D. Jasper and Geoffrey J. Cuming, eds., *Prayers of the Eucharist: Early and Reformed* (Collegeville, MN: Liturgical Press, 1990), 23.

[24] "The Eucharistic Prayer: Content and Function," 128. Kilmartin reproduces the *Didache* text in this article (p. 127). The line he references, which is said as part of the prayer over the cup, is simply: "We thank you, holy Father, for your holy name, which you have made to dwell in our hearts; and for the knowledge and faith and immortality, which you have made known to us through Jesus, your servant. The glory to you forever." See also *Prayers of the Eucharist: Early and Reformed*, 23–24. Jasper and Cuming translate the beginning of the passage as "enshrined in our hearts." Interestingly, the phrase actually refers to the Hebraism of "pitching one's tent" with another, thus dwelling with him or her.

thanksgiving for creation and redemption.[25] This eucharistic prayer is "directed to the Father through the 'name of the Son and the Holy Spirit.' (*Apol. 1*, 65.3; 66:2) and involves the two essential moments of benediction and thanksgiving."[26] The praise offered to God is viewed in connection with the fulfillment of the prophecy of Malachi 1:11, namely, that "from the rising of the sun, even to its setting, my name is great among the nations; And everywhere they bring sacrifice to my name, a pure offering; For great is my name among the nations, says the Lord of hosts." The memorial of the Lord's Supper, as praise offered to Christ, becomes the nexus for understanding the praise offered to God the Father. Justin writes: "So God bears witness in advance that he is well pleased with all the sacrifices in his name, which Jesus the Christ has handed down to be done, namely in the Eucharist of the bread and the cup, and are done in every place in the world by Christians."[27] The impact of the Justinian analysis of the second-century Roman prayers stems from his portrayal of the Eucharist as having a likeness to the historical event of the incarnation: Christ is made present to believers in the celebration and becomes flesh and blood for their sake. Kilmartin argues that the invocation of Christ evokes in the elements a sacramental presence of the incarnation.[28]

Kilmartin notes that by the third century the eucharistic prayers used by the early church increasingly contain sacrificial language, were filled with petitions for the people of God, or were preoccupied with epicletic formulae. Looking at the *Apostolic Tradition*, he recognizes the central role of the institution narrative: it "serves as both object of thanks and authority for what the church does. The thanksgiving which precedes the narrative leads up to it, and the sacrificial prayer and petition which follow depend on it."[29] The final petition after the institution narrative reflects the theological understanding of the prayer itself. The prayer asks not for the consecration of the

---

[25] Kilmartin notes that, depending on his audience, Justin seems to vacillate between depicting the Eucharist as a memorial of the passion and of the incarnation. This vacillation is less a theological structure than it is a practical one, as Justin attempts to appease Jewish audiences by portraying Christ as the fulfillment of the Old Covenant.

[26] "The Eucharistic Prayer: Content and Function," 121–22.

[27] *Prayers of the Eucharist: Early and Reformed*, 28.

[28] "The Eucharistic Prayer: Content and Function," 125.

[29] "*Sacrificium Laudis*," 279.

species *per se*, but rather for the coming of the Spirit on the offering of the church for the sanctification of the faithful. "Hence," asserts Kilmartin, "the Communion petition must be understood to serve as explanation of what the prayer as a whole ultimately intends: the sanctification of the communicants, especially through the communication of spiritual food and drink."[30]

But the centrality of the institution narrative was not a universal constant during this period. Kilmartin noted that both Clement of Alexandria and Origen refer to an Alexandrian eucharistic prayer in which the institution narrative is absent and the prayer itself is referred to as a sacrifice.[31] While conjecture might allow for the recitation of the institution narrative at the end of the prayer, the tenor of this Alexandrian prayer is notably different.[32] The mediation of Christ is still needed for the act of worship to take place, but it is precisely the act of the church that seems to be emphasized. The text of the prayer ("Giving thanks through him to you with him and the Holy Spirit, we offer the reasonable sacrifice and this bloodless service, which all the nations offer you") suggests that Kilmartin's analysis is correct.[33] The mediation of Christ is left intact but, indeed, the emphasis is redirected to the offering of praise by the gathered assembly. The *Anaphora of Addai and Mari* also contains a eucharistic prayer that differs from those seen earlier. While many of the traits of the Hippolytan prayer in the *Apostolic Tradition* are present here, Kilmartin notes that "the narrative of institution does not provide the hinge which unifies the prayer."[34] Instead, what we see is an anaphora dependent on the action of the Holy Spirit: "May your Holy Spirit, Lord, come and rest on this offering of your servants, and bless and sanctify it, that it may be to us, Lord, for the remission of debts, forgiveness of sins, and the great hope of the resurrection from the dead, and new life in the kingdom of heaven, with all who have been pleasing in your sight."[35] Unlike the Alexan-

---

[30] Ibid. For the translation of the text from the *Apostolic Tradition*, see also *Prayers of the Eucharist: Early and Reformed*, 35.

[31] "*Sacrificium Laudis*," 280.

[32] For a complete translation of the prayer found in the Papyrus Strassburg gr. 254 (to which Kilmartin alludes), see also *Prayers of the Eucharist: Early and Reformed*, 52–66.

[33] Ibid., 53.

[34] "*Sacrificium Laudis*," 282.

[35] *Prayers of the Eucharist: Early and Reformed*, 43.

drian prayer, this one diminishes the value of the activity of the church in favor of the words of the epiclesis, and the notion of sacrificial offering is absent.

Kilmartin depicts the development of the eucharistic prayer formulas in the fourth century as taking two divergent and distinctive paths. On the one hand, the West Syrian (or Antiochene) tradition, found in the *Apostolic Constitutions* and the *Prayer of St. James*, contains an extremely detailed and developed prayer that "asks explicitly for the consecration of the gifts in view of the sanctification of the faithful."[36] While both prayers are highly trinitarian, Kilmartin believed that the later *Prayer of St. James* shows a rather nuanced understanding of trinitarian action within the sacrament: "Here the Trinity is presented not simply acting one after the other. Rather, the divine Persons are shown as entering into action and revealing themselves together: specificity of act and unity of action are admirably expressed."[37] This is most clearly seen in the invocation of the Spirit over the gifts. The text of the anaphora reads:

Have mercy on us [Lord,] God the Father, almighty; [have mercy on us, God, our Savior. Have mercy on us, O God, according to your great mercy,] and send out upon us and upon these [holy] gifts set before your [all-] Holy Spirit, (*he bows*) the Lord and giver of life, who shares the throne and the kingdom with you, God the Father and your [only-begotten] Son, consubstantial and coeternal, who spoke in the law and the prophets and in your new covenant, who descended in the likeness of a dove upon our Lord Jesus Christ in the river Jordan [and remained upon him,] who descended upon your holy apostles in the likeness of fiery tongues [in the Upper Room of the holy and glorious Zion on the day of the holy Pentecost; (*he stands up and says privately*) send down, Master, your all-Holy Spirit himself upon us and upon these holy gifts set before you,] (*aloud*) that he may descend upon them, [and by his holy and good and glorious coming may sanctify them,] and make this bread the holy body of Christ, (*People:* Amen.) and this cup the precious blood of Christ (*People:* Amen.).[38]

[36] "*Sacrificium Laudis*," 283.

[37] Ibid. Kilmartin relied heavily on the extended doctoral work of André Tarby, who had reconstructed the original prayer. See also Tarby, *La prière eucharistique de l'Église de Jérusalem*, Théologie historique 17 (Paris: Beauchesne, 1972).

[38] *Prayers of the Eucharist: Early and Reformed*, 93. Parentheses, brackets, and italics are all provided by Jasper and Cuming to allow for the variances in the surviving manuscripts or to demarcate rubrics as opposed to text.

Kilmartin alludes to this invocation because of its insistence on the oneness of the three persons who "[share] the throne and the kingdom," while still recognizing the proper function or activity of the Spirit in salvation history and in the eucharistic celebration. He goes to great lengths to show the importance of this trinitarian scope within the *Prayer of St. James*, asserting (rather dramatically):

> In the theological perspective of this prayer the whole cosmos is called to return to God in a unique liturgy which links heaven to earth. The history of salvation is viewed as animated by the synergism of the three divine Persons and crystallized around the divine image impressed on man the sinner, whom Christ, the full expression of the divine philanthropy, comes to renew in the perfection of his sacrifice. The Eucharist is understood to insert the believer into the economy of salvation, which is fully realized in the effusion of the Spirit. It is the sacrifice of propitiation which the Church, attentive to the fearful return of the Judge, ceaselessly offers to the Father to draw on itself His mercy and pardon. Simultaneously it is, for the participants of the body and blood, the source of communication of the Spirit, who divinizes man progressively in the totality of his being.[39]

In this sense the fully developed Antiochene prayers, especially as seen in the *Prayer of St. James*, move the believer into an unfolding drama of salvation history in which the primary *actors* are the three divine Persons and the faithful are brought into a liturgical offering to the Father and act of sanctification in Christ and through the Holy Spirit.

On the other hand, the Egyptian tradition also developed during this fourth-century period and was marked by increased sacrificial language and a distinct separation between the consecration of the species and the sanctification of those participating in the Eucharist. Kilmartin looked at the *Dêr Balyzeh Papyrus* and the *Anaphora of Serapion*, both of which contain two separated epicleses. He asserts that in the case of the *Dêr Balyzeh Papyrus* prayer the insertion of the first epiclesis (which is the specific invocation of the Holy Spirit to make the bread and wine the body and blood of Christ) "puts the thanksgiving in the background and so changes the orientation of the whole prayer."[40] Whether or not the second epiclesis is equally separated

---

[39] *"Sacrificium Laudis,"* 283.
[40] Ibid., 284.

from the theme of thanksgiving is difficult to determine since there are approximately fifteen lines (or more) missing from the text just before it. The missing text separates the proclamation of the anamnesis from the petition to "provide us your servants with the power of the Holy Spirit, for strengthening and increasing of faith, and for the hope of eternal life to come."[41] In the prayer of *Serapion*, however, the first epiclesis is situated within a sacrificial prayer and is oriented toward the institution narrative. The second epiclesis asks for the transformation of the elements for the sanctification of the communicants. Here, Kilmartin asserted, "the church's sacrificial action is depicted as representing the sacrificial action of Christ at the Last Supper."[42] While the *Anaphora of Serapion* maintains the importance of the Last Supper, the thanksgiving character so prevalent in the first-century eucharistic prayers has been relegated to a much smaller introductory role. Mention is made in the text of the prayer of the "living sacrifice, this bloodless offering,"[43] as seen in earlier prayers, but the use of heightened sacrificial language dominates.

By the beginning of the fifth century one sees that the Western church is highly dependent on this Egyptian tradition. Kilmartin asserts that the Western prayer has a "variable element (thanksgiving) and a stable one (sacrificial prayer enclosing the narrative of institution)."[44] In these first centuries of the church, importance was placed on the acceptance of the offering rather than the consecration of the elements: the whole of the prayer is said to consecrate the offering of the church and no fixed moment of consecration was known. However, in the reform following the Second Vatican Council the new Roman eucharistic prayers do not follow the same orientation as what had eventually been codified as the Roman Canon. A specific epiclesis for the sanctification of the elements appears, as well as one for the sanctification of the communicants. Kilmartin asserts that the "decisive influence on the structure of these prayers was not concern for traditional forms or Eucharistic prayers, much less for modernity, but

---

[41] *Prayers of the Eucharist: Early and Reformed*, 80–81.

[42] *"Sacrificium Laudis,"* 284–85.

[43] *Prayers of the Eucharist: Early and Reformed*, 77. The offering mentioned here is also diminished by the use of the aorist tense, προσενεγκαμεν, implying that it was made in the past but not necessarily in the present.

[44] *"Sacrificium Laudis,"* 285.

the concern of Western theology to fix the moment of consecration in the recitation of the narrative of institution."[45]

This prolonged look at Kilmartin's analysis of the early eucharistic anaphoras leads us to his important conclusions from this study. In his final analysis of these eucharistic prayers, Kilmartin maintained that "[t]he original thanksgiving prayer, which expressed the Church's desire for participation in the covenant relation of Jesus with the Father, was gradually overrun with sacrificial prayers and petitions which emphasized the Church's activity and the Church's confidence in the efficacy of its prayer."[46] Even though the early eucharistic prayers were expressed in a multitude of fashions, Kilmartin believed that "the relational structure of the accounts of institution remains: thanksgiving to God for His mighty works in Christ is the *sacrificium laudis* of the Church undertaken with a view to obtaining deeper communion with the Father, especially through the sacrament of the humanity of Christ."[47] In the Western church, however, the general orientation of the prayer of thanksgiving and the prayer for sacramental incarnation was supplanted by prayers of sacrifice and specific epicleses. While Kilmartin asserts that such a transformation was perhaps predictable, it was not without severe, and perhaps detrimental, consequences: thanksgiving was placed at the margins of eucharistic theology and the lay faithful were relegated to a position of spectators for what became a primarily sacerdotal act. Herein lies the great motivation for the development of Kilmartin's theology of liturgical participation and what it should achieve. For Kilmartin, the liturgy is that unique place where the self-communication of the Trinity is made manifest through the action of the whole church. Participation in the divine life of the Trinity, therefore, becomes inextricably linked to participation in the liturgical life of the church, most notably participation in the sacraments.

In his later works Kilmartin showed that the preeminent form and structure of the eucharistic prayers are precisely oriented toward the active participation of the assembly in the rite, and therefore instead of isolating the institution narrative as the focal point within the liturgy he examined the entire eucharistic prayer and its focus on the sanctification of the elements for the transformation of the communicants.

[45] Ibid., 287.
[46] Ibid.
[47] Ibid.

In this sense "the Eucharistic Prayer provides a global and dynamic vision of this ecclesiastical mystery which requires identifying the epiclesis of transformation of the participants as the key to the ultimate meaning of the celebration."[48] Moreover, the prayer itself points to the lifelong journey all Christians are meant to make in returning to God. In one of the last articles he wrote, Kilmartin maintained that the literary structure of the classical eucharistic prayers "mirrors the dynamic relation of the partners of the new covenant in the history of salvation realized fully through the redemptive work of Christ in the power of the Spirit."[49] This dynamic relation is actualized in the memorial of events presented in the prayer itself. Kilmartin noted:

> The thankful recognition of the Father's action in Christ (anamnesis) is followed by the petition (epiclesis) that the continuing fidelity of the Father to his people be expressed and realized through the sanctifying action of the Holy Spirit by which the communicants are brought to Christ (epiclesis for sanctification of communicants) and by which Christ is brought to the communicants (epiclesis for sanctification of the bread and wine).[50]

This dynamic is liturgically expressed through the celebration of the Eucharist and reveals the single *transitus* of Christ emanating from and returning to the Father. It is this same journey in which the assembly participates "through the medium of the eucharistic celebration"[51] and the action of the Holy Spirit. Thus Kilmartin's extensive look at the form and structure of the early eucharistic anaphoras is meant to underscore the essential dynamic of the self-communication of the Trinity in the liturgical action. From this starting point he was able to develop more fully his trinitarian theology of the liturgy.

Worship as the Point of Sanctification: The Action of Christ and the Church
    Kilmartin's approach to a trinitarian understanding of sacramental action and efficacy is rooted in his understanding of the liturgy as not only the manifestation of the personal missions of the Son and Spirit but also the means by which the human person is able to enter into the

[48] *The Eucharist in the West*, 355.
[49] Edward J. Kilmartin, "The Catholic Tradition of Eucharistic Theology: Towards the Third Millennium," *Theological Studies* 55 (1994): 405–57, at 444.
[50] Ibid.
[51] Ibid.

divine life. Tracing his thought in this particular area is not always easy since he first demarcated a synthesis of sacramental theology before 1979,[52] nuanced that depiction in later articles and in the publication of *Christian Liturgy I* (1988), and then revised and honed it further in subsequent articles[53] as well as in *The Eucharist in the West*, published posthumously in 1998. One could be tempted to look at this last work as his summary of sacramental theology, but because it deals specifically with one sacrament and not sacraments in general, and because of its relatively disproportionate treatment of some authors, it does not provide the best medium for understanding the final synthesis of Kilmartin's thought. Rather, the best overview of Kilmartin's sacramental theology can be gained by analyzing the development of four central aspects of his modern approach to sacraments: the recognition of the sacramental church as the place of encounter with the divine, the relationship of the Spirit to word and sacrament in the life of the church, a broadening of the understanding of the institution of the sacraments, and a pneumatological understanding of the modes of Christ's presence in the church.

Foremost in Kilmartin's understanding of sacramental operation and efficacy is a fundamental distinction: the church provides the medium through which God communicates himself to the world. Kilmartin approaches this truth from the perspective of the Second Vatican Council's declaration that the church acts as a sacrament for the life of the faithful.[54] The council specifically states that "the Church, in Christ,

---

[52] Kilmartin's first complete attempt to tackle a comprehensive theology of the sacraments occurred with the publication of his extended article in the Theological Institute volume on sacraments. See Edward J. Kilmartin, "A Modern Approach to the Word of God and Sacraments of Christ: Perspectives and Principles," in *The Sacraments: God's Love and Mercy Actualized.* Proceedings of the Theological Institute 11, ed. Francis A. Eigo (Villanova, PA: Villanova University Press, 1979), 59–109.

[53] These articles would include: Kilmartin, "The Catholic Tradition of Eucharistic Theology" (1994); *Culture and the Praying Church* (Ottawa, ON: CCCB, 1990); "Sacraments as Liturgy of the Church," *Theological Studies* 50 (1989): 527–47; "The Sacrifice of Thanksgiving and Social Justice," in *Liturgy and Social Justice*, ed. Mark Searle (Collegeville, MN: Liturgical Press, 1989). Also of note are the works cited earlier in this text that were written before *Christian Liturgy*.

[54] The first references the council makes to the church *qua* sacrament are in *Sacrosanctum Concilium* 5, 26, but the bulk of Kilmartin's thinking is derived from the later Constitution on the Church, *Lumen Gentium*.

is in the nature of a sacrament—a sign and instrument, that is, of communion with God and of unity among all men," and that the church is a "visible sacrament" of the salvific unity implied by its communion with Christ.[55] Kilmartin, however, nuances this understanding of the church as sacrament of Christ by looking at the notion of encounter and adding a pneumatological dimension to the council's formulation.

Kilmartin begins to distinguish his concept of church as sacrament by introducing a positive anthropological model of human encounter.[56] For him, an encounter between two persons leads to the opening of a new relational understanding that resists specific definition or limitation because it is dependent on the level or gradation of willingness to communicate oneself to another or open oneself to the experience of another. On this basis he maintains that encounter necessarily implies engagement as well—engagement that is defined as the commitment one person can have toward another.[57] For Kilmartin the sacramental encounter between God and the human person is essentially a declaration of " 'Christ for us! We with Christ!' " that must take place within the church.[58] Here, there is a recognition not only of the union that takes place between the individual and Christ but also of the unity of the church itself, of believers with other believers. Kilmartin argues that the paradigm for such an encounter of engagement is the Last Supper. For him the church becomes the locus for the divine-human encounter; believers are united in self-offering "in, with, and through the self-offering of Christ, and with Christ and one another in the communion of his body and blood. But believers are in Christ's Body 'in the Spirit.' "[59] The sacramental reality of the church has to be seen through this pneumatological lens, both for the believing individual and for the church as a whole.

---

[55] LG 1, 9.

[56] "A Modern Approach," 69. Kilmartin cites within the text Martin Buber's use of the term *Begegnung* as a positive understanding of encounter between I and Thou from which a new awareness arises. For the sake of his argument Kilmartin does not detail the extent of Buber's thesis but merely shows the possibility for a nonnegative understanding of the word *encounter* in English.

[57] Ibid., 69–70. Kilmartin repeats this discussion in *Christian Liturgy*; see *Christian Liturgy I. Theology and Practice* (Kansas City: Sheed & Ward, 1988), 220–21.

[58] "A Modern Approach," 70. See also *Christian Liturgy*, 221.

[59] *Christian Liturgy*, 222.

At first Kilmartin maintains that the church is more properly called a sacrament of Christ. In his article "A Modern Approach to the Word of God and Sacraments of Christ" he applies the council's relation of the Spirit to the sacramental structure of the church to his own synthesis. While he admits that *Lumen Gentium* points to the Spirit as a "constituent factor" of the sacramentality of the church, he wants to maintain that the Spirit is inextricably linked to Christ within the church.[60] He depicts the church as a sign of Christ, but one whose signification is made possible by the Spirit. He writes: "The church is the corporate social sign and instrument of the past saving work of Christ which is rendered present and operative through the Spirit of Christ."[61] Citing the work of Walter Kasper[62] and returning to the council's presentation of the church in *Lumen Gentium*, Kilmartin notes that the church, like the incarnate Word, is comprised of human and divine elements and that the basis of the animating unity of those elements is the Spirit. The church, then, is called sacrament in an analogous sense to the same demarcation of Christ as sacrament. Just as the humanity of Christ is seen as the instrument of the divine Logos that is united to it, the church can also be understood as a subject that is not ontologically autonomous in itself. Rather, while the organism of the church admits to a unity of activity by various individuals exercising their gifts for the sake of the whole, "the social structure of the Church is fashioned ultimately by the Spirit who works through it, or, more precisely, through the activity of the members. Those who form the social organism are ontically united to the Spirit and serve as instruments of the Spirit. Hence the activity of the Spirit depends on them."[63] In this sense he maintains that the church can adequately be called a "sacrament of the Spirit" as well as "sacrament of Christ."

[60] "A Modern Approach," 70–71.

[61] Ibid., 71.

[62] See Walter Kasper and Gerhard Sauter, *Kirche, Ort des Geistes*, Ökumenische Forschungen: Ergänzende Abteilung. Kleine ökumenische Schriften 8 (Freiburg: Herder, 1976), 41–52.

[63] *Christian Liturgy*, 225. Kilmartin makes similar claims elsewhere in discussing the unity of the church in the sacrament of the Eucharist. See especially his "The Eucharist: Nourishment for Communion," in *Populus Dei II: Ecclesia. Studi in onore del Card. Alfredo Ottaviani*, ed. Giuseppe d'Ercole (Rome: Communio, 1967), 1043–85 .

The importance of that Spirit is seen in Kilmartin's second fundamental characteristic of sacramental theology: the role of the Spirit in
the preaching of the word and the celebration of the sacraments. In "A
Modern Approach" he notes that the relationship of the Spirit to the
preaching of the word and the sacraments of Christ is one of causality,
at least in their ecclesial dimensions. Both word and sacrament can be
construed as ecclesial expressions of faith in which the source is Christ
in the Spirit.[64] Kilmartin asserts that the "mediation of the Church,
which has the goal of bringing the individual into direct fellowship
with God, is effective because of the personal mission of the Spirit. It is
from this personal mission that the ecclesial word and sacraments can
be called 'means' of salvation."[65] In this understanding he maintains
that the Spirit acts as the "primary efficient cause of the communication of salvation through word and sacrament."[66] But Kilmartin also
wishes to assert that the Spirit functions in a way that is analogous to a
formal cause, that is, the Spirit is (in some way) responsible for determining the content of the communication itself. Within the scholastic
approach to sacramental theology the signification of the sacraments is
maintained by divine ordination. Here, Kilmartin simply wishes to assert that the Spirit is the divine principle of that ordination.[67] The Spirit
then acts as the primary efficient cause of the instrument of salvation
(word and sacrament) and also produces the milieu in which word
and sacrament can be grasped by faith. Kilmartin summarizes the
overarching influence of the Spirit in the sacramental action:

> It is in the Spirit that the sacramental words and gestures form a
> sacrament and are efficacious. By the exercise of the intellect and
> will illumined by faith which is granted by the Spirit, the individual

[64] "A Modern Approach," 71.

[65] Ibid. Although he does not cite Heribert Mühlen at this point in "A
Modern Approach," it is clear that Kilmartin is playing off of the notion of
"mediated immediacy." As we will see later, he uses this analogy to speak of
the Spirit's action in manifesting Christ's presence in the sacramental action.

[66] Ibid.

[67] Ibid., 71–72. It is perhaps interesting to note here that in "A Modern Approach" Kilmartin begins with his description of the Spirit as efficient cause
and then moves into the discussion of formal causality. However, in *Christian
Liturgy* he begins by establishing the Spirit as a quasi-formal cause and then
proceeds to a discussion of efficiency.

accepts the gift of the Spirit. Hence, if the Spirit is both giver and gift, a positive refusal to recognize the Spirit in the external sacramental celebration renders the participation meaningless from the viewpoint of salvation. On the one hand, the Spirit alone makes the exterior sacrament to be an efficacious sign of salvation and, on the other hand, the Spirit does not touch the heart without the collaboration of the participant and without faith having prepared him for the sacraments of faith.[68]

At every turn in the sacramental act, the Spirit is active. In the later adaptation of this same material in *Christian Liturgy*, Kilmartin expands the analogy of formal causation with reference to the Spirit. In this case the formal cause of the sacraments is depicted as the Spirit, who helps establish the very form and shape of the sacramental celebration. It is the Spirit who inspires the church to determine its sacramental form. This aids Kilmartin's demarcation of "sacraments of the Spirit" to develop its fullest meaning. He describes the sacraments as "Spirit-endowed realities of the Church."[69] As the church actualizes itself through the celebration of the liturgy it most clearly shows its sacramental character as the visible sign (in its members) of an invisible reality (the Spirit who unites them and infuses the celebration). This understanding of the church as "sacrament of the Spirit" allows not only for a "clearer vision of the basically sacramental character of all the activity of the Church" but also for a "description of the dynamics of sacramental celebrations in categories of symbolic interaction of the participants."[70] It opens the way to a discussion of sacramental theology in an arena of pneumatology and trinitarian theology. The Spirit allows for participation not only in the mystery being celebrated in the sacramental event but also in the divine life of the Trinity, which is communicated through that action.

The third fundamental element of Kilmartin's sacramental theology—the broadening of the traditional understanding of the institution of the sacraments in Christ—allows for an interpretation that acknowledges the faith response of the church. In making this determined move toward speaking of the church's constitutive authority in determining sacraments Kilmartin is able to place the sacraments

[68] "A Modern Approach," 73.
[69] *Christian Liturgy*, 232.
[70] Ibid.

more aptly within the trajectory of salvation history. He notes that with the Second Vatican Council's declaration of the church as a kind of sacrament[71] the liturgical celebrations of the sacraments take on the function of representing "the deepest concentration of the sacramentality latent in all church activity, including preaching and other forms of liturgical celebration."[72] In this sense sacraments can be viewed not only as acts of Christ in the Spirit but also as acts of the church. In his article "Sacraments as Liturgy of the Church," Kilmartin goes to great lengths to demonstrate this ecclesial dimension of sacramental activity. In discussing the modern controversy over whether or not the earthly Jesus historically spoke words that instituted each sacrament of the church before the church's formation in the Pentecost event Kilmartin surmises that it is possible to speak of the sacraments in a way that maintains their institution "in Christ" but also points to a more credible origin for them in the faith life of the church. He wished "to situate the origin of the sacraments in that phase of the economy of salvation in which, through the mission of the Holy Spirit, the disciples accepted through faith their incorporation into the Church of the risen Lord."[73] Such a reformulation does not deny that Christ still acts as the primary mode of reference for determining sacramental development. In fact, the church becomes the living consciousness of the ministry of Jesus and defines itself by the very sacraments it performs. Kilmartin notes that

> in the remembrance of Jesus' words and works, under the inspiration of the Holy Spirit, and at different times and places, the Church discovered appropriate ways to manifest and realize herself as the Body of Christ (baptism-confirmation and Eucharist) and to establish ministry of leadership in a way that corresponds to the sacramental nature of the Church (orders), ways that are fitting and necessary for the life of faith of the individual (penance, sacrament of the sick) and for individuals entering into the married state (matrimony).[74]

Moreover, this formulation maintains the teaching that the church is the place where the presence of Christ abides, in and through

---

[71] LG 1.
[72] *Christian Liturgy*, 280.
[73] "Sacraments as Liturgy of the Church," 533.
[74] Ibid.

the Spirit. The church is actualized in its sacraments. It is precisely through this expanded notion of sacramental institution that one can fittingly describe the reality of Christ's presence within the church and the church's ability to mirror that presence to the world. Kilmartin concludes succinctly: "Christ himself is the prototype of the sacrament. The Church, on the other hand, is sacrament as fruit of salvation: the social situation of the abiding presence of Jesus Christ."[75]

Finally, Kilmartin further underscores the trinitarian dimension of his sacramental theology by redefining the modes of Christ's presence within the church in pneumatological terms. Within *Christian Liturgy* he offers a comprehensive review of the teaching and theological interpretation of the notion of Christ's presence in the liturgy.[76] Here we will look at his concluding formulations in *Christian Liturgy* and in subsequent articles.

Citing the Constitution on the Sacred Liturgy, Kilmartin notes that the liturgy of the church here on earth is primarily the work of the glorified Christ acting as Head of his Body and united to that Body in the Spirit.[77] As the eternal High Priest, Christ is present in the liturgical activity of his church, especially in the sacraments. Kilmartin asserts that "this working definition of the liturgy affirms that the glorified Lord has bound the Church to himself in the Spirit" and that this abiding presence of the Lord is made possible by the "mediated immediacy" of the Spirit.[78] Such a presence is unique to Christ. Kilmartin explains that "Christ's presence in the members of the Church is more intimate and intense than the personal presence of one human being to another; for the Holy Spirit, whom Christ possesses in fullness, is given to believers whereby they are united to Christ in the one Spirit."[79] In his article "Sacraments as Liturgy of the Church," Kilmartin describes this relationship in more detail. He avers: "the immediacy of Christ to the individual believers, and through them in the community as such,

[75] Ibid.

[76] *Christian Liturgy*, 303–26. Such a review is not the purpose of this work, but mention of the extensive work Kilmartin did in this area is warranted. What is central to my discussion is the insertion of a pneumatological character into the discussion of Christ's presence in the liturgy and the implications that has for the liturgical action.

[77] Ibid., 350. Kilmartin cites SC 7.

[78] Ibid.

[79] Ibid., 330–31.

is not that of the immediacy of two persons to one another through a third person who stands between them. The Holy Spirit is not a bridge between Christ and the Church."[80] Again, Kilmartin wants to avoid an overidentification of the Body of Christ (*qua* church) with Christ as Head. What is needed is an understanding of immanent transcendence. Kilmartin writes: "The Holy Spirit, whom Christ possesses in fulness, was sent by him from the Father to form believers into the Church. Hence the same Spirit in Christ and in the communion of believers enables the immediacy of Christ to believers, and yet an immediacy that is mediated."[81] Elsewhere he notes that this description of the Spirit's role is essential to the Eastern understanding of the function of the Spirit in the unfolding of salvation history. Referring to the various epicletic formulas in the church's liturgy, he remarks: "The Spirit is invoked both to bring Christ to the Church and over the assembled Church in order to bring it to Christ. Both movements are essential. If Christ is not brought to the assembly there is a purely human ceremony; if the Church is not brought to Christ the liturgy is meaningless."[82] Thus in the exercise of faith, specifically in sacramental words and actions, Christ is made present because he is united to his church through the power of the Spirit. Because of this unity of Head and members created by the immediate mediation of the Spirit, Kilmartin can assert that "all liturgical accomplishments have a dialogical character, in which the action of Christ and the action of the assembly in the same Spirit constitute together the full mutual presence of the Church."[83] This dialogical character can be seen in the twofold dimension of the liturgical act we have noted earlier: sanctification in the self-communication of the triune God through Christ in the Holy Spirit to the church (katabatic) and worship in the church's offering of itself (both individually of its members and collectively as church) through Christ as Head in the Spirit to the Father (anabatic). Kilmartin writes that the "worship of God, and the sanctification of the worshipers, are aspects of the one event of grace offered, bestowed, and accepted."[84] United to the one act of Christ (both katabatic and

---

[80] "Sacraments as Liturgy of the Church," 535.

[81] Ibid., 536.

[82] "The Catholic Tradition of Eucharistic Theology: Towards the Third Millennium," *Theological Studies* 55 (1994): 405–57, at 435.

[83] Kilmartin, *Christian Liturgy*, 350.

[84] Ibid., 336.

anabatic), the church enters into the movement of Christ to the Father that is made present in the liturgical celebration. Such a movement is realized, says Kilmartin, "in the power of the Spirit sent by the *Kyrios*, who configures believers to Jesus, communicating the human attitudes that enable those who are in Christ to participate in his self-offering to the Father."[85] Elsewhere he notes that such a description of Christ's presence in the liturgy preserves the divine action inherent in the sacraments that gives them their efficacy. He writes: "The prayer of the Church through, with, and in Christ to the Father for the Holy Spirit is the way in which the offer of salvation is given visibility. The response of the Church is not the offer of salvation but the way in which the offer is proclaimed in the Church."[86] Because Kilmartin successfully formulates Christ's presence within the church and its liturgical actions in terms of the special mediation of the Holy Spirit, he opens the way to discuss the unique relationship between the members of the church united to Christ in the Spirit and their participation not only in the earthly liturgy of the church's worship but also in the heavenly liturgy characterized by participation in the divine life of the Trinity.

The Self-Communication of the Trinity in the Liturgy

In his opening "Foreword" to Jean Corbon's *The Wellspring of Worship*, Kilmartin presents a very helpful, though brief, overview of liturgical theology and its relation to the Trinity.[87] He begins with a central tenet of Christian anthropology: "that humanity was created in order to live forever in personal communion with the Holy Trinity."[88] The revelation of that purpose came through the person of Christ and the mission of the Holy Spirit that manifested itself after the death and resurrection of Christ. Kilmartin notes that "with the sending of the

---

[85] Ibid., 350.

[86] "Sacraments as Liturgy of the Church," 537.

[87] While Kilmartin uses the "Foreword" of Corbon's book to commend him for what he has done within its text, he does not necessarily agree with Corbon's analysis. Four years after the publication of *The Wellspring of Worship*, Kilmartin commented in his lectures at Creighton University that Corbon "thinks only in terms of descending Christology." See "The Holy Spirit in the Liturgy" (Creighton University, 1992), 2.

[88] "Foreword," in Jean Corbon, *The Wellspring of Worship*, trans. Matthew J. O'Connell (New York: Paulist Press, 1988), v.

Spirit from the Father through the risen Lord to bind believers to the beloved Son, and so bring them into personal communion with the Father of all, the ecclesial body of Christ was born."[89] That ecclesial body proclaims the revelation of the triune God every time it is gathered in the liturgy of the church, in that "the Father's self-communication through his only Son and his Holy Spirit finds a free response of praise and thanksgiving."[90] Thus in understanding this fundamental meaning of Christian liturgy, the goal of all liturgical theology has a simple demarcation: "A comprehensive explanation of the meaning of the liturgy must take the path that leads back to the life work of the Triune God."[91] In his own work and writings, especially in the last two decades of his life, Kilmartin sought to present a systematic theology of the Trinity in the liturgy. While the trajectory of that theology can be seen quite easily in his *magnum opus, Christian Liturgy: Theology and Practice*, it also permeates nearly all of his writings and teachings from 1980 until his death. The remainder of this chapter will follow that trajectory through *Christian Liturgy*, while at the same time noting the significant developments Kilmartin made in other writings.

Kilmartin's theology of the Trinity in the liturgy, and what serves as his theology of liturgical participation, progresses through six stages. An initial discussion of the place of the liturgy within the whole of salvation history, and thus an understanding of liturgical theology as a theology of the Trinity, leads into an exposition of the economic and immanent Trinity. Kilmartin follows this with two alternate ways of viewing the immanent Trinity—a descending Christology marked by the procession model and an ascending Christology marked by the bestowal model. By presenting the benefits of both, he is then able to discuss the proper missions of Christ and the Holy Spirit in the sacraments, especially the Eucharist. Through his recognition of those dual missions, Kilmartin opens the discussion to the means by which the human person is included in the activity and mission of both. He can then solidify the liturgy as the primary point of sanctification for humanity, where sanctification is defined as participation in the divine life of the Trinity. Here, the soteriological understanding of grace is dominant, but what Kilmartin achieves is to link that soteriological

[89] Ibid.
[90] Ibid.
[91] Ibid.

emphasis with his depiction of liturgical participation. In so doing he locates the liturgy as the focal point of the human response to the unfolding of salvation history. In this sense a certain necessary character accompanies any liturgical participation of the sacraments because of their central role as the lived expression of the salvific acts of Christ. While the first five stages are outlined above, a fuller explanation of the final stage now follows.

Participation, Trinitarian Action, and Sacramental Efficacy

Kilmartin wanted to argue that the primary means for participation in the divine life is found in the liturgical celebration, especially that of the Eucharist. His analysis of the early eucharistic anaphoras exposes the mesh and framework for all liturgical celebrations. Since the content and form of the early eucharistic anaphoras all point to defining the manner in which Christ gives worship to the Father, Kilmartin asserts that "through that medium of liturgical ritual activity believers are enabled to express their own psychological conformity to the worship of Christ grounded on the Spirit's transmission of the spiritual attitudes of Christ, which correspond to the content of the concrete liturgical celebration."[92] Linking his own study of the early eucharistic prayers with the work of Cesare Giraudo,[93] Kilmartin sought to identify the basic form of the prayers—anamnesis and epiclesis—with the fundamental attitude of Christ inherent in the prayers. Giraudo's work had looked exhaustively at a theology of the Eucharist derived from the *lex orandi* and noted that there were two basic types of eucharistic prayers in the early church: those that placed the institution narrative of the Lord's Supper in an anamnetic section and those that placed it in an epicletic section of the anaphora. Giraudo's contribution to Kilmartin's theology is to show that the institution narrative acts as an embolism in a way that is consistent with, or at least comparable to, Jewish liturgical prayer. In Giraudo's view the two aspects of anamnesis and epiclesis form a representation of the mystery that transcends time and space: "the event that at the level of space-time is passed—but that now surges to the eternal present—and projects

[92] *The Eucharist in the West*, 360.

[93] See Giraudo, *Eucaristia per la chiesa: Prospettive theologiche sull'eucharistia a partire dalla "lex orandi,"* 382–517. Giraudo's analysis covers nearly every ancient anaphora as well as those revised after the Second Vatican Council.

us eschatologically toward the completion of the future kingdom."[94] In this sense, through the act of memorial and the invocation of the Holy Spirit, Kilmartin saw a complete restructuring of the traditional notion of eucharistic sacrifice and thereby viewed the structure of the anaphoras in terms of the dynamic relationship of the Trinity in its action in salvation history.

In such an understanding of the form and content of the anaphoras and their relation to the liturgical celebration, the role of the Holy Spirit is not only augmented but in fact becomes pivotal. Kilmartin argues that "[i]n the power of the Holy Spirit the sacramental communion with Christ becomes the medium of spiritual, personal communion with the risen Lord."[95] The communion Kilmartin describes here is a communion in faith between the response of Christ in his sacrifice and the response in faith of the church as it offers its sacrifice of praise. The Holy Spirit is viewed as the essential factor uniting the katabatic and anabatic movements of the liturgical celebration: it is the Holy Spirit who allows worship and sanctification to happen simultaneously. In the union of those two movements the Spirit also fulfills a vital function of uniting the faithful to the *transitus* of Christ and thereby allowing them to enter into the divine life through participation in the mystery that is celebrated. Kilmartin argues that the "ritual act serves as a medium through which the faithful are rendered present in memory to the self-offering of the Son of God in his humanity, which culminated in his Passover from suffering to glory."[96] Here the relationship between the faithful and the real and active presence of Christ is neither incidental nor purposeless. Kilmartin maintains that "the community is rendered present under the formality, not of passive spectators, but of active participants in Jesus' uniquely acceptable response to what the Father has done in him for the salvation of the world."[97] In this sense the active presence of Christ involves a personal relation to the believers mediated by the immediacy of the Holy Spirit to Christ and the church: the Holy Spirit brings the faithful to Christ and Christ to the faithful.

[94] Ibid., 615.
[95] *The Eucharist in the West*, 370.
[96] Ibid., 371.
[97] Ibid.

Kilmartin describes personal engagement and fruitful participation in the liturgy as two proverbial sides of the same coin. The concise, almost terse, way in which he expresses this notion in *Christian Liturgy* is expanded and elaborated in other works, most notably "A Modern Approach" and *Eucharist in the West*.

The discussion of personal engagement in the sacraments begins with Kilmartin's clarification of the role and activity of the faith of the church vis-à-vis the individual. He writes: "Sacraments, above all, manifest the relationship between the word of God, in the form of the expression of the faith of the Church, and the response of faith that the word of God claims."[98] That word of God, as it is spoken through the supplication of those gathered for the sacramental celebration (i.e., the faith of the church), should correspond in some way to the faith and commitment of the individual. Kilmartin demonstrates that if the liturgical action is "source and summit" of the life of the church it can also be such for the individual when he or she completely acts in accord with the action of the church. Thus the personal engagement of the individual not only gains value but takes on a quality of necessity stemming from the correlation between the engagement of the individual and the action of the Trinity through the church. Kilmartin explains: "Sacraments are forms of response of faith of the community and individual subject and, at the same time, are saving events which happen to the participants. In other words, the action placed by the participants and the divine action form an indissoluble unity."[99] The worship of God as declaration of faith and the sanctification of the human person as action of the Trinity are linked by the sacramental encounter itself.

As seen earlier in this text, Kilmartin notes that the encounter with God in the sacraments necessarily implies an engagement. His previous work all comes to play now in his concept of the sacramental encounter and the necessity for personal engagement. He asserts that "in all true personal engagements there is an indissoluble unity between the action which a person places and the human and humanizing event that happens. Analogously, we can speak of sacramental celebrations as dependent on the human engagement for their salutary effect."[100] In the case of the sacraments Kilmartin notes that their effi-

---

[98] *Christian Liturgy*, 357.
[99] Ibid., 358.
[100] *Christian Liturgy*, 358. See also "A Modern Approach," 93–94.

cacy has to be tied to the willingness of the participant to enter into the sacramental action because "we do not address ourselves to a sacrament fully constituted and so somehow unlock its mechanism by our faith and thus cause the source of salvation to flow forth."[101] Rather, that efficacy is made manifest by the process of personal engagement, with its connection between the action that is placed and the event that happens to the actor. Kilmartin explains his stance in his essay "A Modern Approach to the Word of God and Sacraments of Christ," in succinct but illuminating fashion:

> In ordinary daily life personal engagement leads to a real experience (love, beauty, truth, etc.) in the measure of the intensity of the engagement. The experience does not find its most profound cause in the human engagement. Rather the experience is mediated through the symbol encountered. It comes as a gift. But the human engagement, through the dispositions which accompany it, makes possible the event which happens to us (e.g., the experience of beauty on an autumn day). A similar thing can be said of sacramental celebration. We do not initiate the celebration independently of the Spirit of Christ. But the measure in which we enter into it determines our personal growth in the life of faith.[102]

Within Kilmartin's schema of sacramental celebration, then, personal engagement forms the fundamental locus for understanding not only the way in which the encounter with Christ in the sacramental action has a direct effect on the participant but also the manner in which the participant is drawn into sacramental action through the invitation and action of Christ in the Spirit.

Kilmartin argues for an intimate connection between personal engagement and the most basic condition for fruitful participation in the sacraments, namely, that one is bound to the teaching of Christ. He maintains, as was noted earlier, that the fundamental paradigm for understanding Christian engagement is found in the Lord's Supper and baptism.[103] Within this paradigm he sees the conformity of the

---

[101] "A Modern Approach," 94.

[102] Ibid.

[103] *Christian Liturgy*, 359. While Kilmartin makes this assertion with reference to the understanding of the early church, in every other instance within *Christian Liturgy* when he speaks of the paradigm for Christian engagement

individual to Christ through the Spirit as a manifestation of the "basic condition of the human being: a being bound to instruction, in need of a word, and so fundamentally answerable to a word."[104] Kilmartin wishes to argue that through the sacramental celebration Christ "instructs" the faithful and "binds" them to the life of the gospel and the trajectory of his own witness and life. In this manner "the subjects of the sacraments are touched in the measure that they recognize themselves as instruction-bound and respond in the obedience of faith under the movement of the Spirit."[105] Kilmartin's argument here seems somewhat flawed, since the introduction of being bound to the teaching of Christ could imply a passivity that would counter both the ideas of communication and of participation. However, if one looks at the earlier paradigm of the Lord's Supper as the hallmark of Christ's teaching, then the *mandatum* of Holy Thursday plays a significant role. The act of love, specifically an act for others, is both revelatory and constitutive for the person of Christ. Christian believers are bound by the *mandatum*. But to be bound by that specific instruction necessarily implies engagement, activity, and the movement toward a sacramental ethic. Kilmartin details his argument more fully in "A Modern Approach" when he speaks of the relationship and perspective Christ brings to the sacramental encounter. The sacraments of the church *are* Christ's instruction; indeed, "Jesus' history shows he understood that instruction corresponds to his being."[106] Here he maintains that "Christian sacraments can be understood only from Christ, from his

---

he refers only to the Last Supper/Lord's Supper. The inclusion of baptism should be linked to the early church's understanding of these two sacraments as fundamental to the expression of the life of the church, and the entrance into the *mysterion* expressed by the sacraments. (See *Christian Liturgy*, 359.) For a detailed look at baptism and the understanding of the commitment to Christ made *per sacramentum*, see also "A Modern Approach," 96–100.

[104] *Christian Liturgy*, 359. See also Ludwig Hödl, "Kirchliches Sakrament— Christliches Engagement," *Zeitschrift für katholische Theologie* 95 (1973): 1–19. In his detailed analysis of the term *sacramentum*, Hödl maintains an Augustinian viewpoint that "the cultic and ritual sacrifice is always only an indication and an obligation to true inner surrender in penance and devotion" (Das kultische und rituelle Opfer ist immer nur ein Hinweis und eine Verpflichtung zur wirklichen inwendigen Hingabe in Buße und Frömmigkeit.). See esp. pp. 6–7.

[105] *Christian Liturgy*, 359.

[106] "A Modern Approach," 100.

decision for us, from his sacrifice and engagement for us. We become engaged through him insofar as we accept his instruction, understand it as binding and perceive it as a promise of salvation."[107] Kilmartin notes that such an understanding of Christian sacraments is not necessarily easy to accept. On the contrary, the human person repeatedly attempts to deny such an instruction-bound existence and instead is more often motivated by drives toward self-assertion and autonomy—in a postliberal world, freedom seems to reign over and above regulation.[108] But Christian life tends toward a different paradigm. In fact, the instruction-bound character of human existence and its fulfillment in sacramental engagement form the imperative for Christian living. Kilmartin makes clear the connection between sacramental action and sacramental ethic: Christian action "results from the graceful instruction received in the sacraments which nourish the faith and so grants to us space for living in which the ethical-religious virtues necessary for Christian life can grow."[109] In this sense the fundamental condition for fruitful participation in the sacraments, the instruction-bound existence of humanity, becomes also the source for the fostering of virtue and hope in the fulfillment of the promise inherent in the teaching of Christ.

In his later works Kilmartin associated the individual response of faith in the sacraments with the theological concept of participation—a participation in the life of Jesus through participation in the sacrament itself. The response of faith is not to be viewed as somehow the articulation of the human person's self-communication but rather points to the willingness and openness of the individual to receive God's self-communication, i.e., sacramental grace, and thereby participate in the divine life of the Trinity. Kilmartin strengthens this notion by stating:

> Through the revelation of God in Jesus Christ the divine gift is identified as the self-communication of the Father through the Son in the Holy Spirit, which consists in the so-called divinization of human persons. Moreover, according to the gospel of Jesus Christ, this trinitarian self-communication admits of degrees. The progressive deepening of personal communion with the individual persons of the Trinity

[107] Ibid.
[108] Ibid.
[109] Ibid., 101.

happens through the exercise of the psychological aspect of the life of faith: the life of trust and hope in, and love of, the triune God.[110]

In this rendering, participation in the divine life is actualized in the liturgical action (*ex opere operato*) but is brought to fruition only through individual engagement with the sacrament (*ex opere operantis*). That individual engagement is not manifested in a semi-Pelagian sense of personal achievement but rather is activated and animated through the power of the Holy Spirit. Participation is not identified as the effect of personal virtue or empowerment in the sacramental action. Instead, Kilmartin avers, participation "is based on the working of the Holy Spirit, who is the mediation of the personal immediacy of believers to Christ and of the divinely transmitted conformity to the spiritual attitudes of Christ."[111]

Here, the personal mission of the Holy Spirit (as seen above) becomes paramount for understanding Kilmartin's dynamic between liturgical participation and participation in the divine life. This "mediated immediacy" of the Holy Spirit, which Kilmartin adapted from his study of the work of Heribert Mühlen, forms the basis for understanding the Holy Spirit as the divine source of sanctification for the human person. Mühlen asserts that "because the Spirit of Christ is not incarnate in one specific human person, it is also not the 'Mediator,' but it is quite accurate to call it the mediating agency."[112] Such sanctification can be viewed ontologically, in the sense that the sacraments re-create individual believers as adopted children of God, and at the same time it must be viewed from a psychological or behavioral lens in that one is conformed to Christ *qua* incarnate Son.[113]

---

[110] *The Eucharist in the West*, 356.

[111] Ibid.

[112] Heribert Mühlen, *Una mystica persona. Die Kirche als das Mysterium der Identität des heiligen Geistes in Christus und den Christen: Eine Person in vielen Personen*, 2d rev. ed. (Munich and Vienna: Schöningh, 1967), 454.

[113] *The Eucharist in the West*, 358. See also "Sacramental Theology: The Eucharist in Recent Literature," 260–61. In this article Kilmartin explains the Eastern church's approach to divinization through the Spirit and the notion of "filial adoption" as a means to being drawn up into the life of the Trinity. For the notion of psychological conformity, see Mühlen, *Una mystica persona*, 454–56. Kilmartin notes Yves Congar's correction of Mühlen's thesis to provide a more suitable integration of the twofold mission of the Spirit and Christ. See also

The primary work of the Holy Spirit in the sacramental celebration, therefore, is to make possible the participation of the individual and the church in the New Covenant inaugurated by Christ. Kilmartin maintains that the effect of this participation in the New Covenant is the "integration into the single *transitus* of Jesus to the Father, a gradual process that takes place through response to the concrete situations of life that are conformed to the attitudes of the Jesus of history in virtue of the inspiration of the Spirit working in the believing disciples of Christ."[114] He believed that the primary role and action of the Spirit is to communicate to the believer the attitudes of Christ in such a way that the believer is conformed to Christ and can respond to that communication in faith. What is significant here in his formulation is the understanding of the human will freely responding to the work of the Holy Spirit. In no way is the communication of the Spirit forced upon the believer and, likewise, while that communication requires a response of faith, the response only comes as a free act of the believer. When such an act is made, the "action of the Spirit attains its goal."[115]

Kilmartin explains his assertion regarding the communication of the attitudes of Christ in "Sacraments as Liturgy of the Church." In this important article he wrote that the incarnate Son loves and knows God in a specifically human way, so that in his human act of faith he, in a sense, is responding to the very mystery that is his incarnation. The Spirit, as the animator of the incarnate Son, makes human knowing and loving possible in the earthly Jesus.[116] Kilmartin asserts that "[I]n the power of the Holy Spirit he [Christ] knows by faith what he knows by divine knowledge in the inner-Trinitarian life; he loves in his humanity the only object of his love in the inner-Trinitarian life, i.e., the Father."[117] Moreover, that response of faith on the part of Jesus is unique because of what Kilmartin terms the "incarnation" of the love of the Son for the Father in the action of Christ's human love: it is the Spirit who is incarnated in the response of faith and the act of love of the human Jesus.[118]

Kilmartin, "The Active Role of Christ and the Holy Spirit in the Sanctification of the Eucharistic Elements" *Theological Studies* 45 (1984): 225–53, at 237.

[114] *The Eucharist in the West*, 358.

[115] Ibid.

[116] "Sacraments as Liturgy of the Church," 541.

[117] Ibid.

[118] Ibid., 541–42.

In Kilmartin's estimation, then, Jesus' response of faith becomes the only acceptable and viable response to the New Covenant. Such a response is both universal and utterly distinctive. Kilmartin avers that Jesus' faithful response to the Father is unique precisely because of his incarnation as the God-man: his response is both individual and universal (as the exemplar for all humanity).[119] This perfect response becomes the one *transitus* that all humanity must emulate through the power of the Spirit. By participation in Christ's response of faith the believer enters into the mystery of the New Covenant. What is necessary in Kilmartin's schema, therefore, is a participation in the faith of Christ, since it is *that* faith that serves as the only way, the only *transitus*, to the Father. Such a participation in the faith of Christ becomes the vehicle toward participation in the inner-trinitarian life itself. Kilmartin warns that such a participation is neither a subjective remembering of the events of Christ nor a supposed ontological participation that would erase the distinction between God and humanity.[120] He explains the tension inherent in his notion of participation in Christ's response of faith: "the believer grasps the faith of Christ and is thereby united to the incarnate Son, and in him with the Father."[121] The Holy Spirit's action makes the communication of the faith of Christ possible and serves as the unifying principle for participation in such faith while still maintaining the real distinction between Christ as Second Person of the Trinity and the church as the living Body of Christ.

For Kilmartin, then, the connection between liturgical participation and the active roles of the Holy Spirit and of Christ in the sacraments centers on the relationship between causality and the understanding of grace as participation in the divine life. He sought to redefine notions of sacramental causality in order to accommodate the twofold mission of Christ and the Holy Spirit and to account for the need for active participation by the faithful in the liturgical celebration. For Kilmartin such participation is not optional. Here, he bases his argument on *Lumen Gentium*'s depiction of the church and its intimate relationship to the transformation of the human person through the power of the Holy Spirit and the continual activity of the glorified Christ in the world. The council asserts:

---

[119] Ibid., 542.
[120] Ibid.
[121] Ibid.

Christ lifted up from the earth, has drawn all men to himself (cf. Jn. 12:32). Rising from the dead (cf. Rom. 6:9) he sent his life-giving Spirit upon his disciples and through him set up his Body which is the Church as the universal sacrament of salvation. Sitting at the right hand of the Father he is continually active in the world in order to lead men to the Church and, through it, join them more closely to himself; and, by nourishing them with his own Body and Blood, make them partakers of his glorious life. The promised and hoped for restoration, therefore, has already begun in Christ. It is carried forward in the sending of the Holy Spirit and through him continues in the Church in which, through our faith, we learn the meaning of our earthly life, while we bring to term, with hope of future good, the task allotted to us in the world by the Father, and so work out our salvation (cf. Phil. 2:12).[122]

This promised restoration of sharing in the divine life, of participation, occurs through the continued mission of the Holy Spirit acting through the church in sacramental celebrations, both communally and individually. What Kilmartin envisioned was a renewal of the scholastic connection between *ex opere operato* and *ex opere operantis*, which also can account for the vital role and mission of the Holy Spirit in the sacramental activity. Such an inclusion mirrors the structure and form of the early church's understanding of sacramental action. In creating this reconnection Kilmartin noted, in his later works, that one must view the active subject of the liturgical action in terms that are both communal and individual; thus the sacraments are corporate acts of the faith of the church and individual acts of the believer entering into the liturgy.[123]

The work of the Holy Spirit in forming the church and its faith response to God's self-communication forms a central component of Kilmartin's theology of the communal action of the church in the sacraments.[124] He argues in *Christian Liturgy* that the "liturgical community itself is the proper active subject of the sacramental celebrations.

---

[122] LG 48.

[123] Kilmartin makes this assertion in a number of places: see esp. "The Catholic Tradition of Eucharistic Theology," 454–57; *Christian Liturgy*, 361–75; *The Eucharist in the West*, 370–83; "Sacraments as Liturgy of the Church," 534–47; "Theology of the Sacraments," 165–74.

[124] While it is not repeated here, one should keep in mind the intimate connection between Christ and the church through the mediated immediacy of the Spirit. In this case the action of the community of faith is linked to the

Its role in the efficacy of the sacraments must be thought through, together with that of the presiding minister and the person in whose favor the celebration takes place."[125] Part of his argument here centers on the simple fact of the performance of the liturgical rite: that no sacramental or liturgical action can be enacted in a theoretical vacuum. Rather, such rites must be performed within and by a living body. Kilmartin's analysis, however, also points to a more substantial and significant distinction—the liturgical rites of the sacraments are the response of faith by the church through the power of the Holy Spirit who forms it. Kilmartin writes:

> Sacraments are a human activity in which the faith of the Church as a whole and the faith of the concrete assembly is (sic) expressed. Such rites cannot be conceived of vis-à-vis the worshipping community. Rather, they are the human language and symbolic actions by which the community expresses itself, and through which God's self-communication takes places and is received in a fruitful way.[126]

Elsewhere Kilmartin notes that this self-communication of God is intimately tied to the liturgical act, so much so that it can only be approached through the sacraments as acts of the community of the faithful.[127] Thus, because of the immediacy of the Christ to the church by the mediation of the Spirit, the community of faith is joined to the act of Christ, which forms the fundamental basis of each sacrament. This is not an overidentification of the church with Christ but rather a recognition that the same Spirit of Christ is shared. The community can be viewed as the subject of the sacraments both as the organ that helps accomplish the sacrament through its performance (in what it gives to the celebration) and also as the communal recipient of grace

---

action of Christ in the sacrament. See esp. *The Eucharist in the West*, 537; "Sacraments as Liturgy of the Church," 262.

[125] *Christian Liturgy*, 366. He specifies elsewhere that with the exception of the Eucharist, in which the objective reality of the sacrament is meant to be shared with all who participate in the sacramental action, other sacramental celebrations occur in favor of particular individuals (i.e., in baptism, for the one to be baptized; in anointing, for someone ill or near death; in marriage, for those joined in union, etc.). See also "Theology of the Sacraments," 169.

[126] *Christian Liturgy*, 367.

[127] "Theology of the Sacraments," 165.

(in what it receives). The sacraments are envisaged as communal dialogues between God and the assembly in which believers respond in faith to the revelation of Christ. The "human giving and receiving" inherent in each sacramental celebration is always responsive; such liturgies are marked by a "response of praise and thanksgiving for what God has done and is doing now in the liturgical assembly, and a petition for a new advent of the saving grace of the Holy Spirit."[128] In this way the faith of the community is both made manifest and strengthened. The sacramental act presupposes the promise of salvation made by God's self-communication but also necessitates the action of the community as the active subject of the liturgy.

While Kilmartin emphasizes the connection between the communal action of the church and the activity of Christ in the sacrament, he also seeks to advocate an understanding of sacramental causality that will argue for the necessity of individual participation as well. In *Christian Liturgy* he states succinctly that through participation in the sacrament "the individual subject is enabled to transcend one's limited commitment of faith, to really experience the offer of God's grace within the ecclesial context, and to accept it gratefully."[129] Kilmartin's argument centers on those who are meant to be the favored recipients of the sacramental action. He notes that it would be erroneous for the individual to assume that the sacramental celebration is an expression of thanksgiving for what God has done in the past (either to the individual or the community of faith to which he or she belongs). Rather, "one's previous spiritual condition is transcended" in the sacramental action.[130] In this sense the sacrament goes beyond whatever capabilities or sense of faith commitment the individual has in coming to the sacrament; to say otherwise is to view the sacraments as juridical formulations of a natural-law obligation whereby the sacramental celebration is nothing more than the individual/communal affirmation of what God has already done. Kilmartin laments that such a formulation, indicative of the scholastic and reformation theologies on sacraments, hindered any reformulation of sacramental theology in the West before the council.[131] Instead, the sacraments pose opportunities whereby the in-

---

[128] *Christian Liturgy*, 368.

[129] Ibid., 370. For a capsule view of the same material, see also "Theology of the Sacraments," 170.

[130] *Christian Liturgy*, 369.

[131] "Sacraments as Liturgy of the Church," 539.

dividual willingly enters into the intentionality of the sacrament, to transform the individual through grace. The individual subject is able to accept God's offer of self-communication and, in so doing, is able to participate more fully in the divine life that is offered in the sacramental celebration. Kilmartin asserts that the individual subject is brought into the *opus operatum* of the church:

> This favored subject of the celebration is drawn into the upward move-
> ment of the prayer of the Church and thereby into the self-offering of
> the communion, which has as its goal the active reception of God's
> self-communication. The sacramental celebration has an anabatic
> orientation in its external form. Through it the assembly responds to
> realize itself as worshiping community at prayer on behalf of an in-
> dividual. The subject for whom the sacrament is celebrated can do
> no less than engage in this movement, agree with the prayer of the
> Church, and respond freely by offering self to receive the meaning of
> life from the divine source.[132]

In this sense the sacramental celebration is a conscious and free act of the individual who, by the indwelling of the Spirit, has assimilated the Spirit of Christ in the act of worship. The transformation of the human person through sacramental grace, by the very nature of the sacramental action, cannot take place against the individual's will; participation in the liturgical unfolding of the sacrament is necessary.

The practice of the life of faith is not directed toward some future reality or promise to be fulfilled, but rather toward the promise as self-communication that occurs in the sacrament; the specification of grace is directly related not to the individual's or the community's transient need in a given situation, but to the divine promise that through the work of the rite (*ex opere operato*) God's divine life is communicated. Such a communication helps the individual and the community meet the needs of both their current life situation and a Gospel-related ethic. It is both the expression of God's love (sanctification) and the witness of faith of the believer in the power of the Spirit of Christ (worship). Both actions are works of God but, as Kilmartin points out, "the scholastic synthesis developed a theory of sacramental sign that placed it on the side of God vis-à-vis the community . . . the fatal flaw in this theology lies in the sharp distinction between the liturgical spheres of

---

[132] Ibid., 538.

the expression of God's love (the essential sacramental rites) and the response of faith of the community (the surrounding liturgical prayer and ritual activity)."[133]

In this sense the sanctifying grace bestowed by God on the community and the individual is specified by the daily life of faith. Kilmartin argues that such a declaration can be made with the following rationale: if the sacraments purport to bestow a specific grace in relation to the meaning of each sacrament, it follows that for adult participants the efficacy of the sacraments depends on the individual's integration of his or her own commitment of faith into the liturgical articulation of the faith of the church. The structure and nature of the liturgy demands an agreement or there is no possibility for personal engagement with God.[134] Kilmartin disavows a productionist mode of interpreting the sacraments whereby the individual and the community come predisposed to receive grace as if it were an object. Rather, the sacraments act as mediators of both disposition and grace, so that the subjects of the sacrament are disposed to a higher level of participation in the divine life, which is communicated through the bestowal of grace. Kilmartin argues elsewhere: "This implies that the effect proper to the sacrament is extended to daily life in the measure of the activity of the faith of the individual."[135] One's commitment to the life of faith determines, even if indirectly, the communication of grace. That communication is made primarily through the individual and communal encounter with "the mystery presence" of Christ in the sacramental action.

This specification of the faith of the individual and the community can only be accounted for in relation to the mystery presence of Christ in the sacraments, which forms the basis for participation in the divine life. Christ's presence in the sacramental action is what manifests the one *transitus* to the Father. Commenting, in *The Eucharist in the West*, on the work of Odo Casel, Kilmartin asserts: "the mystery of Christian worship, what worship images and so re-presents, or reactualizes, is the very kernel of the redemptive work of Christ, namely, the passage of the Lord (*transitus Domini*) from death to life."[136] Elsewhere he explains that the "ecclesial communion participates in the mystery of

---

[133] *Christian Liturgy*, 371. See also "Theology of the Sacraments," 171.
[134] *Christian Liturgy*, 372–73.
[135] "Sacraments as Liturgy of the Church," 540.
[136] *The Eucharist in the West*, 270.

the substantial covenant of God with humanity, the mystery of Christ, extended in history through the mission of the Spirit."[137] The life of faith of the community and of the individual is the concrete means by which that covenant is expressed and solidified in the believer. But as Kilmartin notes, "The life of faith of the ecclesial communion is not something different from the mystery of Christ, but the way of participation in that mystery."[138] The mystery of Christ is not something to be responded to in the sacramental action, as if its presence dictated a second psychological act on the part of the subject of the sacrament. Rather, Kilmartin maintains that the mystery presence of Christ is in the sacramental celebration itself. Entering into the sacramental action is the engagement with the mystery presence of Christ and therefore the deepening of participation in the divine life.[139] This notion of mystery presence leading to participation is directly influenced by the work of Casel. Kilmartin notes, in explaining Casel's work, that "since the sacraments effect the real presence, though sacramental, of the work of redemption, Casel concludes that the believing members of the Church, those who participate in the liturgy of the sacraments, are made participants in redemption."[140] Kilmartin accepts and accentuates a basic Caselian tenet, namely, that Christian liturgy is centered around the "reactualization of the redemptive act of Christ to the end that believers may participate in it and be glorified with the *Kyrios*."[141] The mystery presence that is constitutive of the liturgy leads to participation in the divine life.

Kilmartin, much like the katabatic-anabatic motif he employs, has come full circle. In the closing remarks of "Sacraments as Liturgy of the Church," he shows not only how his modern approach

---

[137] "Sacraments as Liturgy of the Church," 543.

[138] Ibid.

[139] Ibid., 540–44. See also "The Catholic Tradition of Eucharistic Theology," 454–55.

[140] *The Eucharist in the West*, 271. See also Casel, "Mysteriengegenwart," 145.

[141] *The Eucharist in the West*, 274. This is not to suggest that Kilmartin altogether accepts Casel's theology of the mystery of the liturgy. On the contrary, in *The Eucharist in the West* he undertakes a detailed analysis and critique of Casel's work, noting especially his willingness to appropriate a liturgical theology that is analogous to the understanding of the pagan mystery cults. For Kilmartin's conclusions regarding Casel's thought, see *The Eucharist in the West*, esp. pp. 275–77.

to sacramental theology reinterprets the "scholastic reduction" of the sacraments, but also how he can include two formerly missing elements of such a theology—namely, liturgical participation in the mystery presence of Christ and the work and mission of the Holy Spirit.[142] Those two elements marked the beginning of his research in the field of sacramental theology. Kilmartin uses his early work on the patristic sources to show how the early church viewed the sacramental celebration: conformity to Christ was manifested through participation in his mystery. Such a participation was made possible through the Holy Spirit in the sacraments. Having identified this kernel of theology in the early fathers, he then identified the trinitarian dynamic at work in the early eucharistic prayers, a dynamic whose main intent was seemingly to present a vehicle for the self-communication of the Trinity to humanity. The extensive review of his work on the eucharistic prayers provides a fundamental cornerstone for Kilmartin's sacramental theology: that the trinitarian dimension of the content and structure of the sacraments is meant to mirror the communication of the Trinity itself to believers. Finally, Kilmartin develops a possible theology of the Trinity in the liturgy by means of which he can propose the necessary dimension of liturgical participation for the faithful.[143] In making the connection between the mission and activity of the Holy Spirit (the katabatic movement of the sacrament) and the activity of the faithful in the sacramental celebration, Kilmartin moves the liturgical participation of the individual into the *opus operatum* of the faith of the church. Moreover, by stressing the placement of liturgical participation in the movement of worship—that is, that the individual is brought up into the anabatic movement of the sacramental celebration—he also shows how liturgical participation is intimately linked to participation in the divine life of the Trinity.

[142] "Sacraments as Liturgy of the Church," 546.

[143] Ibid. An excellent synopsis of Kilmartin's reinterpretation of sacramental theology can be found here in his closing argument to "Sacraments as Liturgy of the Church."

Chapter 4

Later Attempts to Articulate
a Trinitarian Theology of Participation

While both Vagaggini and Kilmartin present at least the framework for the development of a trinitarian theology of participation, what is perhaps most surprising about postconciliar theology is its relative silence on the issue. Despite the obvious importance that is given to "full, conscious, and active participation" in the liturgy in the council itself, in the decade that followed it very little was written to elucidate the concept of participation and what it means for the faithful. Invariably, most scholars simply reiterate the various phrases of the Constitution on the Liturgy when they enter into theological debate on the matter.[1] Aidan Kavanagh, in his address to the Glenstal Liturgical Congress (Ireland) in 1973, lamented this development. He noted that a "cursory survey of liturgical literature produced since the council reveals that little has been said over the past ten years about the matter of participation except for repeating council maxims. Most recently, this too has fallen off—the maxims have become . . . unstated first principles in liturgical reform and pastoral action."[2] But Kavanagh

---

[1] There are notable exceptions to this statement, but even these occurred long after the constitution was promulgated. See, e.g., Gratien Bacon, "La participation de l'Église à l'offrande eucharistique, d'après Bossuet," *Revue des Sciences Religieuses* 42 (1968): 231–60; James Dallen, "The Congregation's Share in the Eucharistic Prayer," *Worship* 52 (1978): 329–41; Craig D. Erickson, "Liturgical Participation and the Renewal of the Church," *Worship* 59 (1985): 231–43; Boniface Luykx, "Liturgie et dialogue: psychologie de la participation," in *Message et mission: Recueil commemoratif du Xe anniversaire de la Faculté de Théologie* (Louvain: Nouwelaerts, 1968).

[2] Aidan Kavanagh, "What Is Participation?—or, Participation Revisited," *Doctrine and Life* 23 (1973): 343–53, at 343–44. Kavanagh goes on to note that what has been said about participation within theological reflection has been mostly preoccupied with vocal participation. The obvious emphasis on this type of participation after the reform of the liturgy began was to be expected, since vocal participation could have the most demonstrable results.

realized that if these maxims on liturgical participation had, in fact, become unstated principles, they had done so without accompanying theological reflection and thus had become meaningless to many. After the council it would be difficult to disprove that there was a calculable quantitative increase in the amount of active participation by the faithful, if one solely defines that participation as a matter of singing and dialogic response. This narrow definition of participation seems to have prevailed, and to a large extent it ignores the origins and development of the concept since the earliest part of the century. Kavanagh offered a different definition: participation "is first of all full membership in the church, by conversion, faith, hope and charity: 'one heart in love.' Nothing more. But nothing less."[3] Kavanagh saw the inherent connection between baptism and liturgical participation and realized that such participation is meant to transform myriad believers into one church, a living Body of Christ awakened by the Word and rooted in the theological virtues. Qualitatively, one could argue that the "full, conscious, and active participation" of which the council speaks has yet to be achieved.

Since 2000 the theological debate on the meaning and significance of liturgical participation has reopened, in large part due to changes in liturgical practice, but that debate has also been set in motion again by the anniversaries of the promulgation of different documents and has necessarily reflected on their implementation.[4] As the *Missale Romanum* was promulgated in various revisions in the past three decades its accompanying *Institutio Generalis* and further instructions by the Congregation for Divine Worship and the Discipline of the Sacraments have consistently referred to the significance, necessity, and practical applicability of liturgical participation. In the same way, as the church marked the anniversaries of such pivotal documents as *Tra le sollicitudini*, *Mediator Dei*, and *Sacrosanctum Concilium*, theological reflection on the implementation and effect of those documents became common.

In the first decade after the council finished its work there exists surprisingly little evidence in magisterial pronouncements of attention to the trinitarian motif in the sacraments. It can be surmised that a certain

---

[3] Ibid., 353.

[4] The plethora of symposia and scholarly articles that appeared in 2003 on the subject of active participation will be discussed later in this work. That year marked the hundredth anniversary of *Tra le sollecitudini* and the fortieth of *Sacrosanctum Concilium*.

necessary preoccupation with the revision of the texts of the liturgical rites prevented such theological reflection. Pope Paul VI's encyclical on the mystery of the Eucharist, *Mysterium Fidei*, would seem to have been the most logical place to find an elucidation of the trinitarian mystery in the sacraments. Instead, the bulk of the encyclical is geared toward a defense of the concept of transubstantiation and the celebration of private Masses.[5] The only mention of the communication of divine life is made in *Populorum Progressio*, the same pope's encyclical on the Development of Human Society, and that reference is only fleeting.[6]

Developments in Magisterial Teaching

It was only in the second decade after the council, with the beginning of the pontificate of Pope John Paul II, that a decidedly trinitarian turn in papal teaching can be seen. In fact, one could assert that John Paul II marked his pontificate by distinguishing the proper activity of the divine persons in the world with three encyclicals: *Redemptor Hominis* (1979), *Dives in Misericordia* (1980), and *Dominum et Vivificantem* (1986), referring correspondingly to Son, Father, and Holy Spirit. The pontiff asserted that the three encyclicals take their origin and inspiration from St. Paul's exhortation: "The grace of the Lord Jesus Christ (*Redemptor Hominis*) and the love of God (*Dives in Misericordia*) and the fellowship of the Holy Spirit be with you all (*Dominum et Vivificantem*)."[7] While each of the three encyclicals contains a foundational trinitarian theology, each also seeks to articulate the specific work of the respective divine person in the economy of salvation.[8] One can demonstrate that the three encyclicals taken as a whole point to a detailed theology of

[5] Pope Paul VI, *Mysterium Fidei*, AAS 57 (1965), 753–74, at 753–55. In the early pages of the encyclical Paul VI explains why he is writing the document and the abuses he hopes to correct.

[6] Pope Paul VI, *Populorum progressio*, AAS 59 (1967), 257–99, at 263.

[7] Pope John Paul II admits this in his opening of the third encyclical. See Pope John Paul II, *Dominum et Vivificantem*, AAS 78 (1986), 809–900. Paul's exhortation is taken from 2 Cor 13:13. The pontiff translates κοινωνιά as *communicatio*: " Ἡ χάρις τοῦ κυρίου Ἰησοῦ Χριστοῦ καί ἡ ἀγάπη τοῦ θεοῦ καί ἡ κοινωνία τοῦ ἁγίου πνεύματος μετὰ Πάντων ὑμῶν."

[8] John Paul II even admits in the opening paragraphs of *Dominum et Vivificantem* that he takes his cue and guide from the Eastern churches, noting especially the heritage they had protected for centuries and citing the simultaneous

trinitarian action and human sanctification. The framework for such an analysis is presented in *Redemptor Hominis* as the pope articulates the trajectory of God's self-communication: "the Father is the first source and giver of life from the beginning. That new life, which involves the bodily glorification of the crucified Christ, became an efficacious sign of the new gift granted to humanity, the gift that is the Holy Spirit, through whom the divine life that the Father has in himself and is given to his Son is communicated to all . . . who are united to Christ."[9] In this sense it is the love and mercy of the Father that initiate the self-communicative dialogue with humankind, it is the redemptive work of the Son that unites us to him in his dying and rising, and it is the work of the Holy Spirit to perfect the human will, to make us conform to our re-creation as adopted children in Christ, and to guide the church, both individually and collectively, to participation (*participatio*) in God. The fullness of this theology of trinitarian action is presented in *Dominum et Vivificantem*, which serves as a culmination of the series.

John Paul II asserts that the missions of the Son and the Holy Spirit are inextricably linked: "Between the Holy Spirit and the Christ there thus subsists, in the economy of salvation, an intimate bond, whereby the Spirit works in human history as 'another Counselor,' permanently ensuring the transmission and spreading of the Good News revealed by Jesus of Nazareth."[10] The redemptive work accomplished in Christ is continued in the Holy Spirit. That redemptive work is explained as raising the dignity of the human person through Christ's willingness to unite himself with all of humanity in the incarnation.[11] But the paschal mystery also includes the death and resurrection of Christ, and here the believer is made aware of the reconciling power of the Father of all mercy and the outpouring of the Holy Spirit. At the heart of this redemptive process is the universal call for the human person to participate in the divine God. John Paul II asserts that God "has revealed to man that, as the 'image and likeness' of his Creator he is called to participate in truth and love. This participation means a life in union with God, who is 'eternal life.' "[12]

---

celebration in Constantinople and Rome of the sixteenth centenary of the First Council of Constantinople in 1981.

[9] Pope John Paul II, *Redemptor Hominis*, AAS 71, no. 4 (1979), 257–324, at 310.

[10] *Dominum et Vivificantem*, 816.

[11] *Redemptor Hominis*, 271–72. The encyclical cites GS 22.

[12] *Dominum et Vivificantem*, 849.

During his pontificate Pope John Paul II repeatedly renewed the council's call for the "full, conscious, and active participation of the faithful" in the liturgy but increasingly nuanced the council's statements with his own, hoping to shed further theological light on the subject matter. His apostolic letters "Vicesimus Quintus Annus" and "Spiritus et Sposa" mark the twenty-fifth and fortieth anniversaries of *Sacrosanctum Concilium*, respectively. Both of these apostolic letters simply reiterate what the council has said, calling for the full, conscious, and active participation of the faithful. The former notes how difficult such a participation has been to achieve. The pontiff writes: "It can also be supposed that the transition from simply being present, very often in a passive and silent way, to a fuller and more active participation has been for some people too demanding."[13] Such a demand was met by indifference and even outright rejection of the reform espoused by the council. But John Paul II notes that such a reaction to the demand of the liturgy of the church cannot be tenable or a viable position to hold. Rather, he elucidates a twofold level of participation for the faithful centered on the table of the Word and of the Bread.[14] This participation becomes indicative of the manifestation of the church. He asserts that it is precisely when the church is in the midst of its liturgy and the people of God participate in it that the unity of the church, which comes to it from the Trinity, is revealed to the world.

At the end of 2003 John Paul II issued his second letter concerning the Constitution on the Sacred Liturgy, "Spiritus et Sposa,"[15] marking the need for further education in the midst of the reform. He notes that even forty years after the council's promulgation of *Sacrosanctum Concilium*, "it is more necessary than ever to intensify liturgical life within

---

[13] Pope John Paul II, "Vicesimus Quintus Annus," AAS 81, no. 8 (1989), 897–918, at 909.

[14] Ibid., 904–05. John Paul II notes the centrality of the word of God in the council's reform, but here he uses the Latin *communicanda* to refer to the participation of the faithful in the table of the Word: *christifidelium impensam operam in Verbi communicanda mensa*; he continues by noting the need for the faithful to grow in desire for Christ in both the table of the Word and of the Bread, as did the disciples on the road to Emmaus: *gustatum ipsum precandi ex Psalmis necnon ferventum voluntatem Christum agnoscendi, perinde discipuli in Emmaus fecerunt, ad Verbi panis que mensam.*

[15] It should be noted that the original document was not issued in Latin but in Italian. It is consistently referred to by its Latin title, but no such Latin text ever appears in AAS.

our communities by means of an adequate formation of the ministers and of all the faithful with a view to the active, conscious and full participation in liturgical celebrations desired by the Council."[16] This formation recalls the necessity for a liturgical spirituality among the entire people of God. John Paul characterizes that spirituality in a distinctively trinitarian form. At the end of his letter he urges that a liturgical spirituality may "be developed that makes people conscious that Christ is the first 'liturgist' who never ceases to act in the Church and in the world through the Paschal Mystery continuously celebrated, and who associates the Church with himself, in praise of the Father, in the unity of the Holy Spirit."[17]

Earlier in the same year John Paul II issued his encyclical on the Eucharist, *Ecclesia de eucharistia*, on the occasion of the twenty-fifth anniversary of his pontificate. While the pontiff maintains the formula of "full, conscious, and active participation" throughout the document, he also adds the necessity of the *fruitful* character of participation, which had been virtually ignored in the forty years since the promulgation of the Constitution on the Sacred Liturgy. The pope notes that the church's commitment to the Eucharist and the mystery that is being celebrated, especially since the Second Vatican Council, has allowed "a more conscious, active and fruitful participation in the holy sacrifice of the altar."[18] The call for a fruitful participation of the faithful in the sacramental action returns the discussion to the disposition

---

[16] Pope John Paul II, "Lo Spirito e la Sposa," AAS 96, no. 7 (2004), 419–27, at 422.

[17] Ibid., 426. John Paul II puts "liturgical spirituality" in quotation marks and italics apparently for emphasis; there is no reference for the phrase and it appears nowhere else in the document.

[18] Pope John Paul II, *Ecclesia de Eucharistia*, AAS 95, no. 7 (2003), 433–75, at 439. The call for *fruitful participation* in the sacraments also appears in the pontiff's "Address to the fourth group of bishops from France," AAS 96, no. 6 (2004), 342–438, and in the Apostolic Exhortation "Pastores Gregis," AAS 96, no. 12 (2004), 825–924. See specifically §35 (pages 871–72), where the pontiff refers to the "full, conscious, active and fruitful participation in the holy mysteries called for by the Second Vatican Council." Although he cites paragraphs 11 and 14 of the constitution, the "fruitful" character of participation does not appear in those sections, although it is certainly alluded to in paragraph 11. John Paul II has added this element to the formulaic phrase that appears in paragraph 14.

of the person rather than the objective act of the liturgical rite, that is, what has begun to happen within the pontiff's writings and within the larger theological arena is a reunion of scholastic medieval concepts: *opus operatum* and *opus operans*, the former between the objective act of the liturgical rite and the latter pointing to the disposition of the participants. Such a shift perhaps points to the growing influence of the work of Vagaggini and Kilmartin, both of whom were known to John Paul II and both of whom advocated such a marriage of the two terms. Thus in John Paul II's writings the participation of the faithful in the sacramental action, the *opus operans*, becomes crucial. The fruitfulness of participation is seen as the measure by which the person is affected by grace, whereby the will is transformed by sacramental grace and there exists a more intimate union with Christ. Full, conscious, and active participation must also be fruitful. Participation that is not fruitful denies the very nature and aim of the liturgy, which leads the faithful into the paschal mystery itself and the life of the Trinity.

By the time the *Catechism of the Catholic Church* was promulgated in the early 1990s, the action of the Trinity in the world and in the sacraments especially had moved to center stage. One could argue that it would be impossible to envision the correct makeup of the *Catechism* without this trinitarian motif. In fact, the *Catechism* provides a brief synopsis of the economy of salvation as the work of the Trinity and presents a capsule account of the doctrine of trinitarian action in the world. Such a presentation of the trinitarian motif mirrors the theological orientation of the *Catechism*'s primary editor, Christoph Cardinal Schönborn. Schönborn repeatedly stresses the iconic nature of the person of Christ, that is, that the work of the Son is a manifestation of the will of the Father that can only be ascertained through the work of the Spirit.[19] Not surprisingly, then, the *Catechism* asserts that the Father's plan of loving kindness unfolds in the work of creation, the history of salvation, and the missions of the Son and the Holy Spirit.[20] The *Catechism* also attempts to find a middle ground between the distinction of persons in the Trinity and their proper actions and maintaining a unity of action. Thus it testifies that while the Trinity has one and

---

[19] Christoph Schönborn, *God's Human Face: The Christ-Icon*, trans. Lothar Krauth (San Francisco: Ignatius Press, 1994), 34–43.

[20] United States Catholic Conference, ed., *Catechism of the Catholic Church* (New York: Doubleday Image, 1994), 76 (§257). All further references to this edition will be to CCC, followed by the paragraph number of the *Catechism*.

the same operation, "each divine person performs the common work according to his unique personal property."[21] The final cause (end) of trinitarian action, the self-communication of God for the sanctification of the human person, remains unified. The means by which that self-communication takes place is relative to each divine person. The *Catechism* takes an interesting approach to this declaration of divine action: it attempts to create a supportive juxtaposition of the personal uniqueness of the divine persons and their essential unity: "Being a work both common and personal, the whole divine economy makes known both what is proper to the divine persons and their one divine nature. Hence the whole Christian life is a communion with each of the divine persons, without in any way separating them. Everyone who glorifies the Father does so through the Son in the Holy Spirit; everyone who follows Christ does so because the Father draws him and the Spirit moves him."[22] Such a stance seems to elucidate the church's teaching in terms of the very trinitarian mystery it celebrates; the paradox of divine action, as both personal and common, is allowed to remain.

The promulgation of the *Catechism* also marked a significant development in the church's teaching on trinitarian action in the sacraments. The *Catechism* depicts the liturgy as the work of the three divine persons of the Trinity.[23] By juxtaposing various elements of the Second Vatican Council's trinitarian ecclesiology with an explication of the communication of grace and salvation in the sacraments, and by elaborating on the trinitarian encyclicals of Pope John Paul II, the *Catechism* presents a cogent, if succinct, trinitarian understanding of sacramental action. First, the Father is shown to be the source and goal of the liturgy. This is articulated in terms of the act of blessing, a "divine and life-giving action, the source of which is the Father."[24] The liturgical action centers on the revelation and communication of the divine blessing: the twofold nature of the liturgy, as both worship and sanctification, has as its starting point the recognition of the Father's blessings on the church. Thus the Father acts by blessing the church, which is united to Christ in the power of the Holy Spirit, and the church, in turn, calls upon the Father to bless the offering it extends

---

[21] CCC §258.
[22] CCC §259.
[23] See especially CCC §§1077–90.
[24] CCC §1078.

in the liturgical-sacramental act, that is, the very offering of itself as church, as the Body of Christ.[25] In this sense the Father acts as source and goal of the liturgy.

Second, the *Catechism* reiterates the depiction of the sacraments as acts of Christ, but here that action is intimately connected to the power of the Holy Spirit as well.[26] It asserts that "in the liturgy of the Church, it is principally his own Paschal Mystery that Christ signifies and makes present."[27] Repeating the conciliar declaration of Christ's presence in the liturgical celebration, the document stresses the link between the earthly liturgy and the heavenly one, where Christ's action is united with the action of the church.

Finally, the Spirit is depicted as the divine person who motivates the cooperation and participation of the faithful in the sacramental action. As animator of the church, the Holy Spirit "seeks to awaken faith, conversion of heart, and adherence to the Father's will."[28] In this sense the proper work of the Spirit is to help form the most fruitful disposition in the believer. The *Catechism* maintains that "these dispositions are the precondition both for the reception of other graces conferred in the celebration itself and the fruits of new life which the celebration is intended to produce afterward."[29] The Holy Spirit also acts to enliven the memory of the church to inspire it to praise and thanksgiving, and, through the outpouring of the Spirit, the mystery of Christ is made present.[30] Moreover, the Holy Spirit's power is portrayed with eschatological import: through the Spirit's action in the liturgy a foretaste of the Kingdom of God is presented to believers: "While we wait in hope he causes us really to anticipate the fullness of communion with the Holy Trinity."[31] Finally, the Spirit is depicted as the divine person who unites us to Christ to form the Mystical Body. The *Catechism* asserts:

> The most intimate cooperation of the Holy Spirit and the Church is achieved in the liturgy. The Spirit, who is the Spirit of communion, abides indefectibly in the Church. For this reason the Church is the

[25] CCC §1083.
[26] CCC §1084.
[27] CCC §1085.
[28] CCC §1098.
[29] Ibid.
[30] CCC §§1103–4.
[31] CCC §1107.

great sacrament of divine communion which gathers God's scattered children together. Communion with the Holy Trinity and fraternal communion are inseparably the fruit of the Spirit in the liturgy.[32]

In this manner each of the divine persons is seen to have a specific function and activity within the sacramental celebration: the Father who blesses the church in its action, the Son who unites the church with the heavenly liturgy through his presence, and the Spirit who prepares the faithful to receive the grace of the sacrament.

Elsewhere the *Catechism* augments its understanding of trinitarian action in the liturgy by describing the specific missions of the Son and Spirit. In discussing the nature of prayer it asserts that "in the sacramental liturgy of the Church, the mission of Christ and of the Holy Spirit proclaims, makes present, and communicates the mystery of salvation."[33] Moreover, the proper end of the missions of the Son and Spirit is defined as union with the Father, thereby making the action of the Trinity in the economy of salvation relate back to the inner life of the Trinity in communion with the Father.[34]

This same approach is taken in Pope Benedict XVI's apostolic exhortation "Sacramentum Caritatis." Much of it is a careful juxtaposition of the sacrament of the Eucharist to other elements in theology, but two sections are of special note: his initial discussion of the eucharistic mystery and its relation to the Trinity (and the Son and the Spirit in particular), and his later discussion of the complex nature of the phrase *actuosa participatio*.

Benedict XVI asserts that "the first element of Eucharistic faith is the mystery of God himself, trinitarian love."[35] This mystery is communicated to the believer through the sacramental encounter. The pontiff writes that "Jesus Christ, who 'through the eternal Spirit offered himself without blemish to God,' makes us, in the Eucharistic gift, sharers in the divine life itself."[36] The communication of this grace becomes the focal point of the eucharistic celebration, so much so that it leads to participation in the mystery that is the Trinity. Benedict XVI maintains:

[32] CCC §1108.

[33] CCC §2655.

[34] CCC §737.

[35] Pope Benedict XVI, "Sacramentum Caritatis," AAS 99, no. 3 (2007), 105–80, §7, cited hereafter simply by title and paragraph number.

[36] Ibid., §8.

"The 'mystery of faith' is thus a mystery of Trinitarian love, a mystery in which we are called by grace to participate."[37] In this simple explication of the trinitarian nature of the Eucharist the pontiff articulates the fundamental relationship between *communicare* and *participare*—in the celebration of the Eucharist, the faithful are led to share (*communicat*) in the divine life so as to participate (*participandum*) in the mystery of trinitarian love.

The pontiff further specifies this participation in the Trinity by noting the proper actions of both Christ and the Holy Spirit in the sacrament of the Eucharist. Benedict XVI carefully delineates an understanding of how Christ is made present in the celebration of the Eucharist so that the memorial act allows the faithful to enter into the "hour" of Jesus. Reiterating the words of his earlier encyclical, *Deus Caritas Est*, he asserts: "The Eucharist draws us into Jesus' act of self-oblation. More than just statically receiving the incarnate *Logos*, we enter into the very dynamic of his self-giving."[38] This same Jesus, once risen from the dead, is able to pour out the Spirit upon believers, making them sharers in the mission he received from the Father. This offering of Jesus is twofold: he offers himself in the dynamic of the oblation and he offers the Spirit in the bestowal of love. The Spirit, once given through Christ, continues to work and act, promoting the ministry of Christ through believers. The Spirit is posited as the person of the Trinity who transforms not only the gifts of bread and wine but also the community that offers those gifts: Christ's self-gift is united to the gift of the faithful through the power of the Spirit.

Benedict XVI's discussion of the phrase *actuosa participatio* also helps clarify the relationship between liturgical participation and participation in the divine life. He begins by noting that "participation" must refer to more than simply exterior activity during the celebration of the liturgy. Rather, it revolves around the awareness of the paschal mystery being celebrated and the relationship it has to one's daily living.[39] Such an understanding presupposes catechesis and ongoing liturgical instruction. He also clarifies the concept of active participation by noting that it cannot be "equal to the exercise of a specific

---

[37] Ibid.

[38] Ibid. See also Pope Benedict XVI, *Deus Caritas Est*, AAS 98, no. 3 (2006), 217–79, at 228.

[39] "Sacramentum Caritatis," §52.

ministry" within the liturgical celebration.[40] Each person's participation is not simply relative to his or her role in the gathered assembly—the presider, in the act of presiding, does not necessarily enter into active participation. Active participation is not defined by the fulfilling of ministerial duties, although it can serve as the vehicle toward full, active, and conscious participation.

Instead, Benedict XVI points to various personal conditions that would be necessary for fruitful participation to occur. Active participation in the liturgy begins at a level deeper than mere superficiality. One is called to look closely at his or her life, at the very least at the level of an examination of conscience and reconciliation. He asserts that "a heart reconciled with God restores the fit [person] to true participation."[41] Moreover, this participation in the liturgy cannot simply be qualified by an internal reconciliation with God. The pontiff also asserts that "there can be no active participation in the sacred mysteries without an accompanying effort to participate actively in ecclesial life in its fullness," especially in the missionary activity of Christ.[42] The sacraments demand a real and lived Christian ethic. It appears, in the context of Benedict XVI's exhortation, that active participation requires a disposition for the reception of grace as well as a commitment to continue the work of Christ through the power of the Spirit.

From the combined elements of trinitarian action in the Eucharist and the explication of *actuosa participatio* one can see how Benedict XVI relates the communication of divine life to both liturgical participation and an appreciation for what such participation implies. His conclusions augment the trinitarian language used by his predecessors in speaking of the sacraments and the church. Despite the advances made in the twentieth century in the formulation of a trinitarian theology of liturgical participation, a host of questions remains open for sacramental theologians to consider. To mention only two: What does it mean for the individual and the community to participate in a liturgical action directed to the Father that is also the work of Christ and the Holy Spirit? If the inner trinitarian dynamic is made manifest in the liturgical celebration in reference to the actions of the divine

---

[40] Ibid., §53.
[41] Ibid., §55.
[42] Ibid.

persons, then to what extent can the church (both collectively and individually) enter into that dynamic?

Contemporary Attempts to Identify Active Liturgical Participation

While both Kilmartin and Vagaggini offered cogent and viable springboards for trinitarian theologies of active participation, neither theologian was able to create a full system of thought on the topic. Since 2003, when the church marked the hundredth anniversary of *Tra le sollecitudini* and the fortieth of *Sacrosanctum Concilium*, the debate over the nature of active liturgical participation and how it is to be understood has resurfaced and attracted great interest. Present within much of the debate is a tension between those who view active participation as an avenue to engage the faithful even more fully in the sacramental action and those who view active participation as a means to encourage silent, inner transformation. But even this elementary distinction does not begin to elucidate the vast applications of theology on both sides of the debate. One can begin to appropriate the myriad differences in contemporary theological speculation on the topic of *actuosa participatio* when one looks at the Leuven (Belgium) Conference of 2003, the 2005 *La Maison-Dieu* edition (France) dedicated to the topic, and a series of Italian articles both in *Rivista Liturgica* and in a collection of essays written in honor of Domenic Sartore (Italy), which also took *actuosa participatio* as its theological locus.

The Liturgical Institute of the Faculty of Theology of the Catholic University of Leuven convened the 16th International Liturgical Colloquium at Mont César, the abbey of Keizersberg, in October 2003. The colloquium has historically brought together liturgical scholars and other academics every two years to discuss contemporary issues in sacramental or ritual studies. The 2003 colloquium was dedicated to a dialogue on the subject of active participation. While some of the papers were devoted to simple historical analysis or were particular to specific regions, the work of liturgist Thomas Pott and that of sociologist Liliane Voyé are of note here.

Thomas Pott asserts that any understanding of active participation in the modern world demands a mystagogical initiation and instruction of the faithful.[43] Using the priesthood and sacrifice of Christ as his

---

[43] It should be noted that Pott was specifically asked by the colloquium to address the tendency of many postconciliar liturgists to interpret "active

starting point, Pott notes that any sense of liturgical participation has to take into consideration how much the "Christian liturgy is the offering of ourselves to the Father in Christ's sacrifice. This is our active participation in the liturgy—the most proper and the most personal, the full exercise of our priesthood."[44] But Pott is also quite clear that such a participation is not limited simply to the enactment of the rite or the distribution of ministries. True active participation has to take that next step beyond the rite—the rite and its enactment serve as a means to an end: conformity to the cross of Christ.[45] At the same time, the significant role of the liturgy in achieving this end cannot be ignored. Pott maintains:

> The Christian liturgy is to live in Christ before it is question of a set of texts and rituals. The texts and rituals also certainly have their importance because they constitute the form in which—within the ecclesial community—within the mystical body of Christ—we have received the faith, we celebrate what we are and, in a mystical way, participate anew in the death and resurrection of Christ. In this sense our "earthly liturgy" is also an offering to God, but only insofar as it is the celebration of and participation in the sacrifice of Christ.[46]

In this sense the enactment of the rite is never just the enactment of the rite. The ritual action always points to something more, always invites the participant into something greater than the ritual.

Pott asserts that this understanding of active participation needs to occur on three distinct levels. The first involves the internalization of the mystery of Christ in the faithful. Much in the same line of the thinking as Vagaggini's *sintonia d'anima*, Pott maintains that "every Christian is a real and authentic bearer of the mystery of Christ, and the fact of making them personally aware of that is the first step

---

participation" as simply letting "people do as much as possible." Thus there is a specific agenda set forth by the colloquium to go beyond what they viewed as a misperception of the term. See Jozef Lamberts, "A Colloquium on Active Participation," in *The Active Participation Revisited: La Participation Active 100 ans après Pie X et 40 ans après Vatican II*, ed. Jozef Lamberts (Leuven: Peeters, 2004), 10.

[44] Thomas Pott, "Une réflexion spirituelle et mystagogique renouvelée sur la participation active," in *The Active Participation Revisited*, 70–82, at 76.

[45] Ibid.

[46] Ibid.

toward the restoration of the Christian liturgy as worship in spirit and in truth (John 4,23)."[47] The second level points beyond the personal and incorporates the ecclesial nature of participation. It "is focused on the ecclesial and social form 'of being the Temple of God.' "[48] Here the individual recognizes that the liturgy takes place within the context of the community and directs the individual always outward. Pott asserts that within the context of the church "the liturgy is received here within a person's life as a gift, but also as a mission. In fact, it is much more an accommodation of the person to the liturgy than the contrary."[49] Thus, because the liturgy is the proper expression of the life of faith of the church, the individual believer also becomes aware of his or her connection to the wider church. The third level of participation in Pott's schema centers on the living nature of the liturgy in the life of the faithful. He avers that to participate in the liturgy demands growth in the "awareness that the promotion of the liturgy, its adaptation to the needs of the times and of man, is in our hands."[50] As a living expression of faith, the liturgy is bound to the ecclesial body that celebrates it. Such a responsibility, however, also carries certain demands lest it become self-serving. Pott maintains that "these liturgical adaptations are meaningful only when they accompany a liturgical reform of the inner man."[51]

The import of Pott's assessment comes in his assertion about the nature of liturgy as a whole as determined by his characterization of active participation. Pott argues that the liturgy exists as a special form of reality, one "that cannot be determined or imposed either 'from on high' (from the altar, from the hierarchy) or 'from below' (from the faithful or from the person who accidentally enters the church)."[52] For him the liturgy is iconic (both evoking a reality and making it present) and acting in a symbolic world. Liturgy, when it acts symbolically, demands much more than a textbook or rote conception of the church's ritual actions. Pott argues that the symbolic nature of the liturgy requires, in and of itself, "its own initiation, an appropriation of

[47] Ibid., 77.
[48] Ibid.
[49] Ibid.
[50] Ibid.
[51] Ibid.
[52] Ibid.

the language and of the nature of the symbol which goes much deeper than an intellectual concept."[53]

Even this explanation, he notes, does not suffice. What is required of any true initiation into the understanding of active participation matches the very requirements of mystagogical initiation into the Christian life: a stripping away through purification and enlightenment that leads to an embrace of a new way of living. Pott maintains that nothing imposed from the outside could truly be adequate. Active participation, he argues, "is an irreplaceable dimension of the liturgy, of our 'being liturgy,' and of our 'being in the liturgy.' "[54] He has ostensibly enmeshed the various levels of participation within its core metaphoric meaning: participation at the level of being. Only then can participation be fully realized: "But at each level of this 'being,' deeper within until even more exterior, it has its own characteristics. These characters are organically connected with each other; active participation within the framework of the liturgical celebration—for example, the 'action' of the prayers of the faithful—which is not established on our personal priesthood may be 'truly active' but it is not a 'real participation.' Conversely, communion with the Lord at the altar of our heart that never goes out to encounter the communion at the altar of the community is like a dinner that does not go further than the entrée dish."[55] Active participation in the liturgy implies a way of life, not simply an interior attitude or outward display of ministries and actions within the liturgical celebration.[56]

Similarly, Liliane Voyé moves beyond the typical demarcations of active participation in order to appropriate a fuller sense of the term. Beginning from within her own field of sociology, Voyé explains that participation within a social dynamic has certain inherent problems or challenges. Given any corporate entity, there may be juridical issues about who can or cannot participate, questions about those capable of investing the necessary effort to enter into participation, differences in

[53] Ibid., 78.

[54] Ibid.

[55] Ibid.

[56] Pott uses the example of St. Mary of Egypt, who, after very little ritual experience in the church, goes into the desert for 47 years. At the end of that time she requests the Eucharist from a passing monk but displays knowledge and awareness of the sacrament far beyond her one initial encounter. Pott surmises that she has lived the reality of active participation in the desert.

opportunity, and inequalities in various points of view that may subvert the corporate authority or corporate whole.[57] For this reason, any kind of attempt at fostering participation implies a possible fracturing of the collective body. Voyé asserts:

> Because it leads everyone to express his or her point of view, participation may reveal fractures and lead to "schisms" that heretofore the observance of the authoritarian rule shrouded behind a facade of unanimity, perhaps comfortable in the short term, but potentially dangerous. Thus insofar as it reveals differences of view, if participation rocked the institution, it may also help to renovate and redefine.[58]

When Voyé applies this concept to the ritual action of the church, certain conclusions can be drawn concerning the relationship between and among believers, the church, and the liturgy. First, in order to participate, the individual believer needs to be able to appropriate the rites, understanding "the logic that sustains their production."[59] So Voyé concludes that in order to be accessible to those who desire such participation, the rite itself must be kept open and transparent: "Open—i.e, susceptible to variation and adaptation; transparent, i.e., explained both in its intent and in its form, with the symbols it uses, whose understanding is often much less obvious when they are inserted in other times, other places, and other cultures."[60] Second, Voyé in essence calls for a reform of the rites, and the education and experience surrounding the rites, that will allow for such lucidity and malleability. In doing so she also posits a hierarchy that is motivated less by the imposition of a rite through rules and regulations and more by movement toward the transcendent.[61] In this way the typical tension in a sociological sense of participation may be abrogated because of the proposed end and focus of the ritual action: the transformation of the participants.

---

[57] Liliane Voyé, "Le concept de participation en sociologie et les attentes à l'égard des pratiques rituelles," in *The Active Participation Revisited*, 83–97, at 87–88.

[58] Ibid., 88.

[59] Ibid., 97.

[60] Ibid.

[61] Ibid.

Much as did the Leuven Conference, the Institut Catholique in Paris also initiated a major theological discussion on *actuosa participatio* in 2005 in its theological journal *La Maison-Dieu*.[62] While many of the initial articles in that collection deal with a historical appreciation of the term and its usage, there are two later articles that are worthy of note here. The first, by Olivier de Cagny, traces the euchological significance of participation in the Roman Missal,[63] while the second, by Patrick Prétot, encourages the theologian to rediscover the concept of active participation in the wake of varying interpretations after the council.[64]

Olivier de Cagny asserts that a primary source for understanding the multivalent concept of participation lies in the euchological witness of Paul VI's *Missale Romanum*. He maintains that the corpus of prayers within the *Missale* points to five typical expressions for participation in the liturgy: *participatio, consortium, commercium, societas,* and *communio*.[65] These expressions, while having specific meanings of their own, create a field of meaning for the concept of participation when they are used within the prayer tradition. He notes that each represents a specific facet or nuance of meaning for understanding liturgical participation. For instance, he maintains that within the euchology of the *Missale* the word *consortium* implies that through the Eucharist the human person shares in (participates in) the destiny of the Son of God, namely, that the derivative forms of *consors* "designate a personal communion with God in reference to the mystery of the New Covenant, through which God gives to humanity a share in his proper nature."[66] In similar fashion he describes how each of the

---

[62] It should be noted that these collections of essays are not insular to each institution or region but typically appeal to a wide base of scholarship. In fact, Josef Lamberts, who edited the collection for the Leuven Conference, submitted a historical assessment of the concept of *actuosa participatio* for the Parisian collection as well.

[63] Olivier de Cagny, "La notion de participation dans l'euchologie du Missel Romain," *La Maison-Dieu* 241 (2005): 121–35.

[64] Patrick Prétot, "Retrouver la 'participation active,' une tâche pour aujourd'hui," *La Maison-Dieu* 241 (2005): 151–77.

[65] "La notion de participation," 125.

[66] Ibid., 127. In this case de Cagny cites specifically the Prayer after Communion for the Saturday of the Second Week of Lent, the second preface of the ritual Mass for Marriage, and the third preface for the Nativity.

various terms can illustrate a different meaning or understanding of *participatio: commercium* shows that the Eucharist is a holy exchange between God and humanity that leads to transformation or diviniza-tion; *societas* describes the union of the earthly liturgy with the heav-enly one; *communio* refers to the purpose behind the reception of the Body and Blood of Christ, which is the unification of the recipient with the Mystical Body, namely, participation in the sanctifying reality of the church.[67]

De Cagny uses these various euchological examples to conclude that the theology of the liturgy implies a threefold sense of participa-tion that is "essentially a conjunction of the life of the faithful with the very life of God."[68] Participation, for de Cagny, from its euchological witness implies an "offering of the interior self with the unique sacri-fice of Christ, the transformation of the human nature truly associated with the divine nature, and the germination of eternal life."[69] What de Cagny indicates cogently is that the very *lex orandi* of the church admits that the theology of participation is not univocal but rather elu-cidates various shades of meaning and interpretation.

In his subsequent article Patrick Prétot asserts that what is necessary for the church at present is to rediscover the true meaning of partici-pation, which has been occluded by a pastoral practice that perhaps assumes its meaning. Tracing the term *participatio* through its historical usage (although in a limited way), Prétot then notes that several es-sential aspects of the term come to light in *Sacrosanctum Concilium* (a stance that is somewhat problematic since *participatio* appears, as we have seen, in many other documents from the council). For instance, he asserts that if one takes seriously the declarations of SC 14 and 48 one must admit that "to the extent that participation is required by the 'nature of the liturgy itself,' it derives from baptism and is a right and duty for Christians; it refers, in fact, to the exercise of the priest-hood of Christ that is continued in the assembly. If so, the efficacy of the sacrament cannot be conceived without taking this principle into account."[70] Moreover, derived from this notion of participation is an ecclesiological sense of participation made popular by Yves

[67] Ibid., 128–31.
[68] Ibid., 135.
[69] Ibid.
[70] Prétot, "Retrouver la 'participation active,' une tâche pour aujourd'hui," 166.

Congar—that the gathered assembly is the subject of the liturgical action. Prétot maintains that this idea of participation helps solidify the understanding of the liturgy as the manifestation of the mystery of the church. Finally, he argues that participation also has a profound connection to the theology of Christian worship and especially to its trinitarian dimension because participation, by its nature, refers to the pneumatological effect in the liturgy, namely, that active participation is the ultimate sign of the work of the Spirit within the church.[71]

But while Prétot recognizes the various ways in which a theology of participation can be understood, he also notes that there are certain present difficulties in inculcating this theology in the faithful. He argues that in the decades after the council the contemporary culture has tended to favor an exterior understanding of participation over an interior one. Moreover, this misconception has often led to what he calls the "distribution of roles" within the liturgy, namely, that active participation has been relegated to the activity of a few at the risk of leaving much of the assembly as external spectators.[72] In agreement with Jean-Yves Hameline, Prétot asserts that there is a danger in forgetting that the council called for active and *conscious* participation: "the risk of confusion between 'conscious participation' and being 'conscious of participation' is real."[73] To alleviate this risk Prétot proposes that active participation should correspond to a certain spirit, "a manner of living," that pervades not only the liturgical action but the Christian life as well. Thus active participation can never have simply one form; it links together multiple variations related to situations, groups, persons, and mentalities.[74]

Finally, one can also point to various clusters of articles in *Rivista Liturgica* and the eighteenth volume of Monumenta Studia

---

[71] Ibid., 166–67.

[72] Ibid., 172–73.

[73] Ibid., 174. Prétot acknowledges his debt to Hameline for often writing about this confusion between "conscious participation" and being "conscious of" or "aware of" participation. See specifically the following articles: "Viollet-le-Duc et le movement liturgique au XIXe siècle," *La Maison-Dieu* 142 (1980): 57–86; "Les *Origines du culte chrétien* et le movement liturgique," *La Maison-Dieu* 181 (1990): 51–96; "Le culte chrétien dans son espace de sensibilité," *La Maison-Dieu* 187 (1991): 7–45; "Observations sur nos manières de célébrer," *La Maison-Dieu* 192 (1992): 7–24.

[74] Ibid., 176.

Instrumenta Liturgica (MSIL) to show that the variety of current scholarship on *actuosa participatio* stretches through the theological gamut. Published in 2002, the MSIL edition was a collection of essays in honor of Domenic Sartore and used *actuosa participatio* as the title and central focus of the *Festschrift*. Over forty articles appear within the massive tome, ranging in scope from how a monastic community approaches liturgy differently than a parochial community to the application of René Girard's anthropology on the liturgical action, and even including the role of the organist in the celebration of a sung liturgy. Following the publication of this volume, *Rivista Liturgica* also occasionally contained articles on *actuosa participatio* in 2003 and 2006. For the focus of this study only the work of Achille Triacca is immediately significant.

In his article " 'Partecipazione': Quale aggettivo meglio la qualifica in ambito liturgico?" Triacca attempts to seek clarification of the term *participatio* as it is used in relation to the liturgy. Its standard rendition as "active participation" appears to lack a definitive meaning. He asserts: "There emerges once again a certain confusion or . . . an equivocal homologization of the term *participatio* made within the same ecclesiastical language. Even now it is noted, in the context of that which you are saying, that it is extremely difficult to bring (back) the term *actuosa participatio* into the primitive fount which is trinitarian theology."[75] In the case of *actuosa participatio* Triacca maintains that the connection it makes to the divine life necessitates that the term not be understood in an exterior modality, but rather that such participation in the divine life happens through the sacraments and thus the most appropriate nuancing of the term must be from a liturgical-sacramental reality.[76] Triacca investigates the liturgical motif of participation as thoroughly as he can, citing its root in the mystery being celebrated and in the relationship among the ministers, the faithful, and the divine action. In the end Triacca seems to suggest that the most proper way of qualifying *participatio* is not from the misunderstood modifier *actuosa* but rather from a series of adjectives he gradually constructs. Because the sacramental liturgy is a foretaste of the heavenly liturgy and the

---

[75] Achille M. Triacca, "'Partecipazione': Quale aggettivo meglio la qualifica in ambito liturgico?" in *Actuosa Participatio: Conoscere, comprendere e vivere la Liturgia, Studi in onore del Prof. Domenico Sartore, csj*, ed. Agostino Montan and Manlio Sodi (Vatican City: Libreria Editrice Vaticana, 2002), 573–85, at 575.

[76] Ibid., 575–76.

means by which the faithful are brought into the divine life, Triacca asserts that participation must be understood in an iconic-trinitarian sense.[77] But he also notes that this representation imposes a further qualification on the theologian and the believer. He asserts:

> In this sense the participation in the celebration can only be described as iconic, because it becomes the earthly image-icon of participation in the heavenly liturgy, and trinitarian because it rediscovers that the trinitarian life is the starting point of this same participation and its arrival point. Along the same line, participation in the present is always projected into the future, toward the salvific *eschaton*. The participation happens in the present but already has its offshoots in the future. It might therefore be possible to characterize participation with multiple adjectives: an eschatological-iconic-trinitarian participation.[78]

In the end Triacca notes that such a multivalent sense of participation is perhaps better for both the theologian and the believer. It allows the theologian a broader locus for study and understanding but it also affords the believer a doorway into the greater mystery that is being celebrated and lived.

What becomes obvious for the theologian at the beginning of the twenty-first century is that the theological understanding of participation in the liturgy is hardly codified. Just as the initial occurrence of *actuosa participatio* in 1903 was developed and augmented by later pontifical and conciliar decrees, so now the theology surrounding that phrase is opening up to various modes of interpretation and meaning. The last section of this book will propose a possible line of development for a trinitarian theology of liturgical participation.

[77] Ibid., 582.
[78] Ibid.

Chapter 5

Toward a Trinitarian Theology of Liturgical Participation

Given the contributions of both Kilmartin and Vagaggini, and the various articulations of the idea of active participation in the last few years, one can begin to assess the components of a theological method that can move the church toward a more complete trinitarian theology of liturgical participation. The two primary premises on which this study began—the intricacy of the complex of metaphors surrounding the concept of participation and the articulation of trinitarian action within the sacramental-liturgical act—certainly lie at the center of such a determination. Kilmartin and Vagaggini also point to the use of the liturgical sources as a theological locus, and this also must be taken into consideration. Our final analysis, then, will make some general comments about the necessary methodological restrictions in developing a trinitarian theology of liturgical participation and then look specifically at three ways in which a trinitarian theology can be augmented in the future—namely, the examination of full initiation texts to ascertain the trinitarian dynamic, a recognition of the active presence of the triune persons in the sacramental action, and the admission of a final metaphoric base of participation in the order of purpose.

The parameters and scope of a trinitarian theology of liturgical participation must attain a balance between and among the various metaphors of participation. A theology of active participation in the liturgy cannot isolate its metaphysical, soteriological, or ecclesiological meaning and somehow still remain unaffected. There is a necessary interpenetration of the terms (and their respective meanings). Participation in God implies a participation in grace; a participation in grace implies a participation in the church; a participation in the church implies a participation in its liturgy. The converse is, as we have seen, equally true: a participation in the liturgy leads to participation in

God. Given the necessary balancing act here, one cannot deny the fundamental need for liturgical catechesis especially in understanding the various ways in which the faithful participate in the liturgical action. While much debate has centered on the need for both external and internal participation, what is more necessary is a cogent catechetical framework for understanding the *kind* of external and internal participation the liturgy demands. Louis-Marie Chauvet's insistence on a liturgical language that might aid such a framework is not without warrant or merit. The Roman Catholic Church in the United States is a prime example of this: the promulgation of a new translation of the *Missale Romanum* in November 2011 brought with it an unprecedented awareness of just how much believers lacked a language with which to discuss the liturgy, let alone engage in it.

Inasmuch as a new and articulate theological framework is necessary for the faithful to develop a fuller understanding of a trinitarian theology of liturgical participation, the theologian is also bound by certain strictures as that theology is formed and developed. Given the necessary balancing of the various metaphors of participation, the theologian is equally required to ensure the interplay of those terms in his or her method. As we have seen, those metaphoric understandings of participation are undergirded by a trinitarian narrative that also reflects the economy of salvation history. It is impossible to speak about liturgical action without also speaking about the work or action of the Trinity in the economy of salvation. Thus the theologian is equally bound to speak about that trinitarian action both within the confines of revealed doctrine and in the necessary speculation about divine action where that doctrine is found wanting.

Certainly the recent *Catechism* acts as a starting point or reference for where to begin. But the *Catechism* is also marked by its brevity and lack of detail. It is the theologian's task to provide coherent and cogent possibilities for understanding the link between the active participation of the faithful and the work of the Trinity in the liturgy. This task is made more arduous by the simple fact that the language of trinitarian theology is often convoluted, jargon-laden, and esoteric. Ask the average believer about the possible generation or spiration of Persons in the Trinity or the meaning of "circumincession" and the typical response will be simply a quizzical, if not perturbed, look.

A case can be made here as well for the value of liturgical sources as a starting point. In his 2007 apostolic exhortation, "Sacramentum Caritatis," Pope Benedict XVI provided a methodological approach to mystagogical catechesis that emphasized both a theological and experiential understanding of the liturgy.[1] The pontiff explains that the initial experience of the liturgy needs to be augmented by catechesis that interprets the rites in the light of salvation history, explains the various signs used in the rites, and elucidates the significance and meaning of the rites for Christian living. There is an implicit acceptance here that theological understanding leads to greater participation in the liturgy; both exterior and interior. In a similar vein Archbishop Piero Marini, former master of papal liturgical celebrations (1987–2007), wrote on the importance of looking to the sources of liturgical texts. He argues that "Scripture, the Fathers and the liturgical sources are not simply testimonies of past history, a subject of archaeological interest; they are *testimonials*, in the deepest sense of the term, of a lived story between God and his people. They are the knots in the woven fabric of which we are the newest threads striving to interlace with one another to form new cloth."[2] The validity in looking at liturgical sources lies in the testimonial witness to the truths of faith—*lex orandi, lex credendi*—and the fact that these sources reveal something fundamental about the nature of the celebration itself. Marini continues: "Digging deep into the sources, the theologian and the liturgist aim simply to penetrate the profundity of the mystery of the faith as it has shown itself in the concrete life of the Church all through her history."[3]

Both Vagaggini and Kilmartin followed predictable trajectories in seeking the sources for their theological understanding of liturgical participation—that is, they took the classical model of looking first at the New Testament, then the early church fathers, and then the liturgical sources themselves. It is in their explication and analysis of the various liturgical sources that they depart from each other.

An analysis of the writings of Vagaggini and Kilmartin has the potential of becoming amorphous and unwieldy since both theologians created whole systems of thought in relation to sacramental action,

---

[1] Pope Benedict XVI, "Sacramentum Caritatis," AAS 99, no. 3 (2007), 105–80, §64.

[2] Piero Marini, "Ritorno alle fonti a servizio della liturgia," in *Simposio sulla collana Monumenta Liturgica Tridentini Concilii* (Salesian Institute "S. Cuore," 23 March 2006). This brief article can be found at: http://www.vatican.va/news _services/liturgy/2006/documents/ns_lit_doc_20060323_ritorno-fonti_ en.html (accessed 10 June 2008).

[3] Ibid.

participation, and the self-communication of the Trinity. The critique offered here necessarily limits the discussion to the central question: how does any theology of liturgical participation help elucidate the notion of *why* such participation is crucial for both the life of the individual and the life of the church? In this case both theologies of liturgical participation center on the connection between trinitarian activity and sacramental action. Vagaggini and Kilmartin, to differing degrees and with varying emphases, brought these elements to the foreground in the development of their own approaches to liturgical participation. In order to evaluate adequately the writings of both theologians one must consider the following: their starting points in the liturgical sources of the early church, the consistency between their writings and the trinitarian theology espoused by the Second Vatican Council (especially in relation to the sacraments), and each theologian's attempt to demarcate a theology of liturgical participation for the faithful that maintains the multivalent understanding of participation itself. Thus this analysis will critique both methodologies and then look at a possible solution or direction in which a new methodology may emerge.

Trinitarian Theology and Liturgical Participation in the Early Sources of Initiation

Both Vagaggini and Kilmartin looked to early liturgical sources to articulate a trinitarian reference to the sacramental action of the Eucharist. Vagaggini ascertained a christological-trinitarian dynamic inherent in the liturgy and then identified that dynamic within the various prayer structures of the sacrament, while Kilmartin determined that the content and function of the prayers were decidedly trinitarian and self-communicative of God. However, neither Vagaggini nor Kilmartin took into account the full breadth and value of initiation sources in the early church. For the most part they confined their studies to eucharistic texts.

Vagaggini's demonstrable starting point is the complexus of signs that makes up the liturgical action. Within that complexus he identifies the major role liturgical sources play in his determination of the christological-trinitarian schema that became the hallmark of his theology of liturgical participation. In the course of his tome, *Il senso teologico della liturgia*, Vagaggini traversed three major groups of liturgical texts: orations and collects, doxologies, and anaphoras. It was through this triad of texts that Vagaggini wished to exemplify the christological-trinitarian schema. However, some of his analysis of the sources is either lacking concrete evidence or is, at least in a few cases, flawed. In discussing the ancient orations and collects Vagaggini relied heavily on the work of Joseph Jungmann.[4] Following Jungmann's analysis, Vagaggini asserted that the orations follow a general rule of orientation: namely, that the "rule noted well from the ancient tradition is that the liturgical orations are directed to the Father, through the mediation of Jesus Christ, our supreme mediator."[5] However, two distinct problems emerge from Vagaggini's recourse to this rule. First, he cites the rule as it was formulated at the Council of Hippo (393),[6] a regional synod whose decrees had force and application only within a local region. It can hardly be deemed "universal and absolute."[7] In fact, the African synods and councils of the fourth century often looked to Rome for guidance and clarification. At the Council of Carthage (397), where the same rule was reiterated, direct reference was also made to the verification and authentication that Roman pronouncements could provide. For instance, in determining the scriptural canon the council added: "But let the Church beyond the sea (Rome) be consulted about confirming this canon."[8] Perhaps more problematic is that there is

---

[4] Joseph Jungmann, *Die Stellung Christi im liturgischen Gebet.* Liturgiewissenschaftliche Quellen und Forschungen 19/20 (Münster: Aschendorf, 1962). While Vagaggini repeatedly cites Jungmann's text, he does not actually provide examples from Jungmann's research, so he repeatedly makes claims the reader is forced to accept on the basis of Jungmann's name alone. All further references to Jungmann's work will be to the accepted English translation by A. J. Peeler.

[5] Cipriano Vagaggini, *Il senso teologico della liturgia: saggio di liturgia teologica generale* (Rome: Edizioni Paoline, 1965), 212.

[6] Vagaggini, however, does not cite the original text from the Council of Hippo, which states, *Ut nemo in precibus vel Patrem pro Filio vel Filium pro Patre nominet. Et cum altari assistitur, semper ad Patrem dirigatur oratio. Et quicumque sibi preces aliunde describit, non eis utatur, nisi prius eas cum instructioribus fratribus contulerit.* ("Let no one in praying rename either the Father by the Son or the Son by the Father, and prayer at the altar is always to be addressed to the Father; and whoever copies down prayers for his use, from some other source, is not to say them unless he has first shown them to more well-instructed brethren.") See also Charles Munier, *Concilia Africae, 345–525*, CCL 149 (Turnhout: Brepols, 1991), 39.

[7] *Il senso teologico* (1965), 212.

[8] Munier, *Concilia Africae*, 43. See Canon 36.c: *Ita ut de confirmando isto canone transmarina ecclesia consultatur.*

no indication that collects were even used in the liturgy of Northern Africa. What Vagaggini fails to see here is the multiplicity of acceptable forms and prayers in the early centuries of the church.[9] Recent scholarship notes that the very existence of a rule formulated by the African council suggests the opposite of what Vagaggini posits. Paul Bradshaw asserts: "The fact that North African legislation at the end of the fourth century finds it necessary to stipulate, 'let no one in prayers name either the Father instead of the Son, or the Son instead of the Father; and when one stands at the altar, let prayer always be directed to the Father,' demonstrates just how widespread and persistent the practice was."[10] It is somewhat dubious to suppose that the formulation of a liturgical rule would have manifested itself in anticipation of a doctrinal error in a prayer form that did not yet exist.

Second, Vagaggini misinterpreted Jungmann's citation of the "ancient rule" from the Council of Hippo. Jungmann first mentions this pronouncement not in relation to the *orationes* (by which he means the collects, *secreta* prayers, and the post-communion prayers), but in connection with the *Praefatio*.[11] Only after he has made this initial connection to the Preface prayers does Jungmann admit that it can also be applied to the *orationes* of the Leonine and Gelasian sacramentaries. The uncertainty of the application of the rule appears in the Aachen version of the Gregorian sacramentary, where some collects for the Masses of Advent appear as addressed to Christ. Once the rule had been broken, the number of collects addressed to Christ increased so that by the time of the *Missale Romanum* (1924) more than one-quarter

---

[9] A. G. Martimort asserts that acceptance of diverse liturgical forms was such a norm in the early church that St. Gregory the Great formulated the principle that "as long as there is unity in faith, diversity in usage is not detrimental to Holy Church (*in una fide, nihil officit sanctae Ecclesiae consuetude diversa*)." See Irénée-Henri Dalmais, et al., eds., *Principles of the Liturgy. The Church at Prayer*, vol. 1 (Collegeville, MN: Liturgical Press, 1987), 118. See also Paul Bradshaw, "God, Christ, and the Holy Spirit in Early Christian Praying," in *The Place of Christ in Liturgical Prayer: Trinity, Christology, and Liturgical Theology*, ed. Brian D. Spinks (Collegeville, MN: Liturgical Press, 2008), 51–64, at 53.

[10] Bradshaw, "God, Christ, and the Holy Spirit in Early Christian Praying," 57–58.

[11] Joseph Jungmann, *The Place of Christ in Liturgical Prayer*, trans. A. J. Peeler, 2d rev. ed. (Staten Island, NY: Alba House, 1965), 114.

of the collects either express or imply a direct address to Christ.[12] Also, one is forced to recognize that Vagaggini was seemingly relying on evidence from the sacramentary tradition that is much later than the time period he wished to analyze. In fact, most of his cited examples are commentaries on liturgical texts and practices, necessarily so since few actual texts of the liturgy itself are extant from the early church.

Dependency on Jungmann is less apparent in Vagaggini's analysis of the anaphora. In fact, in his later work on the reform of the Canon he looked more to his own insight than to the opinions of others. Surprisingly, Vagaggini's consideration of the evidence of the eucharistic anaphoras is sparse. In *Il senso teologico* he presents a detail of the Canon of Hippolytus and then makes only cursory comments regarding other eucharistic prayers in the following centuries before tackling the Roman Canon.[13] The lack of evidence from the various liturgical sources of the first few centuries is a serious flaw in Vagaggini's method. It also appears that Vagaggini chose to follow the demarcation of Mario Righetti in his compilation of the various sources of the early eucharistic liturgies, despite criticizing the same text for lacking "a panoramic view of the development of the liturgy in all its constituent elements according to the different epochs."[14] Ironically, Philippe Rouillard notes this same lack in his own critique of *Il senso teologico*, citing Vagaggini's willingness to rely on the scholarship of others. Rouillard argues: "In more than one case, however, one has the impression that the documentation is incomplete or performed a little too quickly."[15] Commenting on the first edition of Vagaggini's *Il senso teologico*, and aware that a second edition was about to be published,

[12] Ibid., 114–21. Jungmann details the collects (*orationes*) addressed to Christ in the MR 1924 on p. 116.

[13] The English translation of the 1965 Italian original is especially problematic in the discussion of the anaphoras. The English makes a comparison between the Roman Canon (Eucharistic Prayer I) and the newly formed anaphoras of the Pauline Missal (Eucharistic Prayers II, III, and IV). Obviously such prayers had not been formed yet at the time Vagaggini wrote, and since Vagaggini was a major architect of the prayers it seems somewhat dubious, at best, from an evidentiary standpoint for the English editor to use them as a way of cementing Vagaggini's thesis.

[14] *Il senso teologico* (1965), 9.

[15] Philippe Rouillard, "Une initiation théologique à la liturgie," *Les Questions Liturgiques et Paroissiales* 39 (1958): 215–20, at 218.

Rouillard noted that many of the shortcomings inherent in the analysis of the liturgical sources, especially in regard to Vagaggini's treatment of the individual sacraments, could be rectified in future editions. While Vagaggini did make some corrections and emendations in his revisions, the final edition shows little change from the original text other than the improvement of some of the footnotes.[16]

Vagaggini's assessment of the Western anaphoras, especially the Roman Canon, in relation to his own christological-trinitarian schema also displays certain inadequacies. This can be seen both in *Il senso teologico* and in his more direct treatment of the Roman Canon in *Il canone della messa e la riforma liturgica*. He admitted that a number of variants are at work in any attempt to establish a working text of the Roman Canon.[17] What is problematic for his analysis is that the majority of the texts that help exemplify his trinitarian model are found only in the variant fragments. For instance, those parts of the "reconstructed" Roman Canon that apply to the Holy Spirit are either speculatively added or exist in the Mozarabic texts, the *Missale Gothicum*, or the Fulgentius text.[18] Without these added elements of the canon it would be difficult to ascertain the christological-trinitarian structure of the anaphora unless one also admits certain preconditions or suppositions about the nature of the liturgy and its purpose. Moreover, the widely accepted notion that the Roman Canon as it existed in the mid-1960s

---

[16] Compare Vagaggini's 1957 version (pp. 186–91) with his 1965 version (pp. 229–35). What is seemingly unexplainable is that Vagaggini responded to Rouillard's critique in the second edition of 1958 and included various references to Eastern sources mentioned in Rouillard's review but then dropped all mention of them in the 1965 edition.

[17] See Vagaggini, *Il canone delle messa e la riforma liturgica: probleme e progetti* (Turin: Leuman, 1966), 28–34; idem, *Il senso teologico* (1965), 225–29. Because early commentaries on the eucharistic celebration often describe elements of the Roman Canon that do not exist in the form that has been passed down through the Sacramentary tradition, Vagaggini posits that there was a fundamental Roman text that predated the Canon used in the Pian Missal. Historical and comparative studies "show that the canon underwent a profound change during this period (fifth to seventh centuries), a change that, ultimately, was very unfortunate. This must in fact have significantly disrupted the primitive text, or at least it must have aggravated the tendential defects already inherent in it." Vagaggini, *Il canone delle messa e la riforma liturgica: probleme e progetti*, 11.

[18] Ibid., 31–33.

was necessarily a hybrid form of a prayer from varying traditions makes it difficult to posit an intentional structure in its formulation. Vagaggini himself admits: "The current Roman canon stands out as a patchwork of many prayers juxtaposed with each other, whose unity and logical connection are difficult to comprehend, even by specialists."[19] In the absence of such logical coherence and unity the fullness of the christological-trinitarian motif Vagaggini suggests is less obvious. While it is evident that "with respect to the Father and to Christ, the christological-trinitarian perspective expressed by the *ad, per, ad* schema, in its view of salvation history, is not less evident than it is in the anaphoras of Hippolytus or in the oriental anaphoras,"[20] such a motif does not seem to manifest itself as readily with respect to the Holy Spirit. Vagaggini's method, then, is somewhat problematic since he limits himself to the fairly predetermined formula of the christological-trinitarian schema and insists on its presence in spite of occasional evidence to the contrary.

In his own way Edward Kilmartin also sought to identify what is unique to the liturgy by looking specifically at the New Testament accounts of the Lord's Supper and the various texts of the early church that show a development of a more formal eucharistic prayer. His preoccupation with the content and structure of the early liturgical sources allowed him to use the operational dynamic he found within the liturgical celebration as his starting point for understanding human participation in the sacraments. The sheer breadth and depth of Kilmartin's look into the content, structure, and function of the early eucharistic prayers far surpasses what Vagaggini presented in his various writings. At the same time, however, Kilmartin's work in this early period of his career was often not scrutinized by his peers.[21]

---

[19] Ibid., 71.

[20] *Il senso teologico* (1965), 227.

[21] No formal response appears to either of Kilmartin's articles on the content and function of the early eucharistic prayers (one in the collection of essays, *The Word in the World*, and the other appearing in *Theological Studies*). The first had an extremely limited publication and audience (of the 170 known copies still in research institutions, only 12 exist outside North America). His other main work on this topic, *The Eucharist in the Primitive Church*, written much earlier, is primarily a derivative text based on the research of other biblical theologians, and the reviews that appeared shortly after its publication tend to highlight Kilmartin's ability to synthesize other theologians' material.

Still, what Kilmartin does bring to the discussion is worth noting here because of the insight he garnered from his look at the liturgical sources of the early church. Unlike Vagaggini, who determined a central schema for liturgical prayer and then tried to identify that schema within the early sources, Kilmartin appears to have begun with an intensive investigation of the sources themselves to see if they elicit any kind of pattern or motif. What he found is the *sacrificium laudis* of the church, the sacrifice of praise that forms the content and function of the early liturgy. A careful assessment of Kilmartin's approach is needed here.

Kilmartin asserted that the theology that developed around and in the early eucharistic anaphoras displays both a malleability and a consistency: although the literary and liturgical traditions may vary over time, there is a certain maintenance of the import and impact of the anaphoras through the first few centuries of the church's existence. A thorough analysis of Kilmartin's use of liturgical sources must look at both his treatment of the Last Supper narratives (as precursors to the anaphoras) and the development he traces through the early eucharistic anaphoras themselves.

One of the primary models for Kilmartin's analysis was shaped by his research on the Last Supper of Jesus as it is presented in the New Testament. A fundamental issue here is that the Last Supper narratives only appeared in written form after a liturgical experience had also developed within the early church. The retelling of the story of the "night before he died" exists only in light of the passion and resurrection of Christ. In this sense the Lord's Supper of the celebration of the Eucharist informs the retelling of the Last Supper. Xavier Léon-Dufour noted that all the New Testament accounts of the Last Supper were "influenced by the liturgy that was celebrated in the various ecclesial communities."[22] For instance, the Pauline account clearly shows that the apostle seeks to correct certain abuses that have become manifest in the Corinthian community's gathering for and celebration of the Eucharist.[23] The vast majority of Kilmartin's exegesis does not take into account the plethora of research that was produced in the late 1970s and 1980s regarding the historical accuracy of the Last Supper

[22] Xavier Léon-Dufour, SJ, *Sharing the Eucharistic Bread*, trans. Matthew J. O'Connell (Mahwah, NJ: Paulist Press, 1987), 83.

[23] Ibid., 82–84.

accounts and the various attempts to ascertain the intention of Christ from the textual evidence of the accounts.[24] These contemporary exegetes, in their multiple quests for the "historical Jesus," provide a more accurate framework in which to examine the Last Supper narrative and its implications for the development of the eucharistic anaphoras. As noted earlier, Kilmartin maintained that the Last Supper accounts reveal that Jesus intended to establish a covenantal relationship with those who kept the memorial he offered. That covenant relationship was founded on the notion of a participation in his body and blood, as seen in the Pauline account of the Last Supper. The vast amount of research contemporary with Kilmartin, however, presents a much more complex motif to the Last Supper narratives even if the basic conclusion—the establishment of a covenant with the community of Jesus' disciples—still holds true.

Kilmartin derived his hypothesis regarding the Last Supper accounts from the dissertation work of Cesare Giraudo, namely, *La struttura letteraria della preghiera eucharistica* (1981). While Giraudo's work is viewed as foundational for modern scholarship, his analysis is limited by its adherence to a strictly literary assessment of the Last Supper narrative and the early eucharistic prayers.[25] What is needed here

[24] All of Kilmartin's work on the content and structure of the prayer of the Last Supper and the early anaphoras was completed by 1974. His later, more detailed analyses of eucharistic and liturgical theology in *Christian Liturgy*, "Theology of the Sacraments," "A Modern Approach," and *The Eucharist in the West* do not take into account the later research of New Testament scholars. Only "A Modern Approach" has a detailed section on the significance of the Last Supper/the Lord's Supper, but this section makes no mention of contemporary scholarship. Kilmartin seems to base most of his post-1975 scholarship on the early Eucharist on Cesare Giraudo's work, *La struttura letteraria della preghiera eucharistica: Saggio sulla genesi letteraria di una forma: tôdâ veterotestamentaria, berakâ giudaica, anafora cristiana*. Robert Daly, in his introduction to *The Eucharist in the West*, notes that this proclivity of Kilmartin to rely heavily on the work of one or two contemporary scholars is a flaw in his method. See *The Eucharist in the West*, xxi.

[25] Kilmartin seems also to have been influenced in his last few publications by Giraudo's later work, *Eucaristia per la chiesa*. See Cesare Giraudo, *Eucaristia per la chiesa: Prospettive theologiche sull'eucharistia a partire dalla "lex orandi,"* Aloisiana 22 (Rome: Gregorian University, 1989). Thomas Talley is especially critical of Giraudo's approach, noting his preference for categorizing all early eucharistic prayers into one of two forms. See also Thomas Talley, "The

is not a complete summarization of the entirety of the research surrounding the Last Supper narratives in the mid-1970s and 1980s, but a willingness to realize that the Kilmartin-Giraudo assessment cannot be viewed as the only portrayal of the literary historicity of the narratives. For instance, Léon-Dufour augments Giraudo's interpretation of the Last Supper narratives in order to produce what he calls a synchronic reading of the various texts.[26] Léon-Dufour takes into consideration that the form and structure of the early narrative could be assessed in terms of how various thematic elements come to the foreground in producing a hermeneutic of interpretation. He articulates a series of three relationships manifested in the Last Supper narrative that have to be looked at synchronically: the relationship of Jesus, the God-man, to both creation (as man) and divinity (as God), his relationship to the disciples and the multitudes who follow, and his relationship to time (both his past and the future that is about to unfold).[27] In each case Jesus' words and actions in the Last Supper narrative form the essential crux of the respective relationship. Léon-Dufour asserts that when the three relationships are regarded simultaneously a dynamic structure to the narrative becomes evident. This structure helps exemplify the transformative change that takes place in those who partake in the supper. Communion is established through the giving (gift) of Christ; the gift of communion leads to covenant with those who are gathered; and, explicating the passion and resurrection of Christ, the supper forms an ecclesial reality of church.[28] When such a synchronic approach is coupled with the more common diachronic reading of the Supper narratives a fuller sense of the purpose and intent of the narratives appears.

One other difficulty arises within Kilmartin's study. Because he relied so heavily on the work of Giraudo, Kilmartin produced a theological assessment of the early eucharistic sources that is limited by Giraudo's literary parameters. Kilmartin often envisions a somewhat organic development within the various eucharistic anaphoras of the first few centuries, but such an assessment is not without opposition.

Literary Structure of the Eucharistic Prayer," *Worship* 58 (1984): 404–20, at 408–19.

[26] Léon-Dufour, *Sharing the Eucharistic Bread*, 46–76.

[27] Ibid., 54–55.

[28] Ibid., 76.

The genius of Kilmartin's methodology lay in his use of the liturgical sources to provide the nexus for understanding how the faithful participate in and are present to the saving acts of Christ in the sacramental experience. Whereas Vagaggini used the early liturgical sources to demonstrate the existence of a christological-trinitarian dynamic, Kilmartin used the content of the early eucharistic prayer texts as a theological starting point in order to determine a viable connection between sacramental presence, faith, and trinitarian action. Commenting on Kilmartin's theology, Edward Hahnenberg notes that "[i]n liturgical celebration, the faithful are rendered present in memory to the self-offering of the Son, an actualization of faith that is nothing less than an incorporation into the trinitarian dynamic of self-gift and response."[29] What Kilmartin identified in the liturgical sources of the early eucharistic prayers, especially in the *Didache* and the works of Justin Martyr, is that the immediate function of the early prayers is to make present the redemptive acts of Christ.[30] In doing so he drew an inherent connection between anamnesis and epiclesis. Kilmartin noted that the early liturgical sources show that the function of the institution narrative cannot be divorced from its position in the rest of the eucharistic prayer: the anamnesis of the narrative necessarily takes on epicletic overtones. In this sense memory through anamnesis leads to presence through the invocation of the Spirit. All anamnesis is epicletic.

In his analysis of Kilmartin's thought Jerome Hall explains how Kilmartin's use of the liturgical sources helps to reorient the discussion of mystery-presence by reevaluating the role of memory in the liturgical act. Hall comments: "In the prayer of memory, then, the Holy Spirit makes Christians present to the mysteries of Christ's humanity."[31] Such a demarcation differs from Odo Casel's notion of

[29] Edward P. Hahnenberg, "The Ministerial Priesthood and Liturgical Anamnesis in the Thought of Edward J. Kilmartin, S.J.," *Theological Studies* 66 (2005), 253–78, at 270.

[30] See especially Edward J. Kilmartin, "The Eucharistic Prayer: Content and Function in Some Early Eucharistic Prayers," in *Word in the World*, ed. Richard J. Clifford and George MacRae (Cambridge, MA: Weston College Press, 1973), 117–34, at 125; idem, "*Sacrificium Laudis*: Content and Function of Early Eucharistic Prayers," *Theological Studies* 35 (1974): 268–87, at 276–77.

[31] Jerome M. Hall, SJ, *We Have the Mind of Christ: The Holy Spirit and Liturgical Memory in the Thought of Edward J. Kilmartin* (Collegeville, MN: Liturgical Press, 2001), 144.

"mystery presence," whereby the sacrifice of Christ is made present to believers who then accept it in faith. Instead, Hall notes that Kilmartin sees within the early liturgical texts a way of broadening Casel's original (and controversial) stance: the liturgy does not simply reveal the mystery presence of Christ; rather, the mystery is inherently trinitarian. Because the early prayer texts highlight the activity of the Holy Spirit that is revealed in Christ, Kilmartin posits a mystery presence that is rooted in the self-communication of the paschal mystery. Hall explains: "The prayer texts, Kilmartin argued, teach that the church's liturgical celebrations are events in which, through the medium of the interpersonal action of the celebration of faith, the Holy Spirit manifests Christ, and therefore manifests the trinitarian self-communication accomplished and revealed through the history of Christ's humanity."[32] Kilmartin recognizes that, at its root, the Christian liturgy reflects the trinitarian life *ad extra* as it operates in the economy of salvation. In this sense he has not attempted to inscribe a trinitarian motif on the early liturgical sources. Instead, he looks at how those sources are meant to function within a liturgical setting: the early church believed that Jesus intended his death to be the means by which the Father could impart the faith of Christ to believers through the Spirit, so that believers, in turn, could respond in union with Christ. The *sacrificium laudis* of the church is "undertaken with a view to obtaining deeper communion with the Father, especially through the sacrament of the humanity of Christ."[33] The liturgical act of praise and thanksgiving is the offering, in memorial, that reveals and makes present the faith of Christ in the Spirit. If every anamnesis is epicletic, then the liturgical memorial is, *ex opere operato*, the way in which God communicates the trinitarian life to believers: Christ is sacramentally present through the Spirit, and in faith the believing church is united to the one *transitus* back to the Father. Here, the very dynamic of the liturgy is highlighted. The dialogical character of the celebration and the two-sided act of adoration and sanctification reflect the self-communication of the Trinity.[34]

[32] Ibid., 153.

[33] Kilmartin, "*Sacrificium Laudis*," 287.

[34] Michael Witczak views this dynamic as primary to the contribution Kilmartin brings to sacramental theology. See Michael G. Witczak, "The Manifold Presence of Christ in the Liturgy," *Theological Studies* 59 (1998): 680–702, at 697.

What is surprising in both the methodologies presented by Kilmartin and Vagaggini is that neither theologian attempts to look at the early liturgical sources outside of eucharistic texts in order to examine the narrative of the self-communication of the Trinity. Given the primary importance of baptism in the early church *and* the liturgical unity of the threefold initiation by baptism, chrismation, and Eucharist, the poverty of baptismal-chrismal texts in the turn to the early sources is especially jarring. For his part, Vagaggini briefly explains why he avoids these early baptismal texts in most of his work. In *Il Canone della Messa* he writes that he has chosen to discuss the prayer of the consecration of holy oils on Holy Thursday found in the Gelasian sacramentary, noting: "Everything suggests that this text (the consecratory prayer over the oils) has come from the most classic and purest euchological tradition of Rome, as opposed to what has happened to some other similar texts, in particular the prayer of blessing of the water of the baptismal font."[35] At least in the analysis of the Gelasian, Vagaggini decided to omit baptismal texts in his study because he could not verify their connection to the early liturgies of Rome. In fact, in all the source work Vagaggini conducted in his various revisions of *Il senso teologico, Il Canone delle messe,* and *Caro salutis est,* he did little to go beyond that simple statement. In *Il senso teologico* he spends less than five pages dealing with the source texts for baptism and chrismation in the early church and makes few to no revisions from the first edition.[36] The primary focus of his treatment of baptismal texts is on the credal aspect of the rite and the profession of faith required of candidates for the sacrament. In this regard Vagaggini's treatment is cursory and selective. He looks only at the exposition of baptism by Irenaeus and evidence from Hippolytus in *The Apostolic Tradition,* with a passing reference to Ambrose and the Gelasian sacramentary. In the course of *Il senso teologico* there are no explicit references to the baptismal texts of the *Didache* or the *Didascalia* or any citations of the commentaries by Justin Martyr, Tertullian, Cyprian, Cyril of Jerusalem,

---

[35] *Il canone delle messa e la riforma liturgica: probleme e progetti,* 27.

[36] In this instance the 1976 English translation of *Il senso teologico* is again problematic. Paragraphs have been added to the sections on baptism and confirmation with references to the postconciliar revised liturgy that was completed only after Vagaggini published his last edition. These paragraphs, obviously, do not appear in the original Italian.

John Chrysostom, or Ambrose, whose text includes an extensive trinitarian exposition of the sacraments of initiation.[37]

Ironically, in 1972, long after he had finished revising *Il senso teologico*, Vagaggini detailed baptismal-chrismal texts and their connection to the trinitarian narrative in a relatively obscure conference paper presented in Salamanca.[38] The paper cites two fundamental issues that arise whenever any theologian attempts to look at pre-Nicene baptismal-chrismal texts. First, there is a poverty of extant sources since so many of the early liturgies were transmitted orally.[39] In the absence of such sources, what eventually do appear *qua* "text" are the various commentaries on the early sacraments. Vagaggini goes to great lengths to warn about the distinction between *faith* and the further *attempts to explain the faith*.[40] In this sense it is difficult to determine what is genuinely part of the received text of the rite and what is left to the theologian who has interpreted the rite. His second difficulty stems from a reluctance to read too much into the early rites. He argues that "in order to understand honestly what the trinitarian perspectives are that lie in the pre-Nicene liturgies, one has to know what the trinitarian perspectives were that were underway in the church in general."[41] In the earliest period in the church's history, the same period in which the liturgical life of the church was born, faith in the Trinity was primarily seen as identical to the germinations of trinitarian thought found in the Scriptures. Vagaggini asserts that this scriptural identification with a

---

[37] Vagaggini did cite Ambrose's *De sacramentis* a few times, but he only refers to the general form of the baptismal rite in terms of triple interrogations, triple responses, and triple immersions. Ambrose has very specific sections on the trinitarian nature of baptism and chrismation that Vagaggini chose not to include within his section on christological and trinitarian activity in *Il senso teologico*.

[38] Cipriano Vagaggini, "La perspectiva trinitari en la liturgia del bautismo y de la confirmación antes del concilio de Nicea," in *Simposio Internacional de Teología Trinitaria*, Colleción Semanas de estudios trinitarios 7 (Salamanca: Ediciones Secretariado Trinitario, 1972), 27–50. The paper is considered "relatively obscure" because it was not published by Vagaggini himself and only eight institutions in the world have copies of the text of the conference proceedings; of those, only six allow public access to their collections.

[39] Ibid., 30.

[40] Ibid., 31.

[41] Ibid.

trinitarian narrative was manifested from two significant experiences: "First, from the increasingly clear persuasion of the disciples of Jesus of the superhuman nature, always more transcendent or even divine, of Christ, who was born, lived, suffered, and died on earth but is now in its glory of the risen Lord; second, from the simultaneous experience of the transforming force, personal and divine, of the Spirit, present and active in believers in the church."[42] Thus the Scriptures gave witness to the experience of the early church that recognized the importance of a divine-human incarnation in Christ and the gift of his Spirit to those who believed in him. As noted, in his earlier works Vagaggini stresses the extra-trinitarian revelation of the three Persons within the sacramental action. Most of what he presents in relation to liturgical sources in the Salamanca paper appears as a recapitulation of what he had written earlier in *Il senso teologico*, now more detailed and with some additional references to material omitted earlier. Taking his cue from Irenaeus's *Demonstratio*, Vagaggini maintains that the rites of the early church seemingly do not concern themselves with the inner life of the Trinity but rather with the operation of the Trinity *ad extra* in creation and salvation in the biblical schema of *a . . . per . . . in . . . ad*.[43]

But what does the trinitarian narrative gain from a look at the early source material for baptism and chrismation that it would not have otherwise? After all, Kilmartin focused all his attention on the celebration of the Eucharist and rarely looks at the trinitarian schema within baptism or confirmation, and Vagaggini only attempted to look closely at those texts late in his career. The answer emanates partly from Vagaggini's research and partly from the work of contemporary theologians. At the end of his conference paper in Salamanca, Vagaggini maintained that "we should still remember that this way of considering the Trinity has posited, in Christian antiquity and in its own biblical simplicity, a force of unparalleled spirituality and practice in the church. Precisely because of this biblical way of seeing or experiencing the Trinity, the trinitarian meaning was then incredibly alive."[44] Such an increased trinitarian awareness emerging from the baptismal-chrismal texts provides a safeguard against a liturgical aloofness. The

[42] Ibid., 32.

[43] Ibid., 37. Vagaggini insists that Irenaeus's *Demonstratio* provides the best synopsis of the theological awareness of the Trinity before the Arian controversy.

[44] Ibid., 49.

central reality of the mystery of the Trinity in the history of salvation cannot be relegated to an exercise in esoteric or seemingly irrelevant musings. The simplicity of the scriptural message elucidating the Trinity has real value for believers: it allows them to enter into the mystery without necessarily trying to "unpack" it.

Contemporary theologians echo this call for a return to the liturgical sources of baptism (and, to some degree, confirmation) that will help flesh out the trinitarian narrative of the paschal mystery in the life of believers.[45] The two most basic representations of baptism in the early church mirror the early experiences of trinitarian awareness: the life, death and resurrection of Christ and the outpouring of the Holy Spirit as a vital force in the life of the church. Taking a similar look at Irenaeus's trinitarian baptismal theology, Jeremy Driscoll asserts that the liturgical text reflects not so much what the participant does in the ritual as what God does in the life and faith of the participant. The inclusion of baptismal sources points to how the *lex orandi* affects and shapes the *lex credendi*. Driscoll maintains a distinct connectedness between the biblical imperative for baptism and Eucharist and the faith life of the church: "Baptism and eucharist—it is the Lord's command that makes these a *lex orandi*. On the foundation of what God accomplishes in these celebrations and from the community's experience of them there developed a history of thought, a history of theology. Some ways of understanding things eventually become normative themselves: a *lex credendi*."[46] Driscoll emphasizes that Irenaeus discovers his trinitarian belief because of his experience; it is "entirely shaped by the *liturgical* experience of baptism. The clue which leads Irenaeus to uncover the trinitarian pattern in the history of salvation—a *lex credendi*

---

[45] See, for instance, Jeremy Driscoll, OSB, "Uncovering the Dynamic *Lex Orandi—Lex Credendi* in the Baptismal Theology of Irenaeus," *Pro Ecclesia* 12 (Spring 2003): 213–25; Maxwell Johnson, "Back Home to the Font: Eight Implications of a Baptismal Spirituality," *Worship* 71 (1997): 482–504; Basil Studer, "Lex orandi—lex credendi: der Taufglaube im Gottesdienst der alten Kirche," in *Oratio: das Gebet in patristischer und reformatorsicher Sicht*, ed. Emidio Campi, Leif Grane, and Adolph Martin Ritter (Göttingen: Vandenhoeck & Ruprecht, 1999), 139–49; Louis Weil, "Reclaiming the Larger Trinitarian Framework of Baptism," in *Creation and Liturgy* (Washington, DC: Pastoral Press, 1993), 129–43. The primary emphasis here is on the initiative act of the early church that includes baptism, confirmation, and Eucharist as a single event.

[46] Driscoll, "Uncovering the Dynamic," 214–15.

for him—comes from the pattern that he discovers in baptism in the name of the Father and of the Son and of the Holy Spirit."[47]

The unity of the initiation sacraments, especially in the early church, makes the trinitarian motif of liturgical participation all the more tangible for the believer and attests to the action of God in the salvific work of the sacraments.[48] Recent calls for the renewed unity of those sacraments also highlight why it would be necessary to include baptismal-chrismal texts in a liturgical source analysis that serves as the starting point for the development of a theology of liturgical participation. Dominic Serra argues that the incorporation into Christ through the Holy Spirit that takes place in the initiation sacraments is not simply a solitary or personal identification with the saving act of Christ. Rather, that salvific operation occurs when one is "incorporated into the salvation history of God's People, that is, by becoming a participant in the paschal mystery by which the world is redeemed in Christ."[49] Such an incorporation has inherent dimensions that are metaphysical, soteriological, ecclesiological, and liturgical: metaphysical in recognizing the likeness in being in the human person of Jesus and the believer; soteriological in the participation in the saving action and presence of Christ; ecclesiological in the *de facto* realization of incorporation in Christ through the Spirit; and liturgical in the enactment of a rite that culminates in participation in the paschal mystery. By determining the trinitarian narrative of liturgical participation throughout all the initiation sacraments one not only recognizes the indissoluble theological unity of those sacraments but also emphasizes the overarching connection between God's activity in the world, the life of believers, and the multiple understandings of participation in the trinitarian God.[50]

[47] Ibid., 219.

[48] Dominic Serra makes a similar observation in his call for the unity of the celebrations of baptism, confirmation, and Eucharist. See Dominic Serra, "Baptism and Confirmation: Distinct Sacraments, One Liturgy," *Liturgical Ministry* 9 (2000): 63–71.

[49] Ibid., 68.

[50] An advantage of such an integration is also that it helps revitalize the current theology of confirmation. Serra asserts: "Rather than seek a new significance for confirmation, we would be better advised simply to re-appropriate its meaning from the baptismal bath. Without chrismation, the bath is not Christianizing" (ibid., 70).

One interesting recent work on this subject comes from Kimberly Hope Belcher's publication, *Efficacious Engagement: Sacramental Participation in the Trinitarian Mystery*. While Belcher's primary focus is on the efficacy of postconciliar infant baptism for participation in the trinitarian mystery, she points to a rationale for why baptismal imagery may be more persuasive for a trinitarian theology. She argues that the rite of baptism "is more pervaded with ritual action and sensory phenomena: gesture, scent, procession, dressing and undressing. Baptism's 'messiness' makes it more difficult to 'extract' the linguistic content and consider the sacramental significance in it alone."[51] Baptism reminds us of the experiential quality of the sacraments: they are rites to be enacted and performed; they are done to us, with us, and in us. Belcher notes that any methodology of sacraments that is preoccupied with text over ritual action and meaning may, in fact, miss the crucial point. She maintains that "the transience of blessing in the baptismal waters . . . highlights the ritual action and the permanent effect of the sacrament resides in the initiand's body. Thus baptism might be a better choice to emphasize the ritual and embodied dynamic of the sacramental economy."[52] The sacraments of initiation, especially baptism, concretize participation in the paschal mystery and articulate the entry of the believer into the one *transitus* of Christ. For the believer, the entry into the trinitarian dynamic begins with the sacrament of baptism. While Vagaggini advocated a *tuning in* to that dynamic in the liturgy, most especially the Eucharist, he missed the crucial locus for developing a theology around that dynamic. The extensive work done recently on early Christian initiation provides a wealth of insight into the trinitarian action and dynamic realized by the fledgling church in the first centuries after Christ. Even Vagaggini himself warned that it is necessary to appropriate the trinitarian context of these initiation liturgies; otherwise the paschal mystery itself is left to become the most "abstract, abstruse, distant, and basically, the most indifferent" to the life of the church.[53]

At the heart of understanding early Christian liturgical sources of initiation lies the representative witness of Jesus' baptism in the Jordan. That distinctively trinitarian event in one sense needs to be

---

[51] Kimberly Hope Belcher, *Efficacious Engagement: Sacramental Participation in the Trinitarian Mystery* (Collegeville, MN: Liturgical Press, 2011), 67.

[52] Ibid., 67–68.

[53] Vagaggini, "La perspectiva trinitari en la liturgia del bautismo," 50.

reinserted into the sacramental theology of the West, and for two reasons. First, the baptism of Jesus in the Jordan takes the trinitarian dynamic of both Vagaggini and Kilmartin and encodes it, writ large, upon the minds and hearts of believers. Because baptism is the entry-way for believers into the *mind of Christ*, it is necessary to recognize the full initiation of the faithful as the moment when active participation in the liturgy and the divine life must begin. Speaking of the baptism of Jesus in the Jordan, Kilian McDonnell writes:

> In the Son and by the power of the Spirit, believers become sons and daughters of God, sharers in the divine life. The baptism constitutes a moment of christological concentration in a trinitarian context, a pneumatological event with trinitarian moorings defining the inner life of the church, a cosmic bath catching up the universe into the trinitarian dynamic moving back to the Father.[54]

McDonnell's description allows us to recognize a second reason for returning to the baptism of Jesus as a focal point for understanding the early initiation liturgies. In the Jordan event the triune presence is clear and unmistakable. This threefold presence authenticates the central role of Christ in the church while simultaneously acknowledging the mission of the Spirit and the sending by the Father. The trinitarian focus of the Second Vatican Council, especially as seen in the opening paragraphs of *Lumen Gentium*, *Gaudium et Spes*, and *Dei Verbum*,[55] is manifested in the baptism of Jesus: here is the Christ as anointed one of the Spirit and the declared Son of the Father. Baptismal initiation catapults the believer into that moment when the triune presence is revealed and places him or her on the same trajectory as Christ. Yves Congar asserts:

> Jesus entered the water, identifying himself with those who repent, and, while he was praying, the Spirit came down on him. In the same way, Christians are plunged into the water as into his death (Rom 6:3) and the Spirit is given. There is a baptism of water and the Spirit, introducing the believer into the body which is the Body of Christ.[56]

---

[54] Kilian McDonnell, OSB, *The Baptism of Jesus in the Jordan* (Collegeville, MN: Liturgical Press, 1996), 236.

[55] See n. 120 on p. 48.

[56] Congar, *I Believe in the Holy Spirit 3: The River of the Water of Life (Rev. 22:1 flows in the East and in the West* (New York: Seabury, 1983), 222.

Understanding that presence and recognizing its value in the other sacraments, especially the Eucharist, becomes the challenge and goal of a contemporary trinitarian theology of liturgical participation.

The Active Presence of Father, Son, and Spirit in the Liturgical Action

The second area of analysis concerns the ability of both Vagaggini and Kilmartin to remain consistent with the trinitarian theology applicable to sacramental interpretation in the West. The inherent difficulty in establishing a trinitarian theology of liturgical participation centers on the necessity of bridging two theological arenas while maintaining the integrity of each, namely, the theology espoused by the Second Vatican Council concerning the action of the triune God in the world and the tendency of theologies of participation to highlight the action or presence of a particular person of the Trinity. As noted earlier in our investigation, it would be erroneous to think that the council advocated the highly Christocentric notion of sacramental action typified by the neo-scholastics of the beginning of the twentieth century. What emerges from the conciliar documents, when one traces the interrelationship between *communicare* and *participare*, is a true broadening of sacramental theology that includes a trinitarian understanding of participation and self-communication. The conciliar agenda makes clear the parameters of trinitarian action in the world: the Father calls the faithful to share in the divine life, the Son offers himself as the way to participation, and the Spirit vivifies the church that it might follow in the path of the Son. Such an action is based on the self-communication of the triune God and the bestowal of grace as participation in the divine life. What the conciliar documents do not tell us is how such self-communication happens, or how one reconciles attempts to speak about the personal missions of Christ and the Holy Spirit while still maintaining the unity of action in the triune God. The following analysis, then, will attempt to look at how well Vagaggini and Kilmartin explicated the trinitarian narratives within their liturgical theologies while remaining consistent with Western notions of how God acts in the world.

The christological-trinitarian narrative Vagaggini identifies within the early liturgies of the church also forms the basis for his understanding of how the Trinity itself acts in the world. As noted earlier, Vagaggini attempted to articulate his understanding of the operation of the Trinity by reversing the typically Western starting point of the unity of the divine nature, which then moves to an articulation of the divine Persons. Vagaggini asserts a twofold rationale for embracing this reversal. First, "the trinitarian consciousness is psychologically more vivid" in those who begin with the distinction of Persons and "it is a fact that in Scripture, in the Greek Fathers, and in the pre-Augustinian Latin Fathers, in the liturgy and especially in the Roman liturgy," this way of thinking is "far and away more prevalent."[57] Vagaggini does not state clearly how such a starting point produces a *psychologically more vivid* awareness or consciousness of the triune God, nor does he adequately explain what he means by that consciousness. Second, Vagaggini operates under the perceived notion that the Scriptures do not concern themselves with the ontological reality of God, but simply with God acting in the economy of salvation.

Such a twofold position presents certain theological difficulties. What Vagaggini has assumed is an incarnational lens through which to view the revelation of the Trinity. While that act is definitive for the revelation of the triune God, it is neither exhaustive nor solitary. Vagaggini presupposes, perhaps too readily, that the Arian controversy is the only reason that the movement from one God to three divine Persons prevailed in the West. He argues that this explanation of the mystery of the Trinity is "a derived and primarily apologetic method. It made its appearance for the sake of an apologetic defense of the faith against the rationalist objections of Arianism."[58] But one can readily point to the Monarchianism of Paul of Samosata or the Modalism of Sabellius and realize that such considerations regarding the Trinity or the nature of the divine Persons had come to the fore in the interpretations of God a century before Nicaea. Also, Vagaggini does admit that although the dominance of trinitarian themes in the Scriptures points to the economic Trinity, such a dominance does not preclude musings regarding the inner life of the Trinity. John's Prologue stands out as the most obvious example of the early church attempting to reconcile the possibility of a nonmonotheistic conception of God.[59]

The inherent danger for Vagaggini in advocating a push toward the economic Trinity in this incarnational lens—a lens that shapes his own

[57] *Il senso teologico* (1965), 200.

[58] Ibid.

[59] In fact, Vagaggini does make a cursory admission of this fact and notes that several intratrinitarian realities are made explicit in the Scriptures. But he relegates the admission to a few lines of text and subsequent footnotes. See ibid., 202.

understanding of how the trinitarian narrative unfolds within the liturgical action—centers on its resemblance to a social trinitarian model akin to tritheism. In positing the relational grammar of the Trinity as the *a . . . per . . . in . . . ad* schema, Vagaggini maintains that he is moving away from a traditional way of speaking about trinitarian action. He asserts:

> Referring to these difficulties, it surely does not seem necessary, theologically speaking, to explain the formula [*a . . . per . . . in . . . ad*] by reducing it purely and simply to what in trinitarian theology is called appropriation. Many theologians believe that this must be done, but to us it seems it is done too superficially. One can be content to interpret the formula in a purely appropriative sense only as such in that it expresses the efficient causality of the Persons in the world.[60]

The doctrine of appropriation maintains the unity of the triune God while "appropriating" certain *ad extra* actions to a specific person in the Trinity. It exists primarily as a way of expressing in human language the mystery of trinitarian action, which lacks an analogous reality in human experience. William Hill describes appropriation succinctly: "What is in reality a common prerogative of the trinitarian members is predicated of one alone to manifest his personal uniqueness in the Godhead."[61] Appropriation, therefore, safeguards the indissoluble unity of the one God while at the same time recognizing that when God acts in the world all three Persons of the Trinity place one action. Hill goes on to assert: "Appropriation is justified because of the awareness in faith that the divine Persons, in the singularity of their unique identities, are involved *as such* in the creative act and so with all creaturely being, whose inner structure mirrors forth mysteriously a personal order in God."[62]

In his demarcation of the christological-trinitarian schema Vagaggini readily admits that he can dismiss the concept of appropriation when looking at the kinds of relations maintained by formal causality. He argues that within an extrinsic approach to the relations of formal causality within the Trinity "it is possible to believe that in the formula

---

[60] Ibid., 204.

[61] William J. Hill, *The Three-Personed God: The Trinity as a Mystery of Salvation* (Washington, DC: Catholic University of America Press, 1982), 283.

[62] Ibid. Italics in original.

[*a . . . per . . . in . . . ad*] there is expression of the special relation creatures have even with what the single Persons of the Trinity have in proper respect to each other, with the *properties* of the individual Persons."[63] However, in maintaining the formulaic schema as revelatory of the properties of the individual Persons within the Trinity, Vagaggini runs the risk of creating three separate conceivable centers of action within the Godhead. Such a demarcation could ostensibly separate the act of sanctifying by the Spirit from the act of sacrifice and offering by the Son. While this is certainly not Vagaggini's intent, it is difficult to see how he can avoid such a problem. Too often his christological-trinitarian schema appears as three distinct Persons acting in tandem.

Vagaggini is not alone in conceptualizing such proper relations within the Trinity. Many theologians in the latter half of the twentieth century offered similar assessments.[64] Karl Rahner posited a proper mission of the Son, since the hypostatic union of the Son is "something which can be predicated only of one divine person."[65] Similarly, Hans Urs von Balthasar, critical of the psychological analogy often attributed to trinitarian theology in the West, presented in *Mysterium Paschale* an unfolding drama of the paschal mystery in which personhood is defined more by a sense of mission (in relation to the other Persons) than in opposition to some sense of subjective consciousness.[66] In so doing von Balthasar can fathom such notions as the abandonment of the Son by the Father. Ghislain Lafont also attempted to revise personhood in the Trinity in terms of reflective communication while still re-

---

[63] *Il senso teologico* (1965), 205.

[64] For an excellent exposition of modern theology's attempt to receive and revise the doctrine of appropriation, see Neil Ormerod, *The Trinity: Retrieving the Western Tradition* (Milwaukee, WI: Marquette University Press, 2005), 99–123.

[65] Karl Rahner, *The Trinity*, trans. Joseph Donceel (New York: Herder & Herder, 1970), 23.

[66] Hans Urs von Balthasar, *Mysterium Paschale: The History of Easter*, trans. Aidan Nichols (San Francisco: Ignatius Press, 1996), 148–81. See also Anne Hunt, *The Trinity and the Paschal Mystery: A Development in Recent Catholic Theology*, New Theology Studies 5 (Collegeville, MN: Liturgical Press, 1997), 57–89; Ormerod, *The Trinity*, 108–13; Hans Urs von Balthasar, "The Descent into Hell," *Chicago Studies* 23 (1984): 223–36. Hunt offers a particularly good reading of von Balthasar's theology in this area; see esp, pp. 68–76 and 152–53 (for her Lonerganian interpretation of von Balthasar's thought).

maining consistent with the Thomistic theology he espouses.[67] In some respects what emerges from all of these theologians is a contemporary attempt to reenvision the interpretation of the personhood of God, especially when speaking of how God acts in the world. Interestingly, the most recent *Catechism of the Catholic Church* embraces this attempt when it argues for the distinct missions of the Son and Holy Spirit in God's action in the world. As noted earlier, the *Catechism* maintains that when the Trinity acts in the world "each divine person performs the common work according to his unique personal property."[68] While the *Catechism* still maintains the Western sense of appropriation, there is an increasing attempt to recognize the distinction of Persons in the Trinity. What has become apparent, however, is that the *Catechism* has attempted to embrace more fully the trinitarian theology espoused by the conciliar documents, which place appropriation and personal action on equal planes.

The other major concern regarding Vagaggini's christological-trinitarian schema revolves around his inability to embrace such a trinitarian model completely. Vagaggini began writing his major tome, *Il senso teologico*, under the influence and shadow of *Mediator Dei*, which maintains a distinctive and high Christology. In the course of *Il senso teologico*, even with its many revisions, Vagaggini never totally divorced himself from that christological model. Immediately after finishing his exposition of the christological-trinitarian formula he proceeds to center the primary action of the sacraments in the person of Christ. He never develops a full sense of pneumatology within his work. In his explication of the central role of the *Kyrios* in the sacramental celebration, Vagaggini goes to great lengths to emphasize the individual action of Christ. In the case of the Eucharist he maintains: "It is enough to recall the biblical thought that all that Christ, who is now glorious at the right hand of the Father, does in the world, He does through the Holy Spirit, whom He himself sends from the Father; thus, the action of Christ and the action of the Holy Spirit are not two diverse actions, but a single action of Christ in the Holy Spirit or through the Holy Spirit."[69] Vagaggini wants to ensure that one could

---

[67] Ghislain Lafont, *Peut-on Connaître Dieu en Jésus Christ?* Cogitatio Fidei 44 (Paris: Cerf, 1969), 290–91.

[68] CCC, §258.

[69] *Il senso teologico* (1965), 257.

emphasize the role of the Holy Spirit in the sacramental action but still regard the action of Christ as primary since Christ acts as high priest to make the acceptable sacrifice to the Father.

There are two significant criticisms of Vagaggini's insistence on this principle. First, while he intended to highlight the paschal sense of each sacrament, by underscoring the sacerdotal role of Christ in the sacrifice of the Eucharist he created a difficult obstacle. How does one speak of Christ's sacerdotal activity in the sacrament of marriage? Or how does one describe the action in the sacrament of baptism, which is certainly paschal in character but noticeably pneumatic in operation? Vagaggini's characterization of the primacy of the action of Christ seemingly only holds for the sacramental celebration of the Eucharist. In fact, in addressing the other sacraments he glossed over them rather quickly, citing only their paschal character.[70]

Second, Vagaggini's emphasis on the sacerdotal activity of the *Kyrios* over and above the action of the Spirit hinders the development of a truly trinitarian theology of the liturgy. It is perhaps telling that Vagaggini never adopts a strictly trinitarian title for the schema he finds in the early liturgical sources; it is always defined as a christological-trinitarian motif. He inadvertently creates a picture of the trinitarian Persons that places the Spirit in quasirelation to the Father and Son. Simply to reiterate that the liturgical action of Christ occurs *through* the Spirit would not adequately meet the challenge of postconciliar theology of trinitarian action in the sacraments, but one must remember that Vagaggini finished most of his revisions of *Il senso teologico* before the council ended. In some ways he knew that his positions needed to be reworked. When the miscellanea *Lex Orandi, Lex Credendi* was written in his honor he admitted that it would be of great benefit to examine the pneumatological significance of many of the symbolic aspects of the liturgy, which were more numerous than often assumed.[71]

---

[70] Ironically, this is a section of Vagaggini's text not found in the original 1957 version. In the 1965 version he notes baptism's special character as a passage from death to life (and thus its paschal nature), characterizes penance as a new baptism, and asserts that the anointing of the sick is an extension of penance. He says nothing of confirmation, matrimony, or holy orders. See ibid., 263.

[71] Achille M. Triacca, "Dom Cipriano Vagaggini, OSB Cam (1909–1999) In Memoriam," *Ephemerides Liturgicae* 113 (1999): 449–65, at 457–58. Triacca writes of a personal letter he received from Vagaggini regarding his submission on the Holy Spirit and the liturgy for the collection of essays in Vagaggini's

While Vagaggini struggled to incorporate a pneumatological theology into his trinitarian schema, Kilmartin recognized the difficulty in speaking about the proper actions of both the Spirit and Christ in the sacramental celebration. The success (and the challenge) of Kilmartin's trinitarian theology of liturgical participation derives from his willingness and ability to demonstrate the agency of the Holy Spirit in the liturgical action. In fact, Robert Taft emphasizes just how much Kilmartin achieved in this endeavor: "The failure to explicate the trinitarian and pneumatological dimensions of liturgy can be considered a major defect of some Western theologies of worship, a defect sedulously avoided by Edward Kilmartin."[72]

Before we examine the content of Kilmartin's trinitarian theology it would be beneficial to get another brief glimpse of his methodology. Kilmartin's tendency to rely heavily on the work of one or two theologians becomes somewhat problematic in the development of his trinitarian thought. For instance, in attempting to articulate the Thomistic viewpoint on sacramental causality and the mystery-presence of Christ, Kilmartin looks to the work of Brian McNamara.[73] But McNamara was not a Thomist and, in fact, approached the issue and his reinterpretation of Aquinas from a Lonerganian point of view. McNamara's reputation as a theologian and scholar is somewhat obscure, although he is seemingly very influential. On the one hand, it appears that, apart from the one article Kilmartin cites, McNamara did not produce any other works on this topic, with the exception of two reviews that also appear in the *Irish Theological Quarterly*.[74] While other theolo-

---

honor. For Triacca's submission, on which Vagaggini is commenting, see also Achille M. Triacca, "Spirito Santo e Liturgia. Linee methodologiche per un approfondimento," in *Lex Orandi, Lex Credendi: Miscellanea in Onore di P. Ciprano Vagaggini*, ed. Gellért Békés and Giustino Farnedi (Rome: Editrice Anselmiana, 1980), 133–64.

[72] Robert Taft, "What Does Liturgy Do? Toward a Soteriology of Liturgical Celebration: Some Theses," *Worship* 66 (1992): 194–211, at 197.

[73] Brian McNamara, "Christus Patiens in Mass and Sacraments: Higher Perspectives," *Irish Theological Quarterly* 42 (1975): 17–35.

[74] Brian McNamara, "Divine Pedagogy: A Patristic View of Non-Christian Religions," *Irish Theological Quarterly* 53 (1987): 78–80; idem, "El Contra Eunomium I en la produccion letteraria de Gregorio de Nisa," *Irish Theological Quarterly* 57 (1991): 84–85. Part of the reason for McNamara's apparent obscurity is that he became ill while teaching at the National Univeristy of Ireland, eventually left his teaching position, and died relatively young.

gians have cited McNamara's work, they often do so only in conjunction with an analysis of Kilmartin's use of it.[75] And yet Robert Daly notes that, along with Cesare Giraudo, McNamara is one of the pillars upon which Kilmartin based his theology in his final work, *The Eucharist in the West*.[76] Nowhere do we see the rationale for why Kilmartin so readily accepted McNamara's positions.[77] Despite this weakness, Kilmartin was able to posit a cogent interpretation of how trinitarian action is linked to the liturgical celebration.

Perhaps the two largest issues Kilmartin confronted in the development of his trinitarian theology stem from the struggle to determine a proper model for explaining the processions or relations both within and outside the Trinity as well as from the attempt to demarcate a possible way to speak about the agency of the Spirit that moves beyond mediation. Thus, in order to analyze Kilmartin's trinitarian theology in comparison to the trinitarian development of the Second Vatican Council, one must necessarily look at the various models (procession-bestowal) Kilmartin investigates and his attempt to reinsert a viable pneumatology into a Western approach to sacramental liturgy.

The katabatic and anabatic movements proposed by Kilmartin's synthesis of the procession and bestowal models of the Trinity help establish a definitive trajectory for a discussion of liturgical participation, but it also raises certain questions regarding the Persons of the Trinity. In the course of the development of his trinitarian theology of liturgical participation Kilmartin, like Vagaggini, ran the risk of too easily embracing a tritheism. While he attempted to advocate a union of the procession and bestowal models, his primary goal was to articulate a means whereby the single trajectory of Christ can be distinguished within the trinitarian narrative. The return of Christ to the Father is the key issue for Kilmartin: the descending Christology of the

---

[75] See especially, Hans Bernhard Meyer, "Eine trinitarische Theologie der Liturgie und der Sakramente," *Zeitschrift für katholische Theologie* 113 (1991): 24–38; Raymond Moloney, "Lonergan on Eucharistic Sacrifice," *Theological Studies* 62, no. 1 (2001): 53–70.

[76] Edward J. Kilmartin, *The Eucharist in the West*, ed. Robert J. Daly (Collegeville, MN: Liturgical Press, 1998), xviii–xxiv.

[77] There is little evidence that McNamara is cited by any other theologians in this regard. Robert Taft briefly mentions McNamara's theological interpretation of sacrifice and causality, albeit in a section of his work dedicated to Kilmartin's thought. See Taft, "What Does Liturgy Do?," 198.

procession model appears obvious to him, but the ascending Christology of the bestowal model is a necessary component for the salvific activity of the sacraments. This bestowal model, however, holds certain distinct difficulties that must be faced if Kilmartin's trinitarian theology is to remain viable.

The first difficulty enmeshed in Kilmartin's embrace of the bestowal model centers on its fundamental divergence from the accepted processional understanding of the Trinity found in the creed and later expounded upon in the Western tradition. The faith statements of the "only-begotten Son" and the Spirit "who proceeds from the Father and Son" found in the creed of Nicaea were articulated into deeper theological awareness by Augustine's use of a psychological analogy to understand the processions and by Aquinas's redevelopment and further nuancing of that analogy.[78] It is important to recognize here that the processions of the Trinity within the psychological analogy are maintained primarily as intellectual processions *ad intra*. In the *Prima pars* of the *Summa theologiae*, Aquinas argues:

> Procession within should be regarded as an action that remains in the agent. This is most clearly seen in the intellect, where its action of understanding remains in the intellect itself. . . . Therefore, procession is not to be understood according to what is in bodies either as local motion or as the action of some cause leading to an exterior effect . . . but according to an intelligible emanation, just as an intelligible word proceeds from and remains in the one speaking."[79]

But Kilmartin conceptualizes the procession model as fundamentally *ad extra*, that is, as a linear going-outward, even when he speaks of the *ad intra* description of Aquinas's psychological analogy. And yet, one of the most important qualities of Aquinas's analogy is his insistence that intelligible emanation is interior to the intellect. When the analogy is applied to the Trinity it implies a relationality of the Persons within the triune God. Kilmartin assumes that the psychological analogy applies readily to the action of God *ad extra*, and so characterizes the procession model of the Trinity as a "descending Christology."

---

[78] Ormerod, *The Trinity*, 80–84. For Kilmartin's synopsis of the two, see also Edward J. Kilmartin, *Christian Liturgy I. Theology and Practice* (Kansas City: Sheed & Ward, 1988), 125–29.

[79] ST Ia, q. 27, a. 1.

As noted earlier in our discussion of his trinitarian theology, Kilmartin sees a correspondence between the economic Trinity and the immanent Trinity in terms of both effect and execution.[80] In assessing the procession model, Kilmartin assumes that the execution of the self-communication of God creates an identity between the missions of Christ and the Holy Spirit and their processions. Aquinas, however, notes a distinction between the mission of a divine person as a temporal expression or term of a procession and the eternal procession that exists in God as part of God's essence.[81] Thus one can speak of a procession in God that is simultaneously eternal and temporal: eternal in its relation to the principle and temporal in its relation to the term of humanity. By transferring the procession model *ad intra* to the way in which God acts in the economy of salvation, Kilmartin has seemingly collapsed the mission of Christ and the Holy Spirit into the temporal term alone.[82] In fact, he asserts that "in the order of grace, in the economic Trinity, the Father determines himself to receptivity and historicity through the missions of the Word and Spirit."[83] Kilmartin insists that Catholic theology must recognize that the concept of the immutable God is limited by God's own self-determination: that the missions of the Word and the Spirit are essentially offers of God's self to be known and loved, which implies a potential for mutual self-communication (and thus a potential for change). What Kilmartin seems to omit is that in the order of this communication of grace the human subject is fully known and loved by God in the act of creation. Creation, is, in fact, the manifestation of that knowledge and love.[84] Thus the only potency for change exists on the part of human-

[80] Kilmartin, *Christian Liturgy I*, 114.

[81] ST Ia, q. 43, a. 2.

[82] Neil Ormerod makes a similar criticism of David Coffey when he critiques Coffey's trinitarian theology by saying that he has conflated the psychological analogy with its implicit realism into a psychological or processional model that raises questions of validity and veracity for the processions themselves. See Ormerod, *The Trinity*, 91. For relevant passages from Coffey's works, see David Coffey, "The 'Incarnation' of the Holy Spirit in Christ," *Theological Studies* 45 (1984): 466–80, at 470; idem, "A Proper Mission of the Holy Spirit," *Theological Studies* 47 (1986): 227–50, at 230–34.

[83] Kilmartin, *Christian Liturgy I*, 145.

[84] At least this is how Aquinas envisions it in his treatise on the Trinity, which shows that the creative act of the Trinity is manifested as the expression in time of the missions of the Word and the Spirit.

ity, which, through God's grace, is brought into closer union with the Godhead (i.e., the potential exists for believers to become saints). Gilles Emery expresses this viewpoint succinctly while commenting on Aquinas's understanding of the missions:

> By the gift of grace, the saints are united to God by knowing God and loving him. When the Son is sent on mission, the saints are "assimilated" to the Son by the illumination of their intelligence (participation in the property of the Son, through an effect of grace appropriated to the Son) which enables them to know God. When the Holy Spirit is sent on mission, the saints are "assimilated" to the Spirit through the ardor of charity (participation in the property of the Holy Spirit, by an effect of grace appropriated to the Holy Spirit), which enables them to love God.[85]

The missions of the Son and Spirit, while analogous to processions *ad intra*, are not identical to them since the missions are defined by their effect (in grace) and the processions are defined by their origin (in relation).

In attempting to reconcile Eastern and Western theologies of the Trinity, Kilmartin also embraces the bestowal model as a way of positing a proper mission of the Holy Spirit.[86] We noted earlier that this proper mission of the Holy Spirit seems to be advocated by the later documents of the Second Vatican Council, as opposed to the more Christocentric focus of *Sacrosanctum Concilium*. Certainly the post-conciliar documents, and especially the *Catechism*, articulate missions that are proper to each of the divine Persons but still maintain the unity of action in the Godhead. As we have seen, much of Kilmartin's theology here is derived from Heribert Mühlen's notion of the "unc-

[85] Gilles Emery, *Trinity in Aquinas* (Ypsilanti, MI: Sapientia Press of Ave Maria University, 2003), 162.

[86] Kilmartin, "The Active Role of Christ and the Holy Spirit in the Sanctification of the Eucharistic Elements," *Theological Studies* 45 (1984): 225–53, at 237. Kilmartin is not alone in his assessment that a proper mission of the Holy Spirit needed to be articulated in the West. See also David Coffey, *Grace, the Gift of the Holy Spirit* (Sydney: Catholic Institute of Sydney, 1979); idem, "A Proper Mission of the Holy Spirit," 227–50; Congar, *I Believe in the Holy Spirit*; Heribert Mühlen, *Una mystica persona. Die Kirche als das Mysterium der Identität des heiligen Geistes in Christus und den Christen: Eine Person in vielen Personen*, 2d rev. ed. (Munich and Vienna: Schöningh, 1967).

tion of the Spirit" and David Coffey's insistence on the lack of purpose in the mission of the Spirit in the procession model. But in his analysis Kilmartin portrays the bestowal model while presupposing that the procession model is exteriorly linear in its movement. He implies a secondary action in the act of God's self-communication but fails to articulate the impetus that allows the procession model to continue into the bestowal model. To him, the descending Christology of the procession model is "completed" by the ascending Christology of the bestowal model. But the bestowal model only seems to come to fruition through a responsive act of the Father's love in the resurrection, whereby the Father sends the Spirit (again?) upon the Son to raise him into glory. This appears as something of a secondary act in God's self-communication. There is also an implied tertiary action here: the acceptance of faith on the part of the human recipient of the self-communication of God.[87] For Kilmartin this is the essential work of the Spirit's mission: to unite believers to the Son that they might accept the revelation of God in faith, and, in turn, to lead them back to the Father. To bring about union with God, the action of the triune God is wed to the action of the believer.

Given the difficulties articulated here about Kilmartin's embrace of the bestowal model, it is necessary to mention that David Coffey, from whom Kilmartin took his cue regarding the bestowal model, revised his theology of the triune movement after Kilmartin's death. In his book *Deus Trinitas: The Doctrine of the Triune God*, Coffey explains how it became necessary to amend his earlier naming of the bestowal model.[88] In his "Introduction," he notes that by calling this model a "return model" he is able to bring out a more definitive contrast with the rationalist model of procession. In defending the return model, he argues, "It also (sic) encompasses the entire process by which Jesus, having been sent forth from the Father, returns to him through his life and death in the power of the Holy Spirit . . . in its developed form it includes the sending forth in the sweep of the larger movement of return."[89] Coffey further insists that his return model allows for the development of a theology of the proper mission of the Holy Spirit,

[87] Kilmartin, *Christian Liturgy I*, 170–76.

[88] David Coffey, *Deus Trinitas: The Doctrine of the Trinity* (New York: Oxford University Press, 1999).

[89] Ibid., 5.

which he finds lacking in the contemporary formulations of the procession model based on scholastic theology.

The crux of Kilmartin's trinitarian theology lies precisely in this proper mission of the Holy Spirit and the relationship between the action of Christ and the action of the Spirit in the world. For Kilmartin, liturgical participation is a radical identification with the faith of Christ made possible by the Spirit. The trinitarian narrative is not only manifested in the liturgical celebration of the church but also intimately tied to that celebration. For Kilmartin the proper mission of the Spirit centers on its action as the animating force of the individual believer and the church (in both its particular and universal instances). As such, Kilmartin argues, the Spirit acts as the efficient cause of the sanctification of humanity.

However, even this quick recapitulation of Kilmartin's theology of the proper mission of the Holy Spirit presents a number of problematic issues for the trinitarian theologian. First, how can one ascribe actions to the Holy Spirit and how is the Spirit's activity differentiated from the action of the Father and the Son? Is Kilmartin's reliance on first quasi-formal causality and then efficient causality in speaking of the Spirit's actions the best schema to use in contemporary sacramental theology? Is Kilmartin actually successful in guaranteeing no separation between the activity of Christ and the activity of the Holy Spirit, or do their agencies seem to exist in a paradoxical tension?

One has to be careful in understanding the precise relationship between the mission of Christ and the mission of the Holy Spirit. The trinitarian theology of the Second Vatican Council is relatively silent on this relationship, and when it does speak, it does so with some equivocation. *Lumen Gentium* asserts that the Holy Spirit is sent only when the Son's mission is accomplished.[90] Such a description is somewhat problematic since it assumes that the mission of the Spirit is a secondary act in the economy of God's action in the world. In the later Decree on Missionary Activity (*Ad Gentes*), the council emends its earlier description and insists that the "Holy Spirit was at work in the world before Christ was glorified."[91] The particular line cited here is given extensive notation in the conciliar document, with reference both to the action of the Spirit in the age of the prophets and

[90] LG 4.
[91] AG 4.

to the continuation of that mission at the event of Pentecost, while even admitting a possible new interpretation of that mission with the Pentecost event. Kilian McDonnell, in looking at the council's demarcation of missionary activity, notes that by making this assertion the document is able "to see parallels between the way Jesus is constituted and identified ('Christ was conceived in the Virgin Mary with the coming of the Holy Spirit'), the manner in which the Spirit is constitutive of Jesus' ministry ('Christ . . . was moved to begin his ministry by the descent of the same Holy Spirit'), and the way the church was 'manifested' (*manifestata*) on the day of Pentecost."[92] In this sense the Spirit's mission fundamentally connects the incarnation of Christ and the life of the church.

Kilmartin's assertion about the interconnectedness of the missions of the Spirit and Son predates the statement of the *Catechism* regarding the joint missions of the two Persons. On the one hand, Kilmartin's theology here is anticipatory of that declaration, but at the same time it is unclear when it seeks to talk about how the Spirit acts in the economy of salvation. The agency of the Spirit in the sacramental action is not always clearly articulated by Kilmartin. He vacillates between characterizing the Spirit as primary efficient cause and quasi-formal cause, the former having the connotation of a viable acting agent and the latter having the connotation of a primary guiding principle. What is clear, however, is the tension that arises when he speaks about the action of the Spirit and the action of Christ. For instance, Kilmartin asserts that the Spirit determines the content of self-communication of the Trinity, but Christ communicates in himself. Similarly, he argues that the Spirit has a personal mission, but that "mission derives from Christ and has a completely Christ-ward reference."[93] Can the mission of the Spirit be personal if it is also derivative? Moreover, the active presence of Christ in the liturgy is manifested by the mediated immediacy of the Spirit. This appears somewhat paradoxical if the presence of Christ can only be active through mediation by the Spirit. Does such an assertion call into question whether or not Christ acts directly upon

[92] Kilian McDonnell, OSB, *The Other Hand of God: The Holy Spirit as the Universal Touch and Goal* (Collegeville, MN: Liturgical Press, 2003), 198.

[93] Edward J. Kilmartin, "A Modern Approach to the Word of God and Sacraments of Christ: Perspectives and Principles," in *The Sacraments: God's Love and Mercy Actualized*. Proceedings of the Theological Institute 11, ed. Francis A. Eigo (Villanova, PA: Villanova University Press, 1979), 71.

the world? Moreover, Kilmartin maintains that the Spirit is viewed as the "principle of sanctification in the individual and corporate life of the Church,"[94] but only in terms of an adherence to the *transitus* of the Son. What we see at every turn in Kilmartin's theology is that the work of the Spirit and that of the Son are so completely and inextricably intertwined that it becomes difficult, at best, to ascertain how these two divine Persons act in the world.

William J. Hill offers some clarification on the relationship of the mission of Christ to the mission of the Spirit, especially in terms of Kilmartin's use of causal language. Hill is especially helpful here because Kilmartin had looked to Hill's notion of procession as a possible link to Coffey's pneumatology but later dismissed Hill's critique of relative divine missions because he did not use the economic Trinity as a starting point. However, Hill does provide a possible solution to Kilmartin's problem: he asserts that the divine Persons are present in the economy of salvation in virtue of their missions:

> This is not merely a presence of God who happens to be triune, in which the trinitarian dimension is explained by appropriation. It is rather a *proper* presence of two Persons in virtue of their being sent into history; the Father is not sent, yet is present—this is demanded by the inseparability of the Three, as well as by the doctrine of *perichoresis*—as the One who sends.[95]

Hill continues to affirm that the theological tradition has maintained that the presence of the Word can be found in the humanity of Jesus and that the Spirit, because it constitutes the People of God, can be discerned as present in believers. What remains unique to Hill's perspective is his assertion that the specific missions are grounded in the essence of the Godhead:

> The divine presence in one mission is an incarnate one proper to the Word; that in the other mission is an ecclesial one proper to the Paraclete. The effect of the former is *manifestive* of God; the effect of the latter is rather *unitive* to God. But both effects are Trinitarian in mode. Each can be proper to the respective member of the Trinity because there is no operation *ad extra* involved. The Word's personification of

[94] Kilmartin, *Christian Liturgy I*, 109.
[95] Hill, *The Three-Personed God*, 287. Emphasis in original.

Jesus' humanity is not the doing of something in the order of efficient causality, but rather an actualization in the order of personal being.[96]

In this sense, Hill begins to question the best way in which agency can be attributed to an act of the Godhead, since all agency in terms of efficient causality seems to be lacking. Kilmartin, in his work, seems to fluctuate between two distinct kinds of agency. In "A Modern Approach," he shows that "it is ultimately the Spirit who structures word and sacrament into intelligible unit, giving them unity of signification."[97] For Kilmartin, one cannot speak about a sacrament without its act of signification; thus he argues that there must be some sort of theological identity between the action of the Spirit and the action of the sacramental celebration. It would be difficult to determine where one ends and the other begins. When one applies the description that Hill gives regarding the action of the Christ to the Holy Spirit, however, the actualization of the personal being of the Spirit begins to emerge. In this case, the language of efficient causality is left wanting. Instead, Hill maintains: "What we are speaking of here can be reduced to the order of formal causality (the form actualizes by its very presence), as long as it is understood that person is not a form but actualizes in a way analogous to that of a form."[98] In this description, then, the Spirit's action is perhaps best understood as a formal cause because of the unitive character that its very presence brings *qua* person. Herein lies the genius of Hill's assertion: he can maintain the trinitarian unity of the Godhead when it acts in the world while at the same time he can make clear distinctions about the presence of the persons, their respective missions, and their effects. Personhood becomes revelatory of this causal presence. Hill asserts: "The Holy Spirit's gathering together of believers is not an agent causality but the very relating in love which constitutes his distinctive personhood."[99] Within this framework, the inner-trinitarian nature of the triune Persons is protected and the immutability of God who can transform creation simply by God's presence to it is also maintained. In this sense, one can view the missions of Christ and the Spirit, not as separate agencies, but as the presence of the trinitarian Persons. In his description, Hill takes

[96] Ibid.
[97] Kilmartin, "A Modern Approach," 72.
[98] Hill, *The Three-Personed God*, 287–88.
[99] Ibid., 288.

this notion one step further by formulating a descriptive role for the Spirit in the life of the believer: as personal love, the Spirit is "union of Father and Son and so if given to men makes them be, by his very personal presence, sharers in divine trinitarian life."[100]

The unity of action between Son, Spirit, and Father in the sacramental celebration also proved to be a difficulty for Kilmartin. Following the traditional formulation of the theology of *Sacrosanctum Concilium*, he maintained that the celebration of the sacramental liturgy is primarily the work and action of the glorified Christ acting as head of his Body and united to that Body in the Spirit.[101] For Kilmartin the sacramental action is the manifestation of the Son's mission in the world as *Kyrios*. While the Spirit is given by the Son and serves to unite the believing community in the faith of Christ, Kilmartin is quick to add that only the Son has an abiding presence in the sacramental action that is the fundamental reason for the efficacy of the sacrament. Yet at the same time, as we have just seen, Kilmartin wants to maintain that the action of the Spirit cannot be separated from the sacramental action. It appears that there are two distinct actions, one made present through the mission of the Son and the other by the mission of the Spirit. Kilmartin wants to insist that Christ acts in the liturgy as head of the Body and the Spirit acts in the liturgy to unite the church to Christ. There is no mention of the Father's action in the liturgy in any of Kilmartin's schemas.

One contemporary theologian, Kilian McDonnell, who has dedicated most of his research and writing to the proper mission and action of the Holy Spirit, offers what may be an important corrective to Kilmartin's theology. He maintains that "there is one economy from the Father constituted by the missions of the Son and the Spirit, each of the missions being present and active at the interior of the other."[102] The two missions are not temporally successive in the operation of the Trinity *ad extra*. Nor can one surmise that they are separated by virtue of their procession, even though this constitutes a real distinction in both Son and Spirit. McDonnell argues that an insistence on such a distinction creates a "danger of conceiving of them as two foci at the ends of an ellipse,"[103] whereby one can conceive of two distinct points of operation

---

[100] Ibid., 291–92.
[101] Kilmartin, *Christian Liturgy I*, 350.
[102] McDonnell, *The Other Hand of God*, 198.
[103] Ibid., 199.

within the divine action in the economy of salvation. Such a conception all too easily leads to an "economic tritheism,"[104] the notion of divine Persons acting separately in the world. Instead, McDonnell surmises that there is both a radical distinction and a relation of the divine Persons from and to each other. Following the trinitarian grammar articulated by Vagaggini, McDonnell notes that the double missions of Son and Spirit are coextensive with each other, but are unmixed and without confusion.[105] At the same time there is a mutuality expressed by the missions that is understood by the very framework of the trinitarian grammar: the reality of the missions of Son and Spirit as originating from the Father also imply a return to the Father—"from the Father, through the Son, in the Spirit, to the Father." The katabatic and anabatic movements so integral to Kilmartin's theology are, in fact, the very thing that should maintain both the distinction and the mutuality of the missions of the divine Persons. McDonnell concludes his study by asserting simply: "Without the Son the Spirit is a finger of God lacking a history to touch. Without the mission of the Son the Spirit is a ladder to nowhere, and history never arrives at the Father."[106]

Any present attempt to articulate a trinitarian theology of liturgical participation must take into consideration the critiques presented here for both Vagaggini and Kilmartin, but also the most recent teachings regarding trinitarian action. Both Vagaggini and Kilmartin had developed their understandings of the action of the Trinity *ad extra* prior to the articulation of the most recent *Catechism*. The theology presented in the *Catechism* is worth repeating here:

> Being a work both common and personal, the whole divine economy makes known both what is proper to the divine persons and their one divine nature. Hence the whole Christian life is a communion with each of the divine persons, without in any way separating them. Everyone who glorifies the Father does so through the Son in the Holy

---

[104] Ibid., 200.

[105] Ibid. Interestingly, McDonnell plays off of his elliptical imagery presented earlier in his critique of an understanding of the personal missions as being too distinct from one another. In imaging something that is coextensive, unmixed, and without confusion, McDonnell suggests visualizing two circles, equal in size and depth, that appear superimposed upon each other and thus seem identical.

[106] Ibid., 229.

Spirit; everyone who follows Christ does so because the Father draws him and the Spirit moves him.[107]

The *Catechism* also makes clear how the personal work of Father, Son, and Spirit specifically in the liturgy is to be interpreted. The Father acts as source and goal of the liturgical action as he blesses the church; the active presence of the Son manifests the paschal mystery, which unites the church to the heavenly liturgy; the Spirit animates the faithful to receive the self-communication of the triune God. To speak of specific agencies of the distinct Persons of the Trinity appears problematic; all divine operation in the liturgy is both common and personal. Any contemporary trinitarian theology of the liturgy must walk this careful line between the articulation of personal properties manifested in the triune action and the insistence on the indissolubility of any action of God *ad extra* in the economy of salvation.

Several theologians, both in America and in Europe, have attempted to take this careful walk through the process of devising a comprehensive approach to sacramentology. All of them, in one way or another, distinguish a distinctly trinitarian hue and tenor to their theology of the sacraments. Following in the same vein as the foundational work of both Vagaggini and Kilmartin, Louis-Marie Chauvet, Hans Bernhard Meyer, and Kenan Osborne all attempt to rearticulate the traditional notion of sacraments. A brief look at each of their methods is helpful at this juncture to determine what elements are necessary in a trinitarian theology of liturgical participation.

At the heart of Louis-Marie Chauvet's reinterpretation of sacramental discourse is an inherent belief that the paschal mystery (precisely the cross event) provides a better locus for understanding how the triune God acts in the world than the scholastic adherence to an incarnational model of divine-triune revelation. For Chauvet, an insistence on the recognition of the divinity of Jesus in the incarnation forces a pretrinitarian concept of God upon the theology of Jesus as well as a necessary instrumental mediation upon humanity.[108] Instead, he argues, the modern theologian must admit that there needs to be a different way of thinking about God altogether that moves theology to a possibility of understanding the humanity and corporeality of God through

---

[107] CCC, §259.

[108] Louis-Marie Chauvet, *Symbole et Sacrement* (Paris: Cerf, 1990), 543–44.

God's absence on the cross. In this view "the mystery of the Church, and at the heart of the Church, the mystery of the sacraments are the great symbols of this mystery of God taking flesh in humanity"[109] through two interconnected poles of Christology and pneumatology. The temptation for sacramental theology is to vacillate between those two poles, creating an understanding of sacraments that is rooted in the particular acts of Christ or one that is grounded in the overarching universality of the operation of the Spirit. In his later, more pastoral treatise on the sacraments Chauvet explains this necessary balancing act:

> It is therefore impossible to erase, in the name of the *universal* of the Spirit (who "blows where it chooses"), the *particular* of God's being written down somewhere: in this particular people, Israel; in these particular Scriptures, Judeo-Christian; in this particular human being, Jesus of Nazareth, confessed as "Christ of God"; in this particular group which is claimed by him, the church; and finally, in these particular ritual acts of the Word that this church effects in memory of him.
>
> But conversely, it is impossible to enclose God's salvation within the particularity of an institution: the Spirit knows no boundaries. The particular character of the grace given by baptism is for believers the concrete way enabling them to give thanks for the universal love of God. For how could they give thanks for this universal if they had not received from it their particular grace? At the same time, the universal character of God's love is the horizon without which they could not give thanks for the particular character of the grace they received.[110]

What Chauvet presents in his sacramental theology is a trinitarian God revealed in the world through the humanity of Jesus, but who, in such a revelation, directs the believer into the deeper mystery of the Trinity itself. The sacraments, in balancing the christological and pneumatological poles of God's revelation, provide the nexus for the place of encounter between radically distinct entities: God and humanity.

Hans Bernhard Meyer also represents a methodological shift in the understanding of trinitarian presence in the sacraments in the

---

[109] Ibid., 547.
[110] Louis-Marie Chauvet, *Les Sacrements: Parole de Dieu au Risque du Corps* (Paris: Les Éditions de L'Atelier, 1997), 185. The emphasis is in the original.

development of his theology on the Eucharist. Following on the work of Giraudo, Meyer posits that the eucharistic celebration can be more adequately qualified as a "memorial-blessing."[111] But here, the memorial-blessing is rooted first in the action of the divine blessing upon the people of God (*eulogische* is seen as blessing/thanksgiving) and then in thanksgiving for God's graciousness. Meyer asserts that such a demarcation of the shape of the celebration is significant for and aptly suited to the Eucharist. For Meyer, the memorial-thanksgiving (*gedenkend-eulogische*) character of the worship allows the theologian to frame his or her understanding of the liturgical act in terms of the self-revelatory gift from God and the human response. That gift is expressed in the offering of the Son—Jesus is viewed as the culmination of the self-communication of God: "he is the 'Yes' of God to the world."[112]

Moreover, Meyer maintains that the commemorative act of worship and the salvific act of blessing in the liturgical action are only rooted together through the action of the Trinity. He asserts that within the execution of the actual liturgical celebration there exist both the soteriological-katabatic action (God blessing humanity) and the cultic-anabatic action (humanity giving praise and thanks to God) that come to expression in word, gesture, and offering.[113] But the integration of the two actions only happens because of the presence and action of the Trinity. He maintains that "all of this can only happen because of the blessing of God's self-gift to us, through Christ in the Holy Spirit, so that we, the church, can in turn give ourselves and our world to the Father with Christ, in the Holy Spirit, in the memorial-blessing of praise."[114] In this sense the shape of the celebration as "memorial-blessing" demands a trinitarian construct to understand and execute the liturgical action.

In a similar vein Kenan Osborne maintains that the liturgical celebration of the sacraments represents a unique and unrepeatable event in their actual celebration. Osborne relies on Heidegerrian categories

---

[111] Hans Bernhard Meyer, et al. *Eucharistie: Geschichte, Theologie, Pastoral, Gottesdienst der Kirche*. Gottesdienst der Kirche 4 (Regensburg: Pustet, 1989), 456–57. In his *The Eucharist in the West*, Kilmartin translates Meyer's "gedenkend-eulogischen Charakter des Wortgottesdienstes" as the "blessing-commemoration character of worship." See also ibid., 341.

[112] Meyer, *Eucharistie*, 457. " . . . er ist das 'Ja' Gottes zur Welt."

[113] Ibid., 455.

[114] Ibid.

of *Ereignis* (the individualized event as it happens) and *haecceitas* (the 'thisness' of the celebration—its uniqueness).[115] He cites the earlier work of Chauvet and notes that when one seeks to speak about sacramental *haecceitas* one must recognize the inherent relation between the proclaimed word and the action of the sacrament. Word and sacrament point to the primacy of divine action, the central role of Christ, and the necessary presence and action of the Spirit.[116] But he also goes beyond Chauvet's assessment to note that the challenge to the postmodern world is to establish a linguistic framework for speaking about sacraments that validates the subjectivity so inherent in postmodern thought. For Osborne, part of the *haecceitas* of the sacraments is dependent on the interaction of specific subjects, which is never the same.

Because the sacramental action includes both the self-disclosure of the triune God and the specific graced transformation of individual believers, Osborne argues that sacraments cannot be discussed simply in terms of universals or generalities.[117] The utter subjectivity of the sacramental action is not a reflection of the participants' relation to or stance toward the rite (*ex opere operantis*), but rather that subjectivity stems from the more basic reality that all sacraments are the work of the Trinity—three divine Persons self-communicating the Godhead— and a unique response to that communication by individual " 'selves' not 'sames' responding."[118] For Osborne it is the exchange between the triune God and the responding individual believers that forms the basis for understanding sacramental action.

What becomes apparent, then, in the postconciliar period, especially as the church has moved into the twenty-first century, is that no one system is in place for an understanding of sacramental action. What began in the works of Vagaggini and Kilmartin and is reflected in more contemporary scholars like Chauvet, Meyer, and Osborne

---

[115] Kenan B. Osborne, *Christian Sacraments in a Postmodern World: A Theology for the Third Millennium* (Mahwah, NJ: Paulist Press, 1999), 58.

[116] Ibid., 160–61.

[117] Ibid., 195.

[118] Ibid., 195–96. Osborne's stance is somewhat problematic since he will go on to argue that a sacramental event only truly occurs when the secondary response of the individual human participant has taken place. This is not to say that the offer of grace in the self-communication of God is dependent on the human participant, but rather that the nature of communication itself necessitates a response to the proposed engagement God initiates with humanity.

indicates a significant paradigmatic shift in sacramental theology. The necessary inclusion of trinitarian language into sacramental discourse in the West, brought about by the work of Vagaggini and Kilmartin and the theology of the council, has prompted theologians to develop and experiment with new possibilities for articulating how and why trinitarian action matters to the sacramental event.

The significance of recognizing a triune presence in the early initiation liturgies of the church centers on the reality of how that presence effects change in the believer. The notion of active presence in the sacraments came to the foreground in sacramental theology after the Second Vatican Council demarcated an expanded notion of Christ's presence in the liturgy.[119] Other than the Tridentine-declared presence of Christ in the eucharistic species, the other three descriptions of Christ's presence—in the actions of the minister, the proclamation of the word, and the gathering of the assembly—all had a markedly active component.[120] This active presence of Christ opened the door to speak more concretely of the agency of the presence of the triune Persons.

Earlier we noted William Hill's description of the presence of the triune Persons in relation to their respective missions. Hill asserts that the presence of the Spirit is a reality whose effect is *unitive* of God. When the Spirit indwells in the believer, that indwelling presence is active: "the mere presence of the *Pneuma* means loving union with God because the third in God is personal love. He is himself the union of Father and Son and so if given to men makes them to be, by his very personal presence, sharers in divine trinitarian life."[121] The question for the sacramental theologian is to determine how that presence of the Spirit is distinguishable from the presence of the Spirit that is specific to the liturgical activity of the church in its sacraments. Kilmartin went to great lengths to articulate the indivisibility of anamnesis and epiclesis in the liturgical action and to assert that every sacrament was a means by which the communion of the faithful could accept the grace of the self-communication of God. As he noted, to ask for the Father to send the Spirit or to pray for a sacramental presence of the Spirit

---

[119] SC 7.

[120] Even the presence of Christ in the eucharistic species can be viewed as active in the sense that the consecrated species are meant to transform those who receive them. They are consecrated as such to be received and consumed.

[121] Hill, *The Three-Personed God*, 291–92.

(*Veni, Sancte Spiritus*—Come, Holy Spirit) is to presuppose an ecclesial reality of communion in the church where that same Spirit is already present. The Spirit-filled church gathers to make memorial (anamnesis) of Christ's saving acts and asks for the Spirit's presence (epiclesis) to be drawn into union with Christ. Here, both Kilmartin's and Vagaggini's understanding of the crucial role of the believing church in the sacramental action is important. For Kilmartin it is the simple recognition that the sacraments are simultaneously actions of Christ and the church. For Vagaggini it is the awareness that the sign value of the church, its sacramentality, is dependent on the activity of the Spirit within it. As *mediated immediacy*, the Spirit's presence forms the link between the human person and the self-communication of God to the church. Hill maintains that the "graced soul relates to the Trinity in inverse order (to the processions): first to the Spirit, then to the Son, and lastly to the Father. If so, this explains the preeminence given to the Spirit in all questions of God's *presence.*"[122] Through the presence of the Spirit, the believer and the communion of the faithful are brought into the dynamic action of God's self-communication.

The active presence of the Spirit as invoked in the sacraments (epiclesis) and the active presence of the Spirit that presupposes the liturgical action (in the gathering of the εκκλεσια) demands some clarification. The indwelling of the Spirit in the baptized, and thus in those who belong to the sacramental life of the church, represents a share in the sonship of Christ. The epicletic action of the liturgy invokes an action of the Spirit that allows the faithful to enter into even more complete union with the faith and mission of Christ, or, in the case of the nonbaptized, to enter that sonship for the first time. The question that is presented by the vast number of epicletic formulae in the sacraments centers on one central issue: whether or not the invocation of the Spirit also implies a call for presence. Congar, for example, suggests that the eucharistic epiclesis is constitutive of the sacramental effect through an active presence of the Spirit. He notes: "The effectiveness of the grace of the sacraments has always been attributed to the effectiveness of the Holy Spirit, the *virtus Spiritus Sancti*, throughout the history of the Church. This means that the sacred action celebrated in the Church's Eucharist calls for the complement of an active coming

---

[122] Ibid., 296. The emphasis is Hill's; the parenthetical clarification belongs to this author.

of the Spirit."[123] Does the repeated call of the believing church for the Spirit to come upon baptismal water, sacred chrism, or bread and wine constitute a recognition that the Spirit is lacking? Perhaps yes—at least in those elements that are used in the liturgical celebration. But does the invocation of the Spirit to transform, for instance, the believers into the living Body of Christ, or a man and woman into a wedded couple, or an infirm body into a healthy one recognize a presence that was previously missing? In the end it is the active presence of the Spirit that communicates the sacramental sanctification of grace.

The active presence of the Spirit must be envisioned in conjunction with the active presence of Christ in the sacraments. John H. McKenna writes that this relationship cannot be conceived as an "either-or" dichotomy, as if the presence and action of Christ were in competition with the presence and action of the Spirit: "We have here a double presence, a double service and mediation, a double action of Christ in the Spirit and the Spirit in Christ serving as 'two hands of the Father' in drawing man into a new life."[124] Here, Kilmartin's understanding of the proper missions of Son and Spirit is helpful, as is the insistence of the *Catechism* that Son and Spirit have missions that are both personal and common. McKenna articulates this double presence as fulfilling the purpose of the paschal mystery. He asserts: "It is the Holy Spirit who accomplishes the sanctification of men, who carries the work of Christ to its fulfillment. Or, to put it another way, it is Christ, filled with the Holy Spirit, who, through his own resurrection and exaltation as Lord (*Kyrios*), is now able freely to communicate this life-giving Spirit to mankind."[125] The offer and attitude of acceptance of grace (as the self-communication of the Trinity) are made real through the active presence of the Spirit and Christ.

In the very articulation of his point on a double presence McKenna also points to a third presence—that of the Father. As the "two hands of the Father," the active presence of the Son and the Spirit manifests the presence of their source and goal in the Father. A truly trinitarian theology must take the Father's presence into account when discussing sacramental action. William Hill notes that the personal presence

---

[123] Congar, *I Believe in the Holy Spirit*, 250.

[124] John H. McKenna, *Eucharist and Holy Spirit: The Eucharistic Epiclesis in 20th Century Theology* (Great Wakering, Essex: Mayhew-McCrimmon, 1975), 199.

[125] Ibid., 200.

of the Father in the Trinity's actions in the world has been explained in various ways; Rahner attempted to posit presence as a quasi-formal cause of salvation in the soul, while Coffey and others articulate a presence of Father and Son that is derived from the abiding presence of the Spirit in the world.[126] None of these attempts, however, seems adequate to explain this notion of active personal presence. Rather, Hill explains the presence of the Triune Persons in terms of *communicatio*—when the Trinity has a causal influence on the created persons (the faithful), it has that influence as Trinity, but it is expressed in terms of their personal presence and the self-communication of their personal identity.[127] In this sense the Father makes himself knowable and lovable through the missions of the Spirit and Son. The Spirit unites the believer to the attitudes and action of Christ, who calls God "Abba, Father."

Eschatological Participation and Sacramental Ethics

The last area for analysis concerns not only how well each theologian is able to uphold the rather intricate metaphoric base for active liturgical participation, but also whether or not each brings a greater understanding or meaning to the cluster of metaphors that surrounds *actuosa participatio*. We have mentioned earlier how any understanding of participation must take into consideration its metaphysical, soteriological, ecclesiological, and liturgical meanings. Furthermore, we have argued that liturgical participation presupposes all the other meanings and, by its very nature, is a reflection of the self-communication of the triune God—so much so that woven through a comprehensive understanding of liturgical participation is a trinitarian narrative that serves as the foundation of the liturgical act. It is appropriate, then, to investigate how well Vagaggini and Kilmartin embrace the multiple nuances of meaning of active participation as each develops his trinitarian theology of liturgical participation. It is also important to articulate possible applications of the theologies or insights they have developed.

At the heart of Vagaggini's trinitarian theology of liturgical participation lies his fundamental concept of *sintonia d'animo interna*—the internal tuning of the soul. He posits that a necessary component of liturgical participation is rooted in the ability of the individual to

---

[126] Hill, *The Three-Personed God*, 292–93.
[127] Ibid., 295–96.

"tune in" to the liturgical signs and actions employed in the celebration by the church. One level of necessity stems from the realm of meaning: simply that the *sintonia d'animo* breaks open the vast array of symbols and signs used in the liturgical celebration. Without this internal tuning of the soul, the full effect and experience of the liturgical action is diminished. Furthermore, through the process of *sintonia d'animo* the individual is united more completely to Christ and to the church. The fundamental narrative to which the soul must attune itself is a trinitarian one that unfolds the self-communication of God. As Vagaggini develops his trinitarian approach to liturgical participation he builds on the various metaphorical understandings of participation.

In the order of being, Vagaggini uses the metaphysical sense of participation in two distinct ways. First, he posits the complexus of signs that makes up the liturgy as a manifestation of the symbolic reality that undergirds the sacramental action. Here, the participation that is implied is not a participation in the divine being directly but rather a participation in the essence of the complexus of signs that is caused or instituted by God. In the metaphysical understanding of participation, an effect participates in its cause. Thus when one enters fully into the complexus of signs that makes up the liturgy one also begins a movement toward participation in the divine being.

Such an understanding of the power of the network of liturgical signs is a distinct revision of the scholastic understanding of signs. Vagaggini himself noted this distinction at the beginning of his major work, *Il senso teologico*. In commenting on Aquinas's developed sense of signification Vagaggini characterizes the scholastic relationship between causality and signifying simply: "Every effect of efficient causality—implying always the realization of an exemplary causality—implies in the effect a participation of the form of the agent, who is first of all God himself. It is for this reason that all things are necessarily and really signs, vestiges, and images of God; they really partake of him and he is really present in them."[128] At the level of being, everything is a sign of God. But Vagaggini also points to the necessity of *tuning in* to the signs that are used in the liturgy in order to recognize the unique activity of the human subject in the act of worship. Here, he begins to build on Aquinas's notion of the meaning of signs for the

---

[128] *Il senso teologico* (1965), 55. The inclusion of exemplary causality in the Aristotelian demarcation of causes is a distinctly Thomistic addition.

faithful. Aquinas maintains that all signs used in the sanctification of the faithful are divinely instituted (*divina institutione*) and therefore are not determined by the individual.[129] Vagaggini's development of this *sintonia d'animo* to the complexus of signs used in the liturgy, however, does have ramifications for the act of worship by the faithful. While the divine component of the liturgy is the act of sanctification, the human component is the act of worship, and thus, for Vagaggini, true and complete worship demands that the believer cognitively understand and appropriate the liturgical signs that have been divinely instituted. The symbolic reality that undergirds the sacramental action reveals the divine.

Second, Vagaggini goes beyond this cognitive notion to imply also that through the medium of sacramental-liturgical signs believers participate metaphysically in God in a unique way. Because he wants to expand the Thomistic notion of sign, Vagaggini maintains that the liturgical sign has four dimensions. It demonstrates to those partaking in the sign: first, sanctifying grace and interior worship; second, God effecting sanctification while being the object of worship; then Christ as the cause of both sanctification and worship in the person; and finally the church as both the object of sanctification and the instrumental cause of worship.[130] The first dimension points to the soteriological value of liturgical acts (participation in grace as the self-communication of God), but the second and third dimensions point to the metaphysical understanding of participation in God in terms of an exemplary cause acting upon its effect. The link between God's transforming sanctification of the human person and Christ's ministry as priest forms the vehicle for metaphysical participation in God's being. Going far beyond what most of his contemporaries would argue, Vagaggini asserts that "when it is said that God sanctifies a man, what is meant is that he actually works a real and physical transformation in his being, allowing him actually to participate in the mode of being and of acting proper to the divinity."[131] He elaborates slightly by arguing that one can see that the eucharistic sacrifice can only occur through a participation in the sacramental and hierarchical priesthood

---

[129] ST III, q. 60, a. 5.
[130] *Il senso teologico* (1965), 87.
[131] Ibid., 268.

of Christ.[132] But this assertion means he is positing that the sanctifying action of God and the offering of Christ are directly revelatory of the *esse* of God. As we will see, that link has significant soteriological and ecclesiological ramifications.

Vagaggini will also posit that the liturgical signs that are instituted by God, namely, the sacraments, transcend time and make present the reality of God's self-communication to the believer. That self-communication is manifested as sanctifying grace, in which, Vagaggini asserts, "We are speaking about a true, though accidental and mysterious participation in the divine nature, of participation in the incarnation and of conformity to Christ, which includes the indwelling within us of the divine Persons and will lead us to the glory of the beatific vision as its natural fulfillment."[133] In this sense Vagaggini maintains the metaphysical sense of participation even if it is one step removed—the believer participates in the sign that effects grace—but also conjoins the metaphysical with the soteriological, since that grace has the self-communication of the divine nature as its cause.

An important observation about Vagaggini's sign theory is appropriate here. One could assert that Vagaggini's formulation of the link between the complexus of signs, grace, and the divine nature serves as a stepping stone from the scholastic notion of sacraments that *effect what they signify* to the modern assessment of sacraments as acts of ritual symbolization as is reflected in the theology of Louis Marie Chauvet. Chauvet deliberately moves away from any sense of metaphysical participation and replaces it with a strictly defined liturgical-ritual participation—the believer participates as part of the body of the faithful in a ritual act that symbolically joins humanity in divinity through grace-filled sacraments—the sacraments "manifest the 'already-there' of grace in the experience of faith."[134] One might argue that the movement toward understanding sacramental efficacy *qua* symbolic ritual actions begins in the work of Vagaggini and finds its highpoint in Chauvet.[135]

---

[132] Ibid.

[133] Ibid., 137.

[134] Chauvet, *Symbole et Sacrement*, 442.

[135] It is worthy of note that Chauvet was selected to inaugurate the *Lectiones Vagagginiaea* (The Vagaggini Lectures) at Sant'Anselmo in 2004. His inaugural address, "De la médiation. Quatre études théologique sur les sacrements," was eventually published in book form in Italy as *Della mediazione. Quattro studi*

Vagaggini also expands the soteriological understanding of participation in his trinitarian theology as he explains how the complexus of signs operates to manifest the mystery presence of Christ. Christ's saving acts are deemed as the merit by which the human person is sanctified in grace and Christ's particular act of worship to the Father, that is, the offering of his life on the cross, becomes the exemplar of all human worship. In asserting the dual impact of his "law of incarnation" Vagaggini maintains that the human person must pass through sensible things in order to receive the divine self-communication of grace and that in the acceptance of that communication the human person is elevated to a divine way of being and acting.[136] In Vagaggini's depiction, that self-communication of grace is connected to the mystery presence of Christ and Christ's priesthood, both of which expand the notion of soteriological and ecclesiological participation. Distinguishing himself from Casel, Vagaggini notes that the mystery presence of Christ is the presence of a continuous divine disposition revealed, as it were, through the medium of Christ's humanity: the mystery presence of Christ is not the singular act of the cross but rather the singular disposition of the Son, the mystery of Christ as redeemer.[137] The liturgical act, which manifests this mystery presence, becomes the vehicle for transformation in grace by union with Christ, both in his disposition as redeemer and in his activity as the eternal priest; worship and sanctification are two sides of the same coin. The *sintonia d'animo* at the heart of Vagaggini's liturgical theology implies a "tuning in" to the liturgical signs and actions of the church that unites the individual to Christ. It is in this union that the soteriological sense of participation opens into the ecclesiological sense.

Vagaggini undergirds his ecclesiological sense of participation by emphasizing the unity of the action of Christ and the action of the church. "Sanctification and worship," he argues, "are nothing but a participation in Christ's sanctity"[138] and a participation in the fleshed-out reality of that sanctity in Christ's worship as a human. Here, Vagaggini's insistence on the corporeality of participation is crucial: the church acts as the living image of the sanctity and worship of

---

di teologia sacramentaria fondamentale. Testo francese a fronte (Assisi: Cittadella, 2006).

[136] *Il senso teologico* (1965), 290.

[137] Ibid., 122.

[138] Ibid., 126.

Christ as its members are radically united to the mystery presence of Christ in the sacraments: the flesh becomes the instrument of salvation. Vagaggini's ecclesiology, then, begins in the nature of the liturgy as signs (metaphysics), is brought to the foreground through the salvific power of the mystery presence of Christ (soteriology), and finds its completion in the unity that believers have with that presence and the church (ecclesiology). Vagaggini asserts that this participation of individuals in the "divine realities that came to pass in Christ"[139] configures the individuals to Christ himself. That configuration allows the sacrifice of Christ to become the sacrifice of the church. In this way Vagaggini is able to create a unique theological impact with his understanding of *ex opere operantis Ecclesiae*, since in his formulation the act of the church cannot be separated from the act of Christ.[140] The offering of Christ and of the Christ-centered church includes a grace-activity that not only discloses the self-communication of God but also establishes the reception of that communication.

Vagaggini uses this amalgamation of the various metaphors surrounding participation to strengthen and nuance his own description of active liturgical participation. Building on the metaphysical, soteriological, and ecclesiological senses of participation, he is able to portray ritual-liturgical participation in full, active, and communitarian terms. As noted earlier in our discussion of his thought,[141] he avers that the fullness of liturgical participation must go beyond both external participation in the rite and internal acceptance of the sanctification and worship of the rite. Rather, Vagaggini's sense of full liturgical participation implies a *tuning in* to the complexus of signs that makes up the liturgy as well as a *tuning in* to the trinitarian narrative that propels it. The fullness of participation directly feeds into the notion of active liturgical participation, since the liturgy by its very nature not only demands the willful action of all who are gathered but also reinforces that action by concretizing the bestowal of grace, not in an internal disposition of readiness or openness but in the enactment of the rite: sacraments cause grace by signifying.

---

[139] Cipriano Vagaggini, "Caro salutis est cardo. Corporeità, Eucharistia e Liturgia," in *Miscellanea Liturgica in onore di sua eminenza Il Cardinale Giacomo Lercaro* (Rome: Desclée, 1966), 73–210, at 165.

[140] Edward J. Kilmartin, "Sacraments as Liturgy of the Church," *Theological Studies* 50 (1989): 527–47, at 529–30.

[141] See page 97.

Finally, Vagaggini's sense of liturgical participation is also communitarian in that it emphasizes the unity between Christ acting as High Priest and Mediator and the church acting in accord with him. Every liturgical action is performed by the church through Christ, in the presence of the Spirit that unites it, and directed to the Father.[142] For Vagaggini, then, liturgical participation incorporates the various metaphors related to participation we have seen thus far.

Vagaggini's careful demarcation of the fullness of the concept of liturgical participation and its embrace of the various metaphorical understandings of participation is not without its shortcomings, especially in regard to the trinitarian narrative. Because Vagaggini maintains that a radical association or union with Christ is made in the liturgical action, he also posits that the same liturgical action provides the vehicle through which one enters into the trinitarian mystery. Any action of Christ is intimately connected to the christological-trinitarian schema of *a . . . per . . . in . . . ad* that Vagaggini finds in the early liturgical evidence of the church. That schema posits not only the self-communication of grace to the world but also the potential for its acceptance. The *a . . . per . . . in . . . ad* dynamic presupposes a return to God the Father manifested also by the reality of the *Kyrios*, the risen and glorified Christ, who acts as High Priest and Mediator. As Vagaggini turns his notion of *sintonia d'animo* upon the trinitarian dynamic itself, one cannot help but notice that he never fully develops this trinitarian motif within his concept of liturgical participation. Rather, in the liturgical celebration the action and presence of Christ, the *Kyrios*, is paramount. The Father is seen as the origin and terminus of Christ's action and the Spirit is depicted as the medium through which the church joins its action to Christ.[143] Despite Vagaggini's insistence otherwise, the trinitarian action within the liturgical celebration seems muted at best because of the overarching identification with Christ: there is "but one liturgist, Christ, and but one liturgy, that of Christ."[144] This is perhaps the greatest irony of Vagaggini's work. He endeavors to identify and develop a christological-trinitarian schema, but he

---

[142] *Il senso teologico* (1965), 765–66.

[143] Ibid., 257. While Vagaggini claims to advocate a distinctive action of the Holy Spirit that is not in contradiction or competition with the action of Christ, he never fully demarcates that action.

[144] Ibid., 249.

never really moves beyond the highly Christocentric approach of the liturgical theology of *Mediator Dei*.

In the end, what we find in the extensive work of Vagaggini is a mixed hybrid of liturgical participation and trinitarian narrative. On the one hand, he has created a nuanced and detailed understanding of liturgical participation, building it slowly but fastidiously upon layers of understanding of the various metaphors related to participation and the divine. On the other, he has attempted to thread throughout that sense of liturgical participation a trinitarian narrative that is never truly developed.

Like Vagaggini before him, Edward Kilmartin also attempted to wed his theology of liturgical participation with the trinitarian narrative he saw at the heart of all liturgical action. Whereas Vagaggini began with a scholastic sense of metaphysical participation and gradually expanded it outward to include the various other metaphorical senses of participation, Kilmartin based his theology on the *de facto* reality of active liturgical participation as a component part of the ritual act. From the acting liturgical subject he opens his theology to varying senses of participation in the church, in Christ, and eventually in the Trinity itself. Unlike Vagaggini, Kilmartin intricately wedded a well-developed trinitarian theology to his theology of participation, but in so doing he perhaps sacrificed some of the detail to the various metaphorical levels of participation.

As we have seen, Kilmartin begins his detailed sacramental theology by placing the liturgical action squarely within the ecclesial arena: all sacraments are acts of the church, which in its own way acts as a sacrament, that is, the church acts as a visible sign of the invisible presence of God. All liturgical participation must therefore assume an ecclesial participation. In order to guard against a humanistic approach to the sacraments, Kilmartin maintains that it is the Spirit who acts as the "primary efficient cause of the communication of salvation through word and sacrament."[145] But he notes that the Spirit is said to function in a way that is analogous to that of a formal cause as well. The Spirit determines the content of the self-communication of God and ordains it within the action of the church, especially in its liturgy. The Spirit establishes the shape and structure of the celebration by inspiring the church in its determination of the liturgy and the

[145] "A Modern Approach," 71.

sacramental form it uses. Kilmartin views the sacraments as "Spirit-endowed realities of the Church,"[146] but perhaps even more significant, he views the church itself as a "sacrament of the Spirit"—that is, the church is the visible reality that signifies the invisible operation and grace of the Spirit. Part of his intent here is to safeguard against an overly christocentric approach to sacraments if, indeed, the purpose of such liturgical actions lies in the self-communication of the triune God. In fact, he maintains that even if one highlights the role of the priest in the sacramental action (acting *in persona Christi*), such an emphasis still points to the reality of the ecclesial body: the priest is ordained to the community, acts for the sake of the community, and represents the church analogously as Christ is head of that church. He argues: "Here the ecclesiological dimension is not short-circuited; it is emphasized. This theological outlook guards against the tendency of scholastic theology toward an exclusively Christological interpretation, which was carried through in classical Reformation theology."[147] If, as Kilmartin surmises, the sacraments are ways in which the church actualizes itself so that it might stand as a sacramental reality in the world, then one has to accept that all liturgical activity begins with an ecclesial participation in the Spirit. Even in the unfolding of the economy of salvation, Kilmartin would argue for this operative ecclesiological participation in the formation of the church itself. He maintains that in their origins the sacraments are manifested in such a way that "through the mission of the Holy Spirit, the disciples accepted through faith their incorporation into the Church of the risen Lord."[148]

For Kilmartin it is precisely this ecclesial participation in the Spirit through the church that serves as the vehicle for a more soteriological participation in the one *transitus* of Christ. He first made this assessment when he looked at the early anaphoras. In the act of memorial (*anamnesis*) and the invocation of the Holy Spirit (*epiclesis*) the structure of the anaphoras not only points to the dynamism at the heart of the trinitarian relations but also points to how that dynamism manifests itself in the world in salvation history. What the church celebrates in its liturgy, Kilmartin argues, centers on a redefinition of the understanding of believers as liturgical subjects. One can argue that

---

[146] *Christian Liturgy*, 232.
[147] "Sacraments as Liturgy of the Church," 529.
[148] Ibid., 533.

the participation in the ecclesial reality and the necessary liturgical participation it implies has soteriological significance because of the trinitarian narrative that lies at the heart of the content and structure of liturgical prayer. Kilmartin asserts that "the community is rendered present under the formality, not of passive spectators, but of active participants in Jesus' uniquely acceptable response to what the Father has done in him for the salvation of the world."[149] Because of the presence and action of the Spirit, the person of Christ is essentially united to the church in the liturgical celebration.

The soteriological union of Christ to the church brought forth by the presence of the Spirit in the sacraments has a twofold dimension. First, that unity can be expressed in terms of the sacrifice of Christ made accessible to humanity through the human act of faith. The once-for-all offering of Christ is joined to the offering of the church in the sacramental action. The mediated immediacy of the Spirit to the church and Christ allows the *sacrificium laudis*, the sacrifice of praise that is the church's offering, to be united to the sacerdotal activity of Christ the High Priest. As Edward Hahnenberg notes, "Christian sacrifice—and thus Christian priesthood in its exercise—is fundamentally an offering of self, an offering rooted in the divine self-offer."[150] Thus, self-offering is at the heart of Christ's identity—and, one can argue, at the heart of the identity of the Trinity in its self-communication. The significance of that offering comes in the liturgical celebration itself. Within the liturgical act the Spirit operates to unite the sacrifice of the lives of the community with the offering that identified the life of the Son. Commenting on Kilmartin's analysis, Hahnenberg asserts, "Believers participate in the priesthood of Christ in their actualization of his sacrificial faith, a faith shaped by the particular acts of love of God and love of neighbor that characterized Jesus' own life."[151] Those acts of love manifest God's self-communication in human form. When the prayer of the church is conducted through, with, and in Christ, "the offer of salvation is given visibility."[152] When the self-communication of God can be identified with the offering of Christ, it enters into the notion of participation in the order of grace.

---

[149] *The Eucharist in the West*, 371.
[150] Hahnenberg, "The Ministerial Priesthood," 258.
[151] Ibid., 267.
[152] "Sacraments as Liturgy of the Church," 537.

Second, the visible aspect of that offer of salvation opens up the way, the single *transitus*, to participation in the divine life through grace. We have noted already that the sacramental celebrations allow Christ to instruct the faithful and bind them to the Gospel; such is the trajectory of his own life and witness through his birth, death, and resurrection. The entry into that one *transitus* is a specifically trinitarian action that has as its root the self-communication of the triune God. While Kilmartin argues that sacraments can only be understood from the reference point of Christ—his offering for, his instruction of, and his engagement with the faithful—he also notes that one only comes to this mystery presence of Christ through the Spirit—to be conformed to the spiritual attitudes of Christ is the proper action of the Spirit, who mediates a personal immediacy between the believers and Christ. That personal immediacy forms the connection between liturgical participation, ecclesiological participation, and soteriological participation: through the liturgical action, enacted by the believing church through the power of the Spirit, the self-communication of God (grace) is made present. Moreover, the human response to the mystery presence in the acceptance of the one *transitus* moves the believer into participation in the covenant with the Father. In fact, Kilmartin would argue that the human response of faith is viewed primarily as a willingness to receive sacramental grace and thereby participate in the divine life of the Trinity.[153]

Participation in the divine life of the Trinity through the single *transitus* of Christ is maintained, in Kilmartin's analysis, by a final metaphysical participation in the Godhead. In this sense the single *transitus* of Christ acts as the exemplary cause of salvation. But the sanctification brought about by that cause has ramifications on the level of being. Because Kilmartin characterizes that *transitus* as the "response of the personality of God in his humanity: the response of the perfect man, which summarizes in itself and grounds the response of faith of all humanity,"[154] participation within that response of Christ ontologically changes those who participate. By participation in the faith response of Christ, believers enter into the mystery of the New Covenant and are united to Christ in a unique way. Commenting on Kilmartin's use of the theology of Brian McNamara, Jerome Hall maintains: "The

---

[153] *The Eucharist in the West*, 306.
[154] "Sacraments as Liturgy of the Church," 542.

historical mysteries of the life of Christ are, then, present in their effect, in the human recipient, as metaphysically affirmed."[155] That meta-physical affirmation must be rooted in the adoption of believers as sons and daughters of the Father in the New Covenant. But that New Covenant is, precisely speaking, the mystery presence of Christ. At the level of being, one enters into participation in the mystery of Christ. Kilmartin is careful not to fall into the fallacy that this participation is an ontological equivalent that erases the distinction between human-ity and God. Rather, such participation is inherently trinitarian: "the believer grasps the faith of Christ and is thereby united to the incarnate Son, and in him with the Father. What explains both the immediacy of the believer to Christ and the distance is the Holy Spirit. As bond of unity between Christ and the believer, the Spirit provides the pneuma-tological link."[156] In this sense Kilmartin comes full circle: liturgical par-ticipation, by culminating in a participation in the mystery presence of Christ, now moves the faithful into the *opus operatum* of the church and back into the fundamental liturgical action where he began.

In looking at the theologies of liturgical participation presented by Vagaggini and Kilmartin one could probably argue that Vagaggini emphasizes a descending christological motif while trying to locate the connection between trinitarian revelation and the liturgical-sacramental act, while Kilmartin highlights an ascending christological schema that leads him from the liturgical action to union with the Trinity. Such a characterization may perhaps be too rudimentary, but it is also inter-esting to note that neither is really complete without the other.

While Kilmartin comes closer to establishing the direct link between active participation in the liturgy and the trinitarian narrative, the full impact and effect of his theology has yet to be determined. After his death in 1994 his papers were collected at Boston College to be placed in one of the institution's research libraries (the Burns Library).[157] To date, however, those manuscripts are available only for limited use and have not yet been made available for public access.[158] The scope

---

[155] Hall, *We Have the Mind of Christ*, 31.

[156] "Sacraments as Liturgy of the Church," 542.

[157] See Robert Daly's comment in Kilmartin, *The Eucharist in the West*, xvi.

[158] The "Kilmartin Papers" have been sorted and catalogued but still remain in the possession of Daly, a professor at Boston College and former student of Kilmartin. This author was fortunate enough to have been granted unlimited access to Kilmartin's papers and notes that were left when he died.

of his final papers, however, does provide some insight into where Kilmartin was taking his developing thought and show as well the various ways in which his theology has been studied and applied. The focus of his work at his death was primarily in two areas: the advantages of a communion ecclesiology and the action of the Holy Spirit in the sacraments.

In the past few years, with the exception of Jerome Hall's *We Have the Mind of Christ*, no extensive study has been published on Kilmartin's work and writings. What one does notice, however, is the growing number of doctoral dissertations and licentiate theses dedicated to one or another element of his thought,[159] despite the dearth of smaller articles devoted to a particular subject of Kilmartin's writings.[160] But

---

[159] See, for instance, Daniel Doherty, "The Development of the Concept of the Ecclesial Nature of the Sacraments from Selected Documents of Vatican II and through the Writings of Karl Rahner, Edward J. Kilmartin and Louis-Marie Chauvet," STL thesis, Catholic University of America, 2006; Joseph Erambil, "The Eucharist, the Holy Spirit, and the Church: A Study of the Pneumatological and Ecclesiological Dimensions of the Eucharist in the Writings of Edward J. Kilmartin," Diss. Pontificia Universitas Gregorianum, 1998; Steven J. Lopes, "From the Trinity to the Eucharist: Towards a Trinitarian Theology of the Sacrifice of Christ and its Representation in the Eucharist of the Church," Diss. Pontificia Universitas Gregorianum, 2005; Carmina M. Magnusen, *Encounter with the Triune God: An Introduction to the Theology of Edward J. Kilmartin, SJ* (San Francisco: Catholic Scholars Press, 1998); Stephen Sauer, SJ, "Naming Grace: A Comparative Study of Sacramental Grace Language in Edward Kilmartin, SJ, and Louis-Marie Chauvet," STD diss., Catholic University of America, 2007; Rodica M. M. Stoicoiu, "The Sacrament of Order in its Relationship to Eucharist, Church, and Trinity in the Theological Writings of Edward Kilmartin and John Zizioulas," PhD diss., Catholic Univeristy of America, 2004; Paul A. Williamson, "Contemporary Approaches to the Ordained Priestly Ministry in Theology and the Magisterium: A Study of Selected Writings of Edward J. Kilmartin, SJ, Hervé-Marie Legrand, OP, and Edward H. Schillebeeckx, OP, in the Light of the Second Vatican Council and Subsequent Magisterium," Diss. Pontificia Universitas Gregorianum, 1983. Magnusen's work was originally her PhD dissertation at Duquesne Univeristy in 1997. Catholic Scholars Press appears to be a self-publishing or desktop-publishing agency.

[160] Surprisingly little has been published in this regard that presents a direct analysis of Kilmartin's thought. See Hahnenberg, "The Ministerial Priesthood," and Peter Sanders, "Pneumatology in the Sacramental Theologies of

the number of theologians who have used Kilmartin as a stepping stone to further theological discussions is exponentially greater. Many of these writings seem to circle around questions of ecclesiology, pneumatology, and the Trinity, but none directly takes up the question of Kilmartin's theology of liturgical participation and its ramifications. A few inferences and conclusions can be drawn here about the impact of Kilmartin's trinitarian theology of liturgical participation that may be helpful in determining the future direction of sacramental participation.

Throughout his works on the liturgy and sacraments Kilmartin has expanded the notion of the ministerial priesthood of Christ and augmented the understanding of the activity and mission of the Holy Spirit. In doing so he has helped articulate the fundamental shift in the role of the laity after the Second Vatican Council, provided theological insight into the need for ecumenism, and reinserted pneumatology into many contemporary theological discussions where even a few decades before it had been noticeably absent.

In order to understand the influence Kilmartin has had on the understanding of the ministerial priesthood one must first look at how his thought on the presence of Christ has been applied to the liturgical action. Michael Witczak uses Kilmartin's theology of presence as a lens through which to analyze other contemporary approaches to understand the presence of Christ in the liturgy.[161] Witczak maintains that it is precisely the dialogic character of the liturgy, its substantial essence as *actio*, that reveals his approach to understanding the various ways in which Christ is present. All liturgy is an intentional movement or action of the Trinity in Kilmartin's theological framework; thus Witczak concludes that Kilmartin "reads the presences in this light, and sees them therefore as anabatic presences (Christ speaking to the Father) and katabatic presences (Christ speaking to us)."[162] The

---

Geoffrey Wainwright, Jean Corbon and Edward Kilmartin," *Worship* 68 (1994): 332–52. Much more has been written using Kilmartin as a foundational stepping stone and branching outward into a particular aspect of eucharistic theology. The overwhelming majority of research or reaction to Kilmartin has been published in English-language journals.

[161] Witczak looks at the interepretations of presence by Edward Schillebeeckx, Joseph Powers, Alexander Gerken, David Power, Robert Sokolowski, and Raymond Moloney.

[162] Witczak, "The Manifold Presence of Christ in the Liturgy," 697.

majority of the literature Witczak studies is "still driven by the Tridentine emphasis on transubstantiation and real presence and ends up dealing with ontological issues surrounding presence."[163] In contrast to this predominance, Witczak articulates the various ways in which the presence of Christ can be viewed as active in the various parts of the eucharistic liturgy. In this sense the active presence of Christ in the liturgy becomes revelatory of the connection between the priest and the assembly. Witczak notes: "Through the priest's service and mediation, the community remembers and petitions God that Christ's sacrifice may be present and shared in communion."[164] Witczak's appropriation of Kilmartin's model has been appropriated by others to articulate an expansion of the understanding of Christ's presence in the eucharistic action.[165]

Perhaps the most distinctive application of Kilmartin's theology of presence in the sacramental action is in the understanding of the priesthood and liturgical sacrifice.[166] For example, Robert Daly uses Kilmartin's notion of the trinitarian self-offering in the sacraments as the basis for a more detailed exposition of the unity between priest and assembly in the eucharistic sacrifice. Daly's point is not to erase the distinction between the ministerial priest and the gathered assembly but rather to emphasize that the prayers themselves point to a "primary ritual agent" in the liturgical assembly.[167] Daly maintains that "the presider never speaks as one above or apart from the assembly, nor does the presider speak or act as a mediator between God or Christ and the assembly."[168] At the heart of Daly's assessment is

---

[163] Ibid., 698.

[164] Ibid., 702.

[165] See Judith Marie Kubicki, CSSF, "Recognizing the Presence of Christ in the Liturgical Assembly," *Theological Studies* 65 (2004): 817–37; John H. McKenna, "Eucharistic Presence: An Invitation to Dialogue," *Theological Studies* 60 (1999): 294–317. McKenna cites Witczak's article at the outset of his discussion, and much of Kubicki's argumentation matches that of McKenna. Both authors attempt to highlight the active notion of presence articulated by Witczak.

[166] See, for example, Robert J. Daly, SJ, "Sacrifice Unveiled or Sacrifice Revisited: Trinitarian and Liturgical Perspectives," *Theological Studies* 64 (2003): 24–42; Hahnenberg, "The Ministerial Priesthood," 253–78; John H. McKenna, "Eucharist and Sacrifice: An Overview," *Worship* 76 (2000): 386–402.

[167] Daly, "Sacrifice Unveiled," 33.

[168] Ibid.

Kilmartin's postulation that the presence of the sacrifice of Christ must be approached from two varying but complementary viewpoints—on the one hand, the sacrifice of Christ is made present in the sacramental action and, on the other, the gathered assembly is made present to the sacrifice of Christ. Daly perhaps oversimplifies Kilmartin's stance since he fails to mention that at the heart of the action that makes the assembly present to the sacrifice of the Christ is the work and agency of the Holy Spirit.[169]

In Hahnenberg's compilation of Kilmartin's thought on priesthood the action of the Trinity comes to the foreground. Echoing the work of Kilmartin, Hahnenberg asserts that "Christ's self-offering response was distinctive, the fullest possible acceptance and response to God's self-communication, an orientation progressively actualized throughout his life and realized on the cross. This sacrifice has its ground in the trinitarian life of God."[170] Because the sacrifice is intimately connected to the self-communication of the Trinity, the priesthood of Christ is similarly set in trinitarian terms. When the assembly then participates in the priesthood of Christ in the liturgical action, that ecclesial action also takes on trinitarian significance. Hahnenberg maintains that the assembly's sacrificial response is nothing other than a "participation in the faith of Jesus, through which human persons experience the Father's love and are united to Christ in his response to the Father—believers are caught up in the Spirit in the saving dynamic of trinitarian life."[171] In creating this dynamic Hahnenberg seeks to extend the notion of priesthood beyond the offering of sacrificial or cultic gifts; priesthood is manifested in the sacrifice determined by self-offering. The ministerial priesthood, therefore, has the unique gift

---

[169] Daly does mention the relationship between the assembly and the Spirit when he describes "the self-offering of believers" (pp. 31–32), but he later notes the limitations of "the second approach to presence," and that the self-offering of believers is a finite, human act (p. 40). The contrasting assertions are problematic. In an earlier article Daly does mention Kilmartin's unique contribution as to the role of the Spirit, but he does not go beyond simply stating that such a role exists. See also, Robert J. Daly, SJ, "Robert Bellarmine and Post-Tridentine Eucharistic Theology," *Theological Studies* 61 (2000): 239–60; McKenna, "Eucharist and Sacrifice: An Overview," 400. McKenna gives an overview of Daly's approach.

[170] Ibid., 258.

[171] Ibid., 263–64.

of leading the assembly in its own self-offering in the priest's kenotic exercise of the "various ministries of prayer, preaching and presiding, counseling and community leadership, active service, teaching, and prophetic witness."[172] In this sense Hahnenberg helps demonstrate how Kilmartin's theology of trinitarian sacrifice can be applied to an understanding of the priest and the assembly both in the liturgical action and in work and life with each other.

The second primary area in which Kilmartin's trinitarian formulations have been applied is in that of understanding the proper role of the Holy Spirit in the liturgy. Here, the ongoing work of David Coffey and the extensive work done by Jerome Hall have been most fruitful. Coffey, for his part, used Kilmartin's theological perspective to hone and clarify his views on the role of the Holy Spirit in the liturgy and in the world.[173] Responding to Kilmartin's 1984 article,[174] Coffey sought to articulate how a proper mission of the Holy Spirit could be understood in the West without falling into the position often cited in the Eastern Orthodox Church, that the Spirit's mission is a replacement of the mission of Christ at Pentecost.[175] Coffey uses Kilmartin's critique to clarify his position regarding the entry of the Holy Spirit into the world and the point at which the same Spirit begins its proper mission at Pentecost. Kilmartin had argued that there were enough dissenting voices in the West about a proper mission of the Spirit to relegate the theological matter to a place of contention.[176] Moving forward from that critique, Coffey seeks to nuance his depiction of the Spirit as the mutual love of the Father and the Son in order to provide a distinction between the grounding of the identity of the Spirit and the grounding of the Spirit's mission; the personal mission of the Spirit appears as "Christ's love for his brethren; and the ultimate ground of this is the

---

[172] Ibid., 277.

[173] In the introduction to *Deus Trinitas*, Coffey dedicates the book to Kilmartin and notes how influential his 1970 visit had been on Coffey's theological formation. Kilmartin played the role of both advocate and critic of much of Coffey's work. See Coffey, *Deus Trinitas*, vii.

[174] Kilmartin, "The Active Role of Christ and the Holy Spirit."

[175] Coffey, "A Proper Mission of the Holy Spirit."

[176] Kilmartin names the diveregent viewpoints of Heribert Mühlen, Yves Congar, and Battista Monden. See "The Active Role of Christ and the Holy Spirit," 237–38.

Father's love for the Son in the Trinity."[177] Coffey asserts that this depiction allows for the possibility of reconciliation between the Western church and the Eastern Orthodox since this approach allows the Spirit to proceed from the Father and also be sent from the Son.[178] For Coffey, then, the proper mission of the Holy Spirit is the manifestation of the love of the Son for the Father after Pentecost as a response to the Father's love of the Son.

Coffey's work certainly advances pneumatology in theological discussions of sacramental theology. In a similar vein, the work of Jerome Hall also serves to take Kilmartin's distinctive theology and apply it even more concretely to the liturgical arena. Hall notes that Kilmartin's use of a trinitarian form and structure to all of his argumentation is "relentless."[179] At the heart of Hall's study is the determination of the Spirit's activity in the liturgical act of anamnesis, which Kilmartin readily paired with epiclesis throughout his work. Hall notes that one of the strengths of Kilmartin's work is his insistence "that theologians should be particularly concerned with detailing the relationship of the Holy Spirit to Christ and to the Father."[180] What is perhaps most interesting about Hall's evaluation of Kilmartin's work is the way in which he succinctly describes the way Kilmartin meshes the liturgical action of the church with the action of the Spirit (and indeed, the dynamic action of the Trinity). Hall asserts:

> Christians' reception of the Spirit, sent by the Father through Christ, is itself a sacrament of the transcendental bestowal of the Spirit on the Son as Spirit of the Father's love. Christians' actions of self-sacrificing love are, in turn, sacraments of the answering return of the Spirit from the Son to the Father within the immanent Trinity. The entire life of the world, for Kilmartin, expresses the activity of the economic Trinity, communicating the divine life in particular human situations that are both sinful and holy.[181]

[177] Coffey, "A Proper Mission of the Holy Spirit," 239.

[178] Kilmartin would assert in his subsequent book, *Christian Liturgy*, that Coffey has successfully made this reconciliation possible. Coffey then later solidifies his thought on this matter in *Deus Trinitas*. See also Coffey, *Deus Trinitas*, 60–65.

[179] Hall, *We Have the Mind of Christ*, 160.

[180] Ibid.

[181] Ibid.

The ecclesial ramifications of such a formulation are significant: the church in communion with the Spirit of the faith of Christ is united to the earthly liturgy, as particular churches are in union with the overarching church of the saints, and to the heavenly liturgy, as the saints in heaven continue their Spirit-filled worship. Such a liturgical ecclesiology demands a movement from liturgical participation to participation in the kingdom of God; it creates a sacramental ethic that makes shared faith a responsibility and not a luxury.[182] The church is a sacrament of the Spirit—the Spirit continues to act in and through the members of the church.

As Peter Sanders notes, this notion of the activity of the Holy Spirit found in Kilmartin's work provides a locus for understanding that individual believers serve as instruments of the Spirit's action in the world.[183] Active liturgical participation, as a reflection of the most basic activity of the church, could never be deemed optional. Sanders envisions Kilmartin's work in this arena as both "assurance and challenge."[184] On the one hand it provides the guarantee that the liturgical activity of the church is guided and directed by the Spirit—that the ecclesial community is iconic of the action of the Spirit. Such an approach, though, also opens up the traditional notions of sacramental theology to present new and provocative avenues for discussion; sacraments can be interpreted in the realm of a symbolic exchange with believers as determined by the Spirit.[185]

While the applications of his work in the various areas of priesthood, sacrifice, presence, and pneumatology are significant, Kilmartin's methodology is not without its shortcomings. He had some difficulty in maneuvering between the trinitarian narrative and the various ways to interpret participation. At times he vacillated between his highly systematic methodology and a more pastoral-liturgical mind-set. Because Kilmartin is *relentless* in his insistence on the trinitarian narrative that undergirds his theology of liturgical participation, he at times favors the narrative over the multivalent understanding of participation. For instance, in his determination to underscore the role and mission of the Holy Spirit in the liturgy he could be said to neglect

[182] Ibid.

[183] Sanders, "Pneumatology in the Sacramental Theologies of Geoffrey Wainwright, Jean Corbon and Edward Kilmartin," 350–51.

[184] Ibid., 352.

[185] Ibid. See also, Kilmartin, *Christian Liturgy*, 232.

the role of the Father in sacramental action. While Kilmartin went to great lengths to make sure that the Holy Spirit is not neglected in any developed theology of the sacraments, one would be hard-pressed to ascertain what exact role is played by the Father beyond the terminology of being both source and goal of the liturgy. In the end, however, he is more successful than Vagaggini in presenting a trinitarian theology that helps further the developing concept of active participation in the liturgy.

A trinitarian theology that recognizes the active presence of Father, Son, and Spirit necessarily integrates a healthy pneumatology back into the theological discussion of both sacramentology and ecclesiology. This integration also helps reframe the liturgical action within an eschatological lens. It is possible and indeed advantageous to speak of participation in the order of purpose, an eschatological understanding of participation that undergirds *actuosa participatio*. Eschatological participation underscores the believer's connection to the glorified Christ, the *Kyrios*. It marks a participation in the kingdom of God as it is realized here and now in the sacramental action and at the same time provides the impetus for the faithful's return to God in beatitude. Eschatological participation moves the faithful outside the liturgical action to enter into the ministry and work of Christ. To speak of an eschatological sense of participation, then, has three primary effects for liturgical action. First of all, it ensures that the action of the church in the liturgy is not stagnant. It removes the misguided notion that somehow the liturgy exists simply for itself. When liturgical participation is connected to its eschatological consequence it preserves the movement of the church toward the building up of the kingdom of God, thus always directing the liturgical action's efficacy toward both the self and the other. Such an eschatological participation refuses to allow a hyperspiritualization of the liturgy in which interior participation is highlighted as seemingly sufficient and similarly disavows the notion that simple performance of the rite suffices for the reception of grace, in which case exterior participation is viewed as the only measure of liturgical efficacy.

Second, an eschatological component to liturgical participation helps maintain and safeguard the pneumatological action and presence in the sacraments that the West has often neglected. While a profound pneumatological awareness exists in the biblical witness,[186] the

---

[186] Kilian McDonnell documents a distinct pneumatology in both the Old Testament and the New Testament. The Old Testatment rooted its pneumatology

early church fathers rather quickly dismissed the Spirit-element from their eschatological theology. Whether that dismissal was due to the delay of the parousia or the need to solidify the identity of Christ after the resurrection is unclear. What is clear is that very quickly in the first centuries of the church eschatology and pneumatology tended to be divorced from each other.[187] Moreover, the scholastics, while trying to articulate a defense for the real presence of Christ in the Eucharist, laid the groundwork for an exclusivity of Christ's action in the sacraments that was never intended by their theological debate. While theologians in the West would readily agree that when one Person of the Trinity is present in the economy of salvation all three Persons are present, the *de facto* reality of sacramental language and theology shows that from the time of Thomas Aquinas to the Second Vatican Council only the presence of Christ and his saving works seem to be a major concern. Eschatological participation reemphasizes the joint missions of Son and Spirit as the "two hands of the Father." Both Vagaggini and Kilmartin point to this sense of participation even if they do not name it as such.

Last, eschatological participation answers our initial question as we first framed our inquiry about *actuosa participatio* at the start of this enterprise: it helps us to know *why* active participation in the liturgy was considered crucial by the Second Vatican Council. Full, conscious, and active participation moves the believer out of the confines of the earthly liturgy to begin to appreciate the one eternal liturgy in the heavenly kingdom. It places the believer firmly in the one *transitus* of Christ—in his ministry and his mission here on earth and in his worship in the heavenly kingdom. Liturgical participation without this eschatological impulse denies the very nature of the liturgy not only as communicating grace to the believing faithful but also as participation in the divine life itself. Full, conscious, and active participation of the faithful in the sacramental-liturgical act cannot be optional. Vagaggini makes this point clear through the notion of *sintonia d'animo*, that by tuning in to the complexus of signs employed in the liturgy one actually gains insight into the heavenly liturgy in which one participates. Similarly, Kilmartin argued that it is the actual personal engagement in

---

in a radical identification with the future while the New Testament offered a more varied association of the Spirit with the identity of Christ and his resurrection. See McDonnell, *The Other Hand of God*, 33–44.

[187] Ibid., 52–53.

the rite itself, a commitment to the covenantal expression of the faith life of Christ and the church, that transcends the earthly act. For him, to be clothed in Christ through the Spirit is not simply a convenient or advantageous sacramental attitude, it is the necessary response of the faithful, as shown by Christ, so that they may participate fully in the divine life. Eschatological participation reminds us that the earthly liturgy is supposed to end. It is only a vehicle for our beatitude, one characterized as a trinitarian participation in Christ, through the Spirit, that leads us back to the Father. In this sense the inclusion of an eschatological understanding of participation completes the trinitarian narrative in salvation history.

In developing a trinitarian theology of liturgical participation one recognizes that the notion of *actuosa participatio* is still open to ongoing interpretation. The most recent debates surrounding the topic help accentuate that fact. If nothing else, the development of a distinctive trinitarian theology of participation in the liturgical-sacramental act helps formulate the dimensions of future discussions. The renewal of a continued *ressourcement* with the early initiation liturgies helps accentuate a baptismal spirituality in the life of the faithful that cannot be disregarded. The recognition of the trinitarian narrative within the initiation liturgies can only augment the understanding of the relationship between *actuosa participatio* and that narrative. Similarly, the acknowledgment of the manifold presence of the triune God in the liturgical action ensures that active participation is also a personal engagement on the part of the believer; the active presence of Father, Son, and Spirit invite and, indeed, demand a commitment on the part of the faithful: to the covenant with the Father, to the one *transitus* demonstrated by the Son, to the communion offered by the Spirit. Last, the inclusion of an eschatological sense of participation within an understanding of *actuosa participatio* prevents a lifeless liturgy devoid of its purpose, safeguards the pneumatological aspect of the self-communication of God, and necessarily directs the faithful outside of the liturgical event.

All of these parameters point to one unmistakable fact: active participation in the liturgy that is rooted in the trinitarian narrative is necessarily connected to the transformation of the believer in grace. Worship and sanctification are two sides of the same liturgical coin. For that transformation to have meaning and purpose, active participation also necessarily implies a sacramental ethic, a way of acting and living in the world that reflects the transforming grace of the sacrament. Full, conscious, and active participation is demanded by the very nature of the liturgy because that liturgy is meant to change us, to mold us and shape us, through the power of the Spirit in order to conform us to Christ so that we, individually and collectively, can be drawn back to the Father. At the heart of understanding active participation is an admission of what God works in us, not a misguided humanism that somehow supposes that participation centers on what we do for God. The inherent eschatological movement of active liturgical participation implies that believers who are united to Christ in the Spirit will, in fact, work for the coming of the kingdom: that the church in its imperfect membership will continually seek perfection in the power of the Spirit, through union with Christ, in its worship of the Father. Active participation ensures that the faithful can accept the grace they are offered in the sacraments and through that acceptance enter into the divine life of the Trinity both here, in an all too imperfect world, and in the perfect beatitude of the world to come.

The Emergence of a Trinitarian Language of Liturgical Participation

This book began by noting the critique of Louis-Marie Chauvet, who asserted the existence of a difficulty in liturgical language preventing the faithful from coming to an easy grasp of the concept of "active participation."[1] Chauvet's assessment of the predicament is coupled with a similar critique about possible solutions, namely, that the process of *understanding* the concept of participation is just as problematic as the concept itself. He maintains that "it is clear that we cannot (and we should not) equate the understanding of the liturgy with an intellectual comprehension."[2] Rather, there is a nonintellectual understanding of the liturgy that resonates with believers in the very mystery that is being celebrated. Chauvet maintains:

> Here the mystery is not an enigma to be solved; it is reality that makes us live. Certainly, its obscure side remains, but in a way that (like the "mystery of life"), the more we live from it, the more we experience its inexhaustible and surprising nature. In this area truth is obviously not the end of a simple reasoning process, when we would have finally understood everything. Here, we "understand, only on condition that we allow ourselves to be grasped from the inside."[3]

While Chauvet recognizes that any kind of anti-intellectualism would not serve the purpose of the liturgy, he readily admits that "it

---

[1] See pages xv–xvi of the Introduction.

[2] Louis-Marie Chauvet, "Are the Words of the Liturgy Worn Out? What Diagnosis? What Pastoral Approach?" *Worship* 84 (2010): 25–37, at 31.

[3] Ibid., 32.

is not first of all to the intellect that the liturgy is addressed."[4] Rather, the liturgy is about experiencing the paschal mystery itself and the "participation in the Passover of Christ that the liturgy offers is indeed in the order of mystery."[5] It is also necessarily and decidedly trinitarian. For this reason Chauvet also asserts that participation in the Christ event, in the mystery of the suffering and death of the revealed God-man, necessitates a kind of respectful distanciation from all that is considered part of everyday occurrence. Thus the very language of the liturgical action is recognized as both commonplace, inasmuch as it is human language, and simultaneously transcendent.[6]

Chauvet's critique presents a valid concern for understanding participation in the liturgy, but one must also consider that the lack of a comprehensible intellectual system runs the risk of producing a symbolic liturgical experience in which the symbols and signs employed remain too embedded in the distance of liturgical language.

At the outset my intent in this book was to present a framework that satisfied the need for both an intellectual and an experiential appreciation of liturgical participation. The contemporary shift in sacramental methodology after the Second Vatican Council produced a correlative shift in symbolic referents. The descriptions of sacramental action from the time of the council to the present have become increasingly trinitarian in nature. Thus any intellectual or experiential framework would need to emphasize this trinitarian element. What this work has sought to accomplish is to tie the language of liturgical discourse, especially in the area of participation, to the language of the Trinity in order to create a realm of meaning that is adaptable to new developments in sacramental theology and yet still holds the experiential node of the liturgical action at the center of that meaning.

In order to create this connection I showed how both Vagaggini and Kilmartin articulated a trinitarian theology of liturgical participation. Vagaggini's detailed development of a liturgical theology not only provides a significant appreciation of the network of signs employed by the liturgy but also advocates a method by which that network can be engaged. In identifying the christological-trinitarian schema within the texts of the early Christian liturgy, Vagaggini links the network of signs to the trinitarian narrative of salvation history. While he perhaps

[4] Ibid.
[5] Ibid.
[6] Ibid., 32–33.

relies too heavily on a christological model for his liturgical theology, he nonetheless adds a vital dimension to the discussion of a trinitarian language of participation, as the positing of the *sintonia d'animo* provides a nexus for entering into liturgical participation. This "sintonation" has both cognitive and affective elements since it encourages an awareness of both the network of signs and the christological-trinitarian schema (in the realm of cognition), and it depends on the experiential appreciation of the sacramental symbols as they are enacted (in the realm of affect). In essence he had already answered Chauvet's critique nearly fifty years before he made it!

In a similar fashion the above presentation demonstrated that Kilmartin's intention to join an ascending and descending Christology also had demonstrable advantages for the development of a trinitarian language of participation. Kilmartin not only brings a well-developed and nuanced pneumatology to the study of the liturgy but also places emphasis on the human experience of *presence* in the liturgical action. He emphasizes that liturgical participation has its root in the active presence of Christ and the Spirit in the church at prayer. To enter into the sacramental celebration is to be engaged in the mystery presence of Christ, which in turn leads to a deepening of participation in divine life. By linking participation and presence Kilmartin shows us that the primary locus for the transformation of the human person in beatitude is the liturgy itself.

By analyzing the works of both Vagaggini and Kilmartin we have seen three important necessities emerge in the formulation of a trinitarian theology of liturgical participation. First, given that the early liturgical sources can reveal something fundamental about the mystery and nature of the celebration, the vast quantity of baptismal and initiation sources warrants serious theological reflection in determining a trinitarian theology of participation. We have argued that the application of baptismal theology to the concept of participation reinforces the understanding of the primacy of God's action in the liturgical event. Moreover, by recognizing the trinitarian narrative of liturgical participation throughout all the initiation sacraments, one not only identifies the indissoluble theological unity of those sacraments but also emphasizes the overarching connection between God's activity in the world, the life of believers, and the multiple understandings of participation in the trinitarian God.

Our analysis also showed that the inclusion of trinitarian language into the sacramental discourse by Vagaggini and Kilmartin has opened a variety of possibilities for discussing the nature of trinitarian action in the liturgy. While no one theology has become predominant in explaining or demarcating that action, what we have seen is a clear movement toward understanding the notion of an active presence of the triune God in the sacraments. Certainly, the Second Vatican Council clearly speaks about the active presence of Christ in the sacraments, especially in the Eucharist. Both Kilmartin and Vagaggini explain this manifold presence in terms of the abiding nature of the Spirit in the church. We have shown, however, that a thoroughly trinitarian theology of participation would necessarily express how the Father, Son, *and* Spirit are engaged in the liturgical action while at the same time defending the unity of God when God acts in the world. Such a trinitarian theology invites the theologian to consider the ways in which both the Father and the Spirit are actively present in the liturgical action in union with the Son.

Last, we concluded that an essential metaphor for participation that safeguards both the trinitarian narrative and the proper end of the sacraments in the sanctification of the human person lies in eschatology. As noted earlier, an eschatological participation underscores the believer's connection to the glorified Christ, the *Kyrios*. Such participation ensures that the liturgical action of the church does not become an isolated exercise unto itself. Rather, when liturgical participation is connected to its eschatological consequence it makes certain that the action of the church in the liturgy does not become torpid. It directs the efficacy of the liturgical action toward the transformation both of the individual believer and of the gathered assembly. This eschatological participation also safeguards the pneumatological action and presence in the sacraments and helps remind the believer why the concept of *actuosa participatio* was so important to the Second Vatican Council: it places the believer firmly in the one *transitus* of Christ. Without this eschatological impulse the believer who engages in liturgical participation runs the risk of forgetting the very purpose of the sacraments: to communicate grace and lead the faithful into the divine life.

Liturgical participation, then, serves as a primary vehicle for the correlative forms of participation we have mentioned—metaphysical, soteriological, ecclesiological, and eschatological. By uniting the various forms of participation to the trinitarian narrative of salvation history we have successfully created a hermeneutical thread that can be drawn through each form of participation and augment its meaning. This trinitarian hermeneutic reminds us that the various metaphors of participation do not stand alone. For instance, ecclesiological participation in the Body of Christ implies a liturgical participation when the church is at prayer, an eschatological participation as the church builds up the kingdom in the Spirit, and a soteriological participation in the saving acts of Christ. We have seen clearly that the trinitarian narrative is linked to the concept of participation in all of its meanings whether it is manifested in the act of creation, the establishment of the covenant, the fullness of the revelation of the triune God in Christ, the work of the Trinity in the sacramental life of the church, or the Second Coming and the revelation of the kingdom. In the end, liturgical participation moves us out of ourselves and into the world around us in the determination of a sacramental ethic by which to live.

Most important, liturgical participation that is wed to the trinitarian narrative not only creates a more accessible liturgical language for the faithful but also maintains a profound respect for the mystery being celebrated. The purpose of a trinitarian theology of liturgical participation centers precisely on these two elements: the creation of an adaptable and viable locus for understanding liturgical language and the maintenance of a paradigmatic system of theology that furthers the paschal mystery. In the end, the participation of the faithful in the liturgy in a full, conscious, and active manner is made more realistically possible by the adoption of a trinitarian approach. Such a participation occurs not simply because an intellectual framework has been established by which the network of signs in the liturgy becomes more comprehensible, nor because an augmented liturgical pneumatology has come to the foreground. Nor does it occur because of sheer human determination to enter into the sacrament. Rather, liturgical participation, in its full complex of meaning as metaphysical, soteriological, ecclesiological, and eschatological, is made possible by being drawn into the trinitarian life through the action of Father, Son, and Spirit. A liturgical participation that is understood as thoroughly trinitarian allows the believer to accept the grace that is offered in the sacramental action, to give a simple *fiat* in response to the self-communication of the triune God.

Bibliography

PRIMARY SOURCES

For Cipriano Vagaggini

Vagaggini, Cipriano. "Caro salutis est cardo. Corporeità, Eucharistia e Liturgia." In *Miscellanea Liturgica in onore di sua eminenza Il Cardinale Giacomo Lercaro*, 73–210. Rome, et al.: Descleé, 1966.

—————. "Contemplazione nella Liturgia e Contemplazione fuori della Liturgia." *Rivista di ascetica e mistica* 7 (1962): 8–35.

—————. *Il canone delle messa e la riforma liturgica: probleme e progetti.* Turin: Leuman, 1966.

—————. *Il senso teologico della liturgia: saggio di liturgia teologica generale.* Rome: Edizioni Paoline, 1957.

—————. *Il senso teologico della liturgia: saggio di liturgia teologica generale.* Rome: Edizioni Paoline, 1965.

—————. "Il valore teologico e spirituale della messa concelebrata." *Rivista Liturgica* 52 (1965): 189–218.

—————. "L'Eucharistia come centro della vita liturgica e l'insegnamento della teologia." *Seminarium* 8 (1968): 49–67.

—————. "La Chiesa si ritrova nella liturgia." *Rivista Liturgica* 51 (1964): 343–54.

—————. "La hantise des *rationes necessariae* de St. Anselme dans la théologie des processions de S. Thomas." *Spicilegium Beccense* 1 (1959): 103–39.

—————. "La messa, sacramento del sacrificio pasquale di Cristo e della Chiesa." *Rivista Liturgica* 56 (1969): 179–93.

—————. "La perspectiva trinitari en la liturgia del bautismo y de la confirmación antes del concilio de Nicea." In *Simposio Internacional de Teología Trinitaria*, 27–50. Salamanca: Ediciones Secretariado Trinitario, 1972.

—————. *Liturgia e pensiero teologico recente.* Rome: Pontificio Ateneo Anselmiano, 1961.

—————. "Lo spirito della Costituzione sulla liturgia." *Rivista Liturgica* 51 (1964): 5–49.

—————. "Riflessioni sul senso teologico del mistero pasquale." *Rivista di Pastorale Liturgica* 2 (1964): 102–12.

—————. "Storia della salvezza." In *Nuovo dizionario di teologia*, edited by Giuseppe Barbaglio and Severino Dianich, 1559–83. Rome: Edizioni Paoline, 1977.

———. "Teologia." In *Nuovo dizionario di teologia*, edited by Giuseppe Barbaglio and Severino Dianich, 1597–711. Rome: Edizioni Paoline, 1977.

———. *Theological Dimensions of the Liturgy: A General Treatise on the Theology of the Liturgy*. Translated by Leonard J. Doyle and W. A. Jurgens. Collegeville, MN: Liturgical Press, 1976.

For Edward J. Kilmartin

Kilmartin, Edward J. "The Active Role of Christ and the Holy Spirit in the Sanctification of the Eucharistic Elements." *Theological Studies* 45 (1984): 225–53.

———. "The Catholic Tradition of Eucharistic Theology: Towards the Third Millennium." *Theological Studies* 55 (1994): 405–57.

———. *Christian Liturgy I. Theology and Practice*. Kansas City: Sheed & Ward, 1988.

———. *Church, Eucharist and Priesthood: A Theological Commentary on "The Mystery and Worship of the Most Holy Eucharist."* New York: Paulist Press, 1981.

———. *Culture and the Praying Church*. Ottawa, ON: CCCB, 1990.

———. *The Eucharist in the Primitive Church*. Englewood Cliffs, NJ: Prentice-Hall, 1965.

———. *The Eucharist in the West*. Edited by Robert J. Daly. Collegeville, MN: Liturgical Press, 1998.

———. "The Eucharist: Nourishment for Communion." In *Populus Dei II: Ecclesia. Studi in onore del Card. Alfredo Ottaviani*, edited by Giuseppe d'Ercole. Rome: Communio, 1967.

———. "The Eucharistic Prayer: Content and Function in Some Early Eucharistic Prayers." In *Word in the World: Essays in Honor of Frederick L. Moriarty, SJ*, edited by Richard J. Clifford and George MacRae, 117–34. Cambridge, MA: Weston College Press, 1973.

———. "The Holy Spirit in the Liturgy." Lecture, Creighton University, 1992. Available in the Edward Kilmartin Manuscript Collection at Boston College.

———. "The Last Supper and Earliest Eucharists of the Church." In *The Breaking of Bread. Concilium 40*, edited by Pierre Benoit, Roland Murphy, and Bas van Iersel, 35–47. New York: Paulist Press, 1969.

———. "A Modern Approach to the Word of God and Sacraments of Christ: Perspectives and Principles." In *The Sacraments: God's Love and Mercy Actualized*. Proceedings of the Theological Institute 11, edited by Francis A. Eigo, 59–109. Villanova, PA: Villanova University Press, 1979.

———. "On the Need to Develop a Communion Ecclesiology Through Integration of Pneumatology." In *"Ecclesiam Suam:" Première lettre encyclique de Paul VI, Colloque International. Rome 24–26 Octobre 1980*, 164–67. Brescia: Istituto Paolo VI, 1982.

―――. "Patristic Views of Sacramental Sanctity." *Proceedings from the Catholic College Teachers of Sacred Doctrine* 8 (1962): 59–82.

―――. "Sacramental Theology: The Eucharist in Recent Literature." *Theological Studies* 32 (1971): 233–77.

―――. "Sacraments as Liturgy of the Church." *Theological Studies* 50 (1989): 527–47.

―――. *The Sacraments: Signs of Christ, Sanctifier and High Priest*. Glen Rock, NJ: Paulist Press, 1962.

―――. "The Sacrifice of Thanksgiving and Social Justice." In *Liturgy and Social Justice*, edited by Mark Searle, 53–71. Collegeville, MN: Liturgical Press, 1989.

―――. "*Sacrificium Laudis*: Content and Function of Early Eucharistic Prayers." *Theological Studies* 35 (1974): 268–87.

―――. "Theology of the Sacraments: Toward a New Understanding of the Chief Rites of the Church of Jesus Christ." In *Alternative Futures for Worship*. Vol. 1: *General Introduction*, edited by Regis A. Duffy, 115–67. Collegeville, MN: Liturgical Press, 1987.

Other Sources

Bacon, Gratien. "La participation de l'Église à l'offrande eucharistique, d'après Bossuet." *Revue des Sciences Religieuses* 42 (July 1968): 231–60.

Baraúna, William. "Active Participation, the Inspiring and Directive Principle of the Constitution." In *The Liturgy of Vatican II*, edited by William Baraúna; English ed. Jovian Lang, 131–93. Chicago: Franciscan Herald Press, 1966.

Beauduin, Lambert. "L'encyclique 'Mediator Dei.'" *La Maison-Dieu* 13 (1948): 7–25.

Békés, Gellért J. "Presentazione." In *Lex Orandi, Lex Credendi: Miscellanea in Onore di P. Ciprano Vagaggini*, edited by Gellért Békés and Giustino Farnedi. Rome: Editrice Anselmiana, 1980.

Belcher, Kimberly Hope. *Efficacious Engagement: Sacramental Participation in the Trinitarian Mystery*. Collegeville, MN: Liturgical Press, 2011.

Benedict XVI, Pope. "Deus Caritas Est." AAS 98 (2005).

―――. "Sacramentum Caritatis." AAS 99/3 (2007): 105–80.

Billy, Dennis J., CSsR, and James Keating. *The Way of Mystery: The Eucharist and Moral Living*. Mahwah, NJ: Paulist Press, 2006.

Botte, Bernard. *From Silence to Participation: An Insider's View of Liturgical Renewal*. Translated by John Sullivan, OCD. Washington, DC: Pastoral Press, 1988.

Bourke, David, ed. *Summa theologiae, Vol 56: The Sacraments*. New York: Cambridge University Press, 1975.

Bouyer, Louis. *Liturgical Piety*. Notre Dame, IN: University of Notre Dame Press, 1955.

―――. *The Liturgy Revived: A Doctrinal Commentary on the Conciliar Constitution on the Liturgy*. Notre Dame, IN: Notre Dame University Press, 1964.

Bradshaw, Paul. "God, Christ, and the Holy Spirit in Early Christian Praying." In *The Place of Christ in Liturgical Prayer: Trinity, Christology, and Liturgical Theology*, edited by Brian D. Spinks, 51–64. Collegeville, MN: Liturgical Press, 2008.

Brinktine, Johannes. "Das Amtspriestertum und das allegemeine Priestertum der Gläubigen." *Divus Thomas* 22 (1944): 291–308.

Bugnini, Annibale. *The Reform of the Liturgy: 1948–1975*. Translated by Matthew J. O'Connell. Collegeville, MN: Liturgical Press, 1990.

Busch, William. " 'Do This in Commemoration of Me.' Popular Participation in the Sacrifice of the Mass." *Orate Fratres* 5, no. 10 (1931): 441–52.

Cagny, Olivier de. "La notion de participation dans l'euchologie du Missel Romain." *La Maison-Dieu* 241 (2005): 121–35.

Campbell, J. Y. "ΚΟΙΝΩΝΙΑ and Its Cognates in the New Testament." *Journal of Biblical Literature* 51 (1932): 352–80.

Cantalamessa, Raniero. *Contemplating the Trinity: The Path to the Abundant Christian Life*. Translated by Marsha Daigle-Williamson. Ijamsville, MD: Word Among Us Press, 2007.

Capelle, Bernard. "Théologie pastorale des encycliques Mystici Corporis et Mediator Dei." *La Maison-Dieu* 47–48 (1956): 65–80.

Casel, Odo. "Das Mysteriengedächtnis der Meßliturgie im Lichte der Tradi-tion." *Jahrbuch für Liturgiewissenschaft* 6 (1926): 8–204.

———. *Die Liturgie als Mysterienfeier*. Edited by Ildefons Herwegen. Ecclesia Orans: Zur Einführung in den Geist der Liturgie, 9. Freiburg: Herder, 1923.

———. "Mysteriengegenwart." *Jahrbuch für Liturgiewissenschaft* 8 (1928): 10–224.

———. *The Mystery of Christian Worship and Other Writings*. Edited by Burkhard Neunheuser, OSB. Westminster, MD: Newman Press, 1962.

Catella, Alceste. "Theology of the Liturgy." In *Handbook of Liturgical Studies: Fundamental Liturgy*, vol. 1, edited by Anscar J. Chapungco, 3–28. Collegeville, MN: Liturgical Press, 1998.

Cattaneo, Enrico. "I recenti insegnamenti di Pio XII sulla liturgia." *Vita e Pensiero* 36 (January 1948): 10–13.

Cavallera, Ferdinand. "L'encyclique 'Mediator Dei' et la piété liturgique." *Revue d'Ascetique et de Mystique* 24 (1948): 105–16.

———. "L'encyclique 'Mediator Dei' et la spiritualité." *Revue d'Ascetique et de Mystique* 24 (1948): 3–30.

Cazaux, Antoine-Marie. "Ordonnance pour l'année de la messe." *La Maison-Dieu* 14 (1948): 129–36.

Chauvet, Louis-Marie. "Are the Words of the Liturgy Worn Out? What Diagnosis? What Pastoral Approach?" *Worship* 84 (2010): 25–37.

———. *Della mediazione. Quattro studi di teologia sacramentaria fondamentale. Testo francese a fronte*. Assisi: Cittadella, 2006.

———. *Les sacrements: Parole de Dieu au risque du corps*. Paris: Les Éditions de L'Atelier, 1997. English: *The Sacraments: The Word of God at the Mercy of the Body*. Translated by Madeleine Beaumont. Collegeville, MN: Liturgical Press, 2001.

———. *Symbole et sacrement*. Paris: Cerf, 1990. English: *Symbol and Sacrament: A Sacramental Reinterpretation of Christian Existence*. Translated by Patrick Madigan and Madeleine Beaumont. Collegeville, MN: Liturgical Press, 1995.

Coffey, David. *Deus Trinitas: The Doctrine of the Trinity*. New York: Oxford University Press, 1999.

———. *Grace, the Gift of the Holy Spirit*. Sydney: Catholic Institute of Sydney, 1979.

———. "The 'Incarnation' of the Holy Spirit in Christ." *Theological Studies* 45 (1984): 466–80.

———. "A Proper Mission of the Holy Spirit." *Theological Studies* 47 (1986): 227–50.

Congar, Yves M.-J. *I Believe in the Holy Spirit*. Translated by David Smith. New York: Crossroads, 1999.

———. "L' 'Ecclesia' ou communauté chrétienne, sujet intégral de l'action liturgique." In *Unam Sanctam, 66: La Liturgie après Vatican II, Bilans, études, prospective*, edited by Jean-Pierre Jossua and Yves M.-J. Congar, 241–82. Paris: Cerf, 1967.

Corbon, Jean. *The Wellspring of Worship*. Translated by Matthew J. O'Connell. New York: Paulist Press, 1988.

D'Eypernon, François Taymans. *La Sainte Trinité et les Sacrements*. Paris: Desclée de Brouwer, 1949. English: *The Blessed Trinity and the Sacraments*. Westminster, MD: Newman Press, 1961.

Dallen, James. "The Congregation's Share in the Eucharistic Prayer." *Worship* 52 (July 1978): 329–41.

———. "Liturgical Spirituality: Living What We Sing About." In *Liturgy and Music*, edited by Robin A. Leaver and Joyce Ann Zimmerman, 169–93. Collegeville, MN: Liturgical Press, 1998.

Dalmais, Irénée-Henri, Pierre Marie Gy, Pierre Jounel, and Aimé Georges Martimort, eds. *Principles of the Liturgy*. Edited by Aimé Georges Martimort. Vol. 1: *The Church at Prayer*. Collegeville, MN: Liturgical Press, 1987.

Daly, Robert J., SJ. "Robert Bellarmine and Post-Tridentine Eucharistic Theology." *Theological Studies* 61 (2000): 239–60.

———. "Sacrifice Unveiled or Sacrifice Revisited: Trinitarian and Liturgical Perspectives." *Theological Studies* 64 (2003): 24–42.

Diekmann, Godfrey. "Conclusions of the Third Congress, Lugano, 1953." *Worship* 28, no. 3 (1954): 162–67.

Dix, Gregory. *The Shape of the Liturgy*. Westminster (London): Dacre, 1945.

Doherty, Daniel. "The Development of the Concept of the Ecclesial Nature of the Sacraments from Selected Documents of Vatican II and through the Writings of Karl Rahner, Edward J. Kilmartin and Louis-Marie Chauvet." STL thesis, Catholic University of America, 2006.

Driscoll, Jeremy, OSB. "Uncovering the Dynamic *Lex Orandi—Lex Credendi* in the Baptismal Theology of Irenaeus." *Pro Ecclesia* 12 (Spring 2003): 213–25.

Ellard, Gerald. "At Mass with My Encyclical." *Orate Fratres* 22 (April 1948): 241–46.

Emery, Gilles. *Trinity in Aquinas.* Ypsilanti, MI: Sapientia Press of Ave Maria University, 2003.

Erambil, Joseph. "The Eucharist, the Holy Spirit, and the Church: A Study of the Pneumatological and Ecclesiological Dimensions of the Eucharist in the Writings of Edward J. Kilmartin." STD diss., Pontificia Universitas Gregorianum, 1998.

Erickson, Craig D. "Liturgical Participation and the Renewal of the Church." *Worship* 59 (May 1985): 231–43.

Fahey, Michael A. "In Memoriam: Edward Kilmartin, S.J. (1923–1994)." *Orientalia Christiana Periodica* 61 (1995): 5–35.

Flicoteaux, Eugène. "Notre sanctification par la liturgie." *Vie spirituelle* 79 (1948): 99–109.

Fliesser, Josef Calasanz. "Allgemeine Messordnung für die volksliturgischen Messfeiern in Österreich." *Heiliger Dienst* 3 (1948): 6–11.

Ford, H. W. "The New Testament Conception of Fellowship." *Shane Quarterly* 6 (1945): 188–215.

Fortman, Edmund J. *The Triune God: A Historical Study of the Doctrine of the Trinity.* 2d ed. Grand Rapids, MI: Baker Book House, 1982.

Franklin, Ralph W. "The Peoples' Work: Anti-Jansenist Prejudice in the Benedictine Movement for Popular Participation in the 19th Century." *Studia Liturgica* 19 (1989): 60–77.

Gelpi, Donald L. "David Coffey's 'Did you Receive the Holy Spirit When You Believed?' A review essay." *Pneuma* 28 (2006): 322–34.

Giraudo, Cesare. *Eucaristia per la chiesa: Prospettive theologiche sull'eucharistia a partire dalla "lex orandi."* Aloisiana 22. Rome: Gregorian University, 1989.

Grillo, Andrea. "Il legittimo e tormento assillo del pensiero moderno: C. Vagaggini tra (e oltre) la teologia monastica e la teologia scolastica." *Rivista Liturgica* 87 (2000): 505–12.

Groeber, Conrad. "Memorandum de S. E. Mgr. Groeber, Archevêque de Fribourg." *La Maison-Dieu* 7 (1942): 97–104.

Hahnenberg, Edward P. "The Ministerial Priesthood and Liturgical Anamnesis in the Thought of Edward J. Kilmartin, S.J." *Theological Studies* 66 (2005): 253–78.

Hall, Jerome M., SJ. *We Have the Mind of Christ: The Holy Spirit and Liturgical Memory in the Thought of Edward J. Kilmartin*. Collegeville, MN: Liturgical Press, 2001.

Hameline, Jean-Yves. "Le culte chrétien dans son espace de sensibilité." *La Maison-Dieu* 187 (1991): 7–45.

———. "Observations sur nos manières de célébrer." *La Maison-Dieu* 192 (1992): 7–24.

———. "Les *Origines du culte chrétien* et le mouvement liturgique." *La Maison-Dieu* 181 (1990): 51–96.

———. "Viollet-le-Duc et le mouvement liturgique au XIXe siècle." *La Maison-Dieu* 142 (1980): 57–86.

Hanssens, John Michael. "La liturgia nell' enciclica Mediator Dei et hominum." *La Civiltà Cattolica* (1948): 242–55.

Hill, William J. *The Three-Personed God: The Trinity as a Mystery of Salvation*. Washington, DC: Catholic University of America Press, 1982.

Hödl, Ludwig. "Kirchliches Sakrament—Christliches Engagement." *Zeitschrift für Katholische Theologie* 95 (January 1973): 1–19.

Hünermann, Peter. " 'The Ignored 'Text': On the Hermeneutics of the Second Vatican Council." In *Vatican II: A Forgotten Future? Concilium* 2005/4, edited by Alberto Melloni and Christoph Theobald, 118–36. London: SCM Press, 2005.

Hunt, Anne. *The Trinity and the Paschal Mystery: A Development in Recent Catholic Theology*. New Theology Studies 5. Collegeville, MN: Liturgical Press, 1997.

Innitzer, Theodor Cardinal. "Response de S. Em. le Cardinal Innitzer au memorandum de S. Exc. Mgr. Groeber." *La Maison-Dieu* 8 (1943): 108–15.

Irwin, Kevin W. *Context and Text: Method in Liturgical Theology*. Collegeville, MN: Liturgical Press, 1994.

———. *Liturgical Theology: A Primer*. Edited by Edward Foley. American Essays In Liturgy. Collegeville, MN: Liturgical Press, 1990.

Jasper, Ronald, and Geoffrey J. Cuming, eds. *Prayers of the Eucharist: Early and Reformed*. Collegeville, MN: Liturgical Press, 1990.

John Paul II, Pope. *Dominum et Vivificantem*. AAS 78 (1986): 809–900.

———. *Ecclesia de Eucharistia*. AAS 95/7 (2003): 433–75.

———. "Lo Spirito e la Sposa." AAS 96/7 (2004): 419–27.

———. *Redemptor Hominis*. AAS 71/4 (1979): 257–324.

———. "Vicesimus Quintus Annus." AAS 81/8 (1989): 897–918.

Johnson, Maxwell. "Back Home to the Font: Eight Implications of a Baptismal Spirituality." *Worship* 71 (1997): 482–504.

Jourdan, G. V. "KOINΩNIA in 1 Cor 10:16." *Journal of Biblical Literature* 67 (1948): 111–24.

Jungmann, Joseph. *Die Stellung Christi im liturgischen Gebet*. Liturgiewissenschaftliche Quellen und Forschungen 19/20. Münster: Aschendorf, 1962.

———. "Einleitung und Kommentar von Univ.-Prof. Dr. Josef Andreas Jungmann, SJ, Innsbruck." In *Das Zweite Vatikanische Konzil, Dokumente und Kommentare*, edited by Heinrich Suso Brechter. Freiburg: Herder, 1966.

———. *The Place of Christ in Liturgical Prayer*. Translated by A. J. Peeler. 2d rev.
ed. Staten Island, NY: Alba House, 1965.

———. "We Offer." *Orate Fratres* 24 (1949–59): 97–102.

Kaczynski, Reiner. "Theologischer Kommentar zur Konstitution über die heilige Liturgie (*Sacrosanctum Concilium*)." In *Herders Theologischer Kommentar
zum Zweiten Vatikanischen Konzil*, edited by Peter Hünermann and Bernd
Jochen Hilberath, 1–228. Freiburg: Herder, 2004.

Kaiser, Albert. "The Historical Backgrounds and Theology of *Mediator Dei*.
Part I: Backgrounds." *American Ecclesiastical Review* 129 (1953): 368–78.

———. "The Historical Backgrounds and Theology of *Mediator Dei*. Part II:
Philosophy and Theology." *American Ecclesiastical Review* 130 (1954): 33–45.

———. " 'Mediator Dei' and the Sacramental Christ." *Homiletic and Pastoral
Review* 54 (1954): 1068–72.

Kasper, Walter, and Gerhard Sauter. *Kirche, Ort des Geistes*. Ökumenische
Forschungen: Ergänzende Abteilung. Kleine ökumenische Schriften 8.
Freiburg: Herder, 1976.

Kavanagh, Aidan. *On Liturgical Theology*. New York: Pueblo, 1984.

———. "What Is Participation?—or, Participation Revisited." *Doctrine and Life*
23 (1973): 343–53.

Keating, James. "A Share in God's Life: Mystical/Liturgical Foundations for a
Catholic Morality." *Logos: A Journal of Catholic Thought and Culture* 8 (2005):
65–88.

Koenker, Ernest B. "Objectives and Achievements of the Liturgical Movement
in the Roman Catholic Church since World War I." *Church History* 20/2
(1951): 14–27.

Kubicki, Judith Marie, CSSF. "Recognizing the Presence of Christ in the Liturgical Assembly." *Theological Studies* 65 (2004): 817–37.

Lafont, Ghislain. *Peut-on Connaître Dieu en Jésus Christ?* Cogitatio Fidei 44.
Paris: Cerf, 1969.

Lamberigts, Mathijs. "The Liturgy Debate." In *History of Vatican II*. Vol. 2: *The
Formation of the Council's Identity, First Period and Intersession, October 1962–
September 1963*. Translated by Matthew J. O'Connell. Edited by Giuseppe
Alberigo and Joseph Komonchak, 107–68. Maryknoll, NY: Orbis, 1997.

Lamberts, Jozef. "Active Participation as the Gateway Towards an Ecclesial
Liturgy." In *Omnes Circumadstantes: Contributions towards a history of the
people in the liturgy presented to Herman Wegman*, edited by Charles Caspers
and Marc Schneiders, 234–361. Kampen: Kok, 1990.

————. "A Colloquium on Active Participation." In *The Active Participation Revisited: La Participation Active 100 ans après Pie X et 40 ans après Vatican II,* edited by Jozef Lamberts, 7–12. Leuven: Peeters, 2004.

Lathrop, Gordon W. *Holy Things: A Liturgical Theology.* Minneapolis: Fortress Press, 1993.

Lécuyer, Joseph. "La Confirmation chez les Pères." *La Maison-Dieu* 54 (1958): 47–51.

————. "Théologie de l'initiation chrètienne d'apres les Pères." *La Maison-Dieu* 58 (1959): 5–26.

Leo XIII, Pope. *Divinum Illud Munus. Acta Sanctae Sedis* 29 (1896–1897): 644–5.

Léon-Dufour, Xavier, SJ. *Sharing the Eucharistic Bread.* Translated by Matthew J. O'Connell. Mahwah, NJ: Paulist Press, 1987.

Lercaro, Giacomo Cardinal. "Active Participation: The Basic Principle of the Pastoral-Liturgical Reforms of Pius X." *Worship* 28 (1954): 120–28.

Lopes, Steven J. "From the Trinity to the Eucharist: Towards a Trinitarian Theology of the Sacrifice of Christ and Its Representation in the Eucharist of the Church." Diss., Pontificia Universitas Gregorianum, 2005.

Luykx, Boniface. "Liturgie at dialogue: psychologie de la participation." In *Message et mission: Recueil commemoratif du Xe anniversaire de la Faculté de Théologie,* 207–23. Louvain: Nouwelaerts, 1968.

Magnusen, Carmina M. *Encounter with the Triune God: An Introduction to the Theology of Edward J. Kilmartin, SJ.* San Francisco: Catholic Scholars Press, 1998.

Mantiero, Antonio. "La partecipazione liturgica." *Rivista Liturgica* 35 (1948): 102–3.

Margerie, Bertrand de. *The Christian Trinity in History.* Translated by Edmund J. Fortman. Still River, MA: St. Bede's Publications, 1982.

Marini, Piero. "Ritorno alle fonti a servizio della liturgia." Contribution to the series *Monumenta Liturgica Tridentini Concilii;* given at the Salesian Institute "S. Cuore," 23 March 2006. Available at http://www.vatican.va/news_services/liturgy/2006/documents/ns_lit_doc_20060323_ritorno-fonti_it.html.

Marsili, Salvatore. "The Mass, Paschal Mystery and Mystery of the Church." In *The Liturgy of Vatican II,* edited by William Baraúna, English ed. Jovian Lang, 4–25. Chicago: Franciscan Herald Press, 1966.

McDonnell, Kilian, OSB. *The Baptism of Jesus in the Jordan.* Collegeville, MN: Liturgical Press, 1996.

————. *The Other Hand of God: The Holy Spirit as the Universal Touch and Goal.* Collegeville, MN: Liturgical Press, 2003.

McKenna, John H. *Eucharist and Holy Spirit: The Eucharistic Epiclesis in 20th Century Theology.* Great Wakering, Essex: Mayhew-McCrimmon, 1975.

————. "Eucharist and Sacrifice: An Overview." *Worship* 76 (2000): 386–402.

————. "Eucharistic Presence: An Invitation to Dialogue." *Theological Studies* 60 (1999): 294–317.

McMurtrie, Kenneth F. "The Liturgy and the Laity." *Orate Fratres* 3 (1929): 414–20.

McNamara, Brian. "*Christus Patiens* in Mass and Sacraments: Higher Perspectives." *Irish Theological Quarterly* 42 (1975): 17–35.

————. "Divine Pedagogy: A Patristic View of Non-Christian Religions." *Irish Theological Quarterly* 53 (1987): 78–80.

————. "El Contra Eunomium I en la produccion letteraria de Gregorio de Nisa." *Irish Theological Quarterly* 57 (1991): 84–85.

Meyer, Hans Bernhard. "Eine trinitarische Theologie der Liturgie und der Sakramente." *Zeitschrift für Katholische Theologie* 113 (1991): 24–38.

————, et al. *Eucharistie: Geschichte, Theologie, Pastoral: zum Gedenken an den 100. Geburtstag von Josef Andreas Jungmann SJ am 16. Nov. 1989.* Gottesdienst der Kirche 4. Regensburg: Pustet, 1989.

Moloney, Raymond. "Lonergan on Eucharistic Sacrifice." *Theological Studies* 62 (2001): 53–70.

Montague, George. "Observations on the Encyclical 'Mediator Dei.'" *Irish Ecclesiastical Record* 70 (July 1948): 577–89.

————. "Recent Encyclical on the Sacred Liturgy: *Mediator Dei.*" *Irish Ecclesiastical Record* 70 (February 1948): 148–58.

Montini, John Baptist Cardinal (Pope Paul VI). "Liturgical Formation." Translation by Leonard Doyle of "Pastoral Letter to the Archdiocese of Milan for Lent, 1958" (February 7, 1958). *Worship* 33/3 (February 1959): 136–64.

Mühlen, Heribert. *Der Heilige Geist als Person in der Trinität bei der Incarnation und im Gnadenbund: Ich, du, wir.* 3d ed. Münsterische Beiträge zur Theologie. Münster: Aschendorff, 1969.

————. *Una mystica persona. Die Kirche als das Mysterium der Identität des heiligen Geistes in Christus und den Christen: Eine Person in vielen Personen.* 2d rev. ed. Munich and Vienna: Schöningh, 1967.

O'Neill, Colman E. *Opus Operans, Opus Operatum: A Thomistic Interpretation of a Sacramental Formula.* Washington, DC: International Pontifical Athenaeum "Angelicum," 1958.

Ormerod, Neil. *The Trinity: Retrieving the Western Tradition.* Milwaukee: Marquette University Press, 2005.

Osborne, Kenan B. *Christian Sacraments in a Postmodern World: A Theology for the Third Millennium.* Mahwah, NJ: Paulist Press, 1999.

Paul VI, Pope. *Mysterium Fidei.* AAS 57 (1965): 753–74.

————. *Populorum Progressio.* AAS 59 (1967): 257–99.

Perrone, Giovanni, SJ. *Praelectiones theologicae* 8. Louvain: Vanlithout & Vandenzande, 1838–1843.

Pius X, Pope. "Tra le sollecitudini." *Ephemerides Liturgicae* 18/3-4 (1904): 129–49.

Pius XI, Pope. "Divini Cultus." AAS 21/2 (1929): 33–41.

Pius XII, Pope. *Mediator Dei*. In *The Papal Encyclicals, 1939–1958*, edited by Claudia Carlen, IHM, 119–54. Ann Arbor, MI: Pierian Press, reprint, 1990.

———. *Mediator Dei*. AAS 39/2:14 (1947): 521–600.

———. *Mystici Corporis*. AAS 35 (1943): 193–248.

Pott, Thomas. "Une réflexion spirituelle et mystagogique renouvelée sur la participation active." In *The Active Participation Revisited: La Participation Active 100 ans après Pie X et 40 ans après Vatican II*, edited by Jozef Lamberts, 70–82. Leuven: Peeters, 2004.

Powell, Samuel M. *Participating in God: Creation and Trinity*. Minneapolis: Fortress Press, 2003.

Prétot, Patrick. "Retrouver la 'participation active,' une tâche pour aujourd'hui." *La Maison-Dieu* 241/1 (2005): 151–77.

Rahner, Karl. "Der dreifaltige Gott als transcendenter Urgrund der Heilsgeschichte." In *Mysterium Salutis. Grundriss heilsgeschichtlicher Dogmatik 2*, edited by Johannes Feiner and Magnus Löhrer. Einsiedeln: Benziger Verlag, 1967.

———. *The Trinity*. Translated by Joseph Donceel. New York: Herder & Herder, 1970.

———. "Zur Theologie des Gottesdienstes." *Theologische Quartalschrift* 159 (1979): 162–69.

Ratzinger, Joseph Cardinal. *The Spirit of the Liturgy*. Translated by John Saward. San Francisco: Ignatius Press, 2000.

Roguet, Aimon-Marie. "The Theology of the Liturgical Assembly." *Worship* 28/3 (1954): 129–38.

Rouillard, Phillippe. "Une initiation théologique à la liturgie." *Les Questions Liturgiques et Paroissiales* 39 (1958): 215–20.

Rusch, William G., ed. *The Trinitarian Controversy*. Sources of Early Christian Thought. Philadelphia: Fortress Press, 1980.

Sacred Congregation for Divine Worship. *General Instruction on the Liturgy of the Hours*. In *Documents on the Liturgy, 1963–1979*, edited by Denis E. Hurley, 1091–1131. Collegeville, MN: Liturgical Press, 1971.

———. "Liturgicae instaurationes." AAS 62 (1970): 692–704.

Sanders, Peter. "Pneumatology in the Sacramental Theologies of Geoffrey Wainwright, Jean Corbon and Edward Kilmartin." *Worship* 68 (1994): 332–52.

Sauer, Stephen, SJ. "Naming Grace: A Comparative Study of Sacramental Grace Language in Edward Kilmartin, SJ, and Louis-Marie Chauvet." STD diss., Catholic University of America, 2007.

Schillebeeckx, Edward. *Christ the Sacrament of the Encounter with God*. Reprint ed. Kansas City, MO: Sheed & Ward, 1963.

Schindler, David C. "What's the Difference? On the Metaphysics of Participation in a Christian Context." *The Saint Anselm Journal* 3 (2005): 1–27.

Schmidt, Herman. *Die Konstitution über die heilige Liturgie: Text, Vorgeschichte, Kommentar*. Freiburg: Herder, 1965.

———. "Il popolo cristiano al centro del rinnovamento liturgico." *La Civiltà Cattolica* 115/1 (1964): 120–32.

Schönborn, Christoph. *God's Human Face: The Christ-Icon*. Translated by Lothar Krauth. San Francisco: Ignatius Press, 1994.

Seasoltz, R. Kevin. *The New Liturgy: A Documentation, 1903–1965*. New York: Herder & Herder, 1966.

Serra, Dominic. "Baptism and Confirmation: Distinct Sacraments, One Liturgy." *Liturgical Ministry* 9 (2000): 63–71.

Sheldrake, Philip, ed. *The New Westminster Dictionary of Western Spirituality*. Louisville, KY: Westminster John Knox, 2005.

Stoicoiu, Rodica M. M. "The Sacrament of Order in its Relationship to Eucharist, Church, and Trinity in the Theological Writings of Edward Kilmartin and John Zizioulas." PhD diss., Catholic University of America, 2004.

Studer, Basil. "Lex orandi—lex credendi: der Taufglaube im Gottesdienst der alten Kirche." In *Oratio: das Gebet in patristischer und reformatorischer Sicht*, edited by Emidio Campi, Leif Grane, and Adolph Martin Ritter, 139–49. Göttingen: Vandenhoeck & Ruprecht, 1999.

Taft, Robert. "What Does Liturgy Do? Toward a Soteriology of Liturgical Celebration: Some Theses." *Worship* 66 (1992): 194–211.

Talley, Thomas. "The Literary Structure of the Eucharistic Prayer." *Worship* 58 (1984): 404–20.

Tanner, Norman P., ed. *Decrees of the Ecumenical Councils*. Vol. 1: *Nicaea I to Lateran V*. Vol. 2: *Trent to Vatican II*. Washington, DC: Georgetown University Press, 1990.

Tarby, André. *La prière eucharistique de l'Église de Jérusalem*. Théologie historique 17. Paris: Beauchesne, 1972.

TeVelde, Rudi A. *Participation and Substantiality in Thomas Aquinas*. New York: Brill, 1995.

Thompson-Uberuaga, William. "Deus Trinitas: The Doctrine of the Triune God." *Theological Studies* 63 (2002): 617–19.

Tillard, Jean-Marie Roger. "Spirit, Reconciliation, Church." *Ecumenical Review* 42 (1990): 237–49.

Torrance, Alan J. *Persons in Communion: An Essay in Trinitarian Description and Human Participation*. Edinburgh: T & T Clark, 1996.

Travers, Jean C.-M. *Valeur sociale de la liturgie d'aprés S. Thomas d'Aquin*. Paris: Cerf, 1946.

Triacca, Achille M. "Dom Cipriano Vagaggini, OSB Cam (1909–1999) In Memoriam." *Ephemerides Liturgicae* 113 (1999): 449–65.

———. "'Partecipazione': Quale aggettivo meglio la qualifica in ambito liturgico?" In *Actuosa Participatio: Conoscere, comprendere e vivere la Liturgia, Studi in onore del Prof. Domenico Sartore, csj*. MSIL 18. Edited by Agostino Montan and Manlio Sodi, 573–85. Vatican City: Libreria Editrice Vaticana, 2002.

———. "Spirito Santo e Liturgia. Linee methodologiche per un approfondimento." In *Lex Orandi, Lex Credendi: Miscellanea in Onore di P. Cipriano Vagaggini*, edited by Gellért Békés and Giustino Farnedi, 133–64. Rome: Editrice Anselmiana, 1980.

United States Catholic Conference, ed. *Catechism of the Catholic Church*. New York: Doubleday Image, 1994.

Vaillancourt, Raymond. *Toward a Renewal of Sacramental Theology*. Translated by Matthew J. O'Connell. Collegeville, MN: Liturgical Press, 1979.

Villalón, José R. *Sacrements dans l'Esprit: existence humaine et théologie sacramentelle*. Paris: Beauchesne, 1977.

Von Balthasar, Hans Urs. "The Descent into Hell." *Chicago Studies* 23 (1984): 223–36.

———. *Mysterium Paschale: The History of Easter*. Translated by Aidan Nichols. San Francisco: Ignatius Press, 1996.

Voyé, Liliane. "Le concept de participation en sociologie et les attentes à l'égard des pratiques rituelles." In *The Active Participation Revisited: La Participation Active 100 ans après Pie X et 40 ans après Vatican II*, edited by Jozef Lamberts, 83–97. Leuven: Peeters, 2004.

Weaver, Ellen. "Liturgy for the Laity: The Jansenist Case for Popular Participation in Worship in the Seventeenth and Eighteenth Centuries." *Studia Liturgica* 19 (1989): 47–59.

Weil, Louis. "Reclaiming the Larger Trinitarian Framework of Baptism." In *Creation and Liturgy*, 129–43. Washington, DC: Pastoral Press, 1993.

Weskamm, Wilhelm. "La participation active au cult et la vie d'une communauté." *La Maison-Dieu* 37 (1954): 25–41.

Williamson, Paul A. "Contemporary Approaches to the Ordained Priestly Ministry in Theology and the Magisterium: A Study of Selected Writings of Edward J. Kilmartin, SJ, Hervé-Marie Legrand, OP, and Edward H. Schillebeeckx, OP, in the Light of the Second Vatican Council and Subsequent Magisterium." Diss., Pontificia Universitas Gregorianum, 1983.

Witczak, Michael G. "The Manifold Presence of Christ in the Liturgy." *Theological Studies* 59 (1998): 680–702.

Zähringer, Damasus, OSB. "Feier der heiligen Messe in Gemeinschaft." *Benediktinische Monatsschrift* 25 (1949): 476–83.

Index

active presence, 47, 83, 127, 165, 186, 199, 204, 208–10, 225, 230, 232, 237–38

actuosa participatio, xvii, xxi–xxiii, 38, 42, 43, 45, 152–55, 160, 163–64, 211, 230, 232, 238

Ad Gentes, 43, 45, 48–51, 198

anabatic movement, 123–24, 127, 138, 140, 141, 193, 203, 206, 224

anamnesis, 89, 113, 115, 126, 177–78, 208–9, 228

anaphora. *See* eucharistic prayer

Apostolicam actuositatem, 43, 45, 48–51

appropriation, 188–90

Aquinas, St. Thomas
    and causality in the sacraments, 67, 69–71
    and *ex opere operato,* 61, 67, 71
    and the personalist view of the Trinity, 79
    on participation, 3, 46
    on the meaning of signs, 64, 212–13
    on trinitarian processions, 58, 194–96

Bacon, Gratien, 143

baptism
    and participation in Christ, 48, 144
    as essential to understanding trinitarian dynamic, 181–85, 232
    as fundamental sacrament, 41, 129–30, 179
    as incorporation into the Body of Christ, 13, 98, 144

as the grounds for participation, 41, 48, 237
    "by virtue of their baptism," 17, 20, 40–41

Baraúna, William, 41

Beauduin, Lambert, 7–8, 22–23

Békés, Gellért, 55, 192

Belcher, Kimberly Hope, 184

Benedict XVI, pope, 58, 152–54, 166–67; *see also* Joseph Cardinal Ratzinger, "Sacramentum Caritatis"

bestowal model, 125, 193–94, 196–97

Botte, Bernard, 8, 30

Bouyer, Louis, 7, 40, 43–44

Bradshaw, Paul, 86, 170

Brinktine, Johannes, 21

Bugnini, Annibale, 40, 54

Busch, William, 9–10

Cagny, Olivier de, 160–61

Campbell, J. Y., 49

Capelle, Bernard, 17–18

Casel, Odo, 11
    and mystery presence, 59–60
    influence on Kilmartin, 103, 106, 139–40, 177–78
    influence on Vagaggini, 215

Catechism of the Catholic Church, 149–50
    on sacraments as acts of Christ and the Spirit, 151
    on the action of the Holy Spirit, 151
    on trinitarian action, 150–51, 152

Cattaneo, Enrico, 24–25

Cavallera, Ferdinand, 25–26

Cazaux, A.-M., 24
Chauvet, Louis-Marie, 204–5, 207,
    214, 223
    and liturgical language, xix–xxiii,
    166, 235–37
christological-trinitarian schema. *See*
    Vagaggini, Cipriano
Christus Dominus, 43–44
Coffey, David, 103, 195, 196, 197, 200,
    211
    adapting the bestowal model,
    227–28
communicatio, its relationship to
    participatio, 45, 49–50
Congar, Yves M.-J., 39, 132, 162, 185,
    196, 209–10, 227
Corbon, Jean, 124, 224, 229

D'Eypernon, François, 47
Dallen, James, 143
Daly, Robert, 103, 105, 175, 193, 222,
    225–26
Dei Verbum, 49, 185
Diekmann, Godfrey, 32
Dives in Misericordia, 145
"Divini cultus," 8
    reaction to, 8–11
Divinum Illud Munus, 48–49
Dix, Gregory, 93
Dominum et Vivificantem, 145–46
Driscoll, Jeremy, 182

Ellard, Gerald, 11, 22
Emery, Gilles, 196
epiclesis, 89, 111–13, 115, 126, 177,
    208–10, 219, 228
Erickson, Craig, 143
Eucharist. *See* eucharistic prayer, Last
    Supper
eucharistic prayer
    and participation, 104, 177
    as memorial, 89
    content, structure, and function,
    88–89, 103–15, 126–27, 141, 168,
    172–73

formation of revised prayers, 54,
    88, 174
    sacrifice and, 75

Fahey, Michael, 101
Flicoteaux, Eugène, 15, 20
Fliesser, Josef C., 24
Ford, H. W., 49
Franklin, Ralph, 7

Gaudium et Spes, 48–50, 146, 185
Giraudo, Cesare, 103, 126, 175–76,
    193, 206
Gravissimum Educationis, 43, 45, 48,
    50–51
Groeber, Conrad, 15–16

Hahnenberg, Edward P., 177, 220,
    223, 225–27
Hall, Jerome, 177–78, 221–23, 227–28
Hameline, Jean-Yves, 162
Hanssens, John Michael, 28–29, 44
Hill, William J., 3–4, 188, 200–201,
    208–11
Hödl, Ludwig, 130
Holy Spirit
    "mediated immediacy," 119, 122,
    132, 135, 199, 209, 220
    proper mission of the Holy Spirit,
    103, 195–98, 227–28
    See also active presence, Trinity
Hünermann, Peter, 37–38, 41
Hunt, Anne, 189

initiation sources, importance of, 168
Innitzer, Theodor Cardinal, 16
Irwin, Kevin, 1, 10

John Paul II, pope, 145–50; see also
    specific documents: *Dominum et
    Vivificantem, Ecclesia de Eucharistia*,
    "Spiritus et Sposa" (alternately, "Lo
    Spirito e la Sposa"), *Redemptor
    Hominis*, "Vicesimus Quintus
    Annus"
Johnson, Maxwell, 182

Jourdan, G. V., 49
Jungmann, Joseph, 23, 40, 85–86, 88, 169–71

Kaczynski, Reiner, 41
Kaiser, Albert, 27, 44
Kasper, Walter, 118
katabatic movement, 123, 127, 140–41, 193, 203, 206, 224
Kavanagh, Aidan, 10, 143–44
Kilmartin, Edward J., 101–3
    action of Christ and the Church in liturgy, 115–24
    content and structure of early eucharistic prayers, 103–15
    sacramental efficacy, 137–41
    self-communication of the Trinity, 124–26
Koenker, Ernest, 15
Kubicki, Judith, 225

Lafont, Ghislain, 189–90
Lamberigts, Mathijs, 38, 43
Lamberts, Jozef, 39–40, 156, 160
Last Supper, 75, 104–8, 113, 117, 130, 174–76
Lathrop, Gordon, 10
Leo XIII, pope, 48–49; see also
    Divinum Illud Munus
Léon-Dufour, Xavier, 174, 176
Lercaro, Giacomo Cardinal, 7, 30, 32, 68, 216
"liturgical pastoral," 94, 96
liturgical theology, definition, 10
Lumen Gentium, 39, 43–44, 48–51, 59, 116–18, 121, 134–35, 185, 198
Luykx, Boniface, 143

Mantiero, Antonio, 24
Marini, Piero, 167
Marsili, Salvatore, 42–44
McDonnell, Kilian, 185, 188, 202–3, 230–31
McKenna, John, 210, 225–26

McMurtrie, Kenneth, 8–10
McNamara, Brian, 192–93, 221
Mediator Dei, participation and, the Mystical Body, 16–21
human suffering, 24–26
non-communitarian approach, 26–29
organized reaction to concept, 29–33
theology of the laity, 21–24
Meyer, Hans Bernhard, 193, 204–7
Moloney, Raymond, 193, 224
Montague, George, 16, 18–20
Montini, John Baptist Cardinal, 33–37; see also Paul VI, pope
Mühlen, Heribert, 103, 119, 132, 196, 227
mystery presence, 59, 139–41, 177–78, 215–16, 221–22, 237
Mystical Body, 12–14, 16–22, 25–27, 29, 33–34, 39, 41, 47, 50, 64, 73–74, 93, 98–99, 151, 156, 161
Mystici Corporis, 11, 16–17, 39, 47

Optatum Totius, 43–45, 50
Ormerod, Neil, 189, 194–95
Osborne, Kenan, 204, 206–7

participation
    active, xviii–xix, xxi, 1, 6–11, 30, 32, 36–47, 50–51, 98, 114, 134, 143–44, 147–49, 153–60, 162–63, 165–66, 185, 211, 222, 230–35; see also actuosa participatio
    ecclesiological, 2, 4, 5, 7, 12, 64, 161, 165, 183, 211, 214–16, 219, 221, 238–39
    eschatological, xxiii, 108, 151, 164, 211, 230–33, 238–39
    external, 19–21, 32, 42, 65, 96, 166, 216
    "full, conscious, and active," xviii, 6, 36, 37–47, 143–44, 147–49, 231, 233, 239

internal, 21, 26, 31, 42, 68, 96–98, 166, 216

and the tuning of the soul, 65, 97, 211–12

metaphoric understanding, 2, 158, 165–66, 211–12, 216–18, 238

metaphysical, 2–3, 5, 33, 62, 165, 183, 211–14, 216, 218, 221–22, 238–39

ritual-liturgical, 2, 4, 216

   contemporary attempts to define liturgical participation, 155–64

soteriological, 2–3, 5, 7, 33, 62, 125, 165, 183, 206, 211, 213–16, 219–21, 238–39

Paul VI, pope, xvii, 34, 145; see also *Mysterium Fidei, Populorum Progressio*

Perrone, Giovanni, 21

Pius X, Pope, 6–9, 30, 32; *see also* "Tra le sollecitudini"

Pius XI, pope, 8–9; *see also* "Divini cultus"

Pius XII, pope, 13–16, 19, 21–22, 24–26, 30, 32–33, 42, 47, 58, 71, 96; see also *Mediator Dei, Mystici Corporis*

Plato, understanding of participation, 2

Pott, Thomas, 155–58

Powell, Samuel, 46

Presbyterorum Ordinis, 43, 45, 48–50

Prétot , Patrick, 160–62

priesthood,

   and sacrifice, 225–27

   baptismal, 28, 43, 220

   ministerial, 29, 39, 220, 224–26

procession model, 124, 194–95, 197

Rahner, Karl, 61, 101, 103, 189, 211

Ratzinger, Joseph Cardinal, 58; *see also* Benedict XVI, pope

Redemptor Hominis, 145–46

Roguet, Aimon-Marie, 30–32

Rouillard, Phillippe, 55, 171–72

sacramental ethics, 23, 60, 68, 130–31, 138, 154, 229–39

"sacraments of the Spirit," 120–22

"Sacramentum Caritatis," 152–53, 166–67

Sacred Congregation for Divine Worship, xviii–xix

sacrifice of Christ

   as sacrifice of the Church, 71, 216, 220

   made present to believers, 178, 226

   participation in, 155–56, 161

sacrificium laudis, 114, 174, 178, 220

Sacrosanctum Concilium, xvii–xix, 1, 37, 39–42, 46–48, 50–51, 59, 74, 96, 116, 122, 144, 147, 155, 161, 196, 202, 208

Sanders, Peter, 223, 229

Schillebeeckx, Edward, 53, 223, 224

Schindler, David, 2

Schmidt, Herman, 38

Schönborn, Christoph, 149

Seasoltz, R. Kevin, 8

Second Vatican Council

   codification of "full, conscious, and active," 37–45

   leitmotif of participation, 45–51

   theological shift regarding participation, xvii–xix

   See also specific documents: *Ad Gentes, Apostolicam Actuositatem, Christus Dominus, Dei Verbum, Gaudium et Spes, Gravissimium Educationis, Lumen Gentium, Optatum Totius, Presbyterorum Ordinis, Sacrosanctum Concilium*

Serra, Dominic, 183

sintonia d'animo, 65, 77, 90, 97, 211–13, 215, 217, 231, 237

Studer, Basil, 182

Taft, Robert, 192–93

Talley, Thomas, 175
Tarby, André, 111
TeVelde, Rudi A., 46
Tillard, J.-M. R., 4
Torrance, Alan, 46
"Tra le sollecitudini," 6–7
transitus, 115, 127, 133–34, 139, 178, 184, 200, 219, 221, 231, 232, 238
Travers, Jean C.-M., 94
Triacca, Achille M., 163–64, 191–92
trinitarian language, 235–37; *see also* Chauvet, Louis-Marie
Trinity
  self-communication of the Trinity, 3, 5, 48, 51, 76, 114–15, 123–24, 131, 141, 168, 178–79, 186, 199, 204, 210–11, 219, 221, 226, 239
  processions of the Trinity, 194–98, 200, 202, 209
  trinitarian action, 46, 48, 51, 55, 76, 78, 94, 96, 111, 126–28, 149–52, 154, 165–66, 184–86, 188, 191, 193, 197, 203, 206–8, 217, 221, 224, 226, 238
  See also Kilmartin, Edward; Vagaggini, Cipriano

Vagaggini, Cipriano

attempts to understand the Trinity, 79–81
christological-trinitarian perspective, 76–78
inability to move beyond the christological pole of schema, 190–92
inaugural lecture for the Pontifical Institute, 56–57
liturgical pastoral, 94–95
network of signs, 57–66
opus operantis Ecclesiae, 71–76
role of the *Kyrios*, 90–92
theology of the body in liturgy, 68–71
trinitarian formula (*ad, per, in, ad*), 82–87, 90, 99, 181, 188–89, 217
Vaillancounrt, Raymond, xx
von Balthasar, Hans Urs, 189
Voyé, Liliane, 155, 158–59

Weaver, Ellen, 7
Weil, Louis, 182
Weskamm, Wilhelm, 24, 30
Witczak, Michael, 178, 224–25

Zähringer, Damasus, 24